SCHOOL CHOICE AND SCHOOL IMPROVEMENT

Edited by

MARK BERENDS, MARISA CANNATA,
AND ELLEN B. GOLDRING

Harvard Education Press
Cambridge, Massachusetts

Library of Congress Control Number 2010942135

Paperback ISBN 978-1-934742-52-5

Library Edition ISBN 978-1-934742-53-2

Published by Harvard Education Press,
an imprint of the Harvard Education Publishing Group

Harvard Education Press
8 Story Street
Cambridge, MA 02138

Cover Design: Perry Lubin

The typefaces used in this book are Sabon, Century Schoolbook, and Helvetica Neue.

Contents

    High School Choice Processes and Outcomes in Chicago
        W. David Stevens, Marisa de la Torre, and David W. Johnson

8   **Communication Breakdown**   147
    Informing Immigrant Families About High School Choice
    in New York City
        Carolyn Sattin-Bajaj

PART IV **Competition and Segregation Effects of Choice**

9   **How Do Principals Respond to Charter School Competition?**   177
    Understanding the Mechanisms of the Competitive Effects
    of Choice
        Marisa Cannata

10 **Shaking Up Public Schools with Competition**   193
    Are They Changing the Way They Spend Money?
        David Arsen and Yongmei Ni

11 **Charter Schools**   215
    Do They Cream Skim, Increasing Student Segregation?
        *Ron Zimmer, Brian Gill, Kevin Booker, Stéphane Lavertu,
        and John F. Witte*

12 **Does Parental Choice Foster Segregated Schools?**   233
    Insights from the Netherlands
        Helen F. Ladd, Edward B. Fiske, and Nienke Ruijs

    Notes   255

    About the Editors   295

    About the Contributors   297

    Index   301

Preface

School choice continues to grow and evolve, and the amount of research on the subject has increased significantly in the past decade. The issues addressed in the research have become more policy relevant, the quality of data has improved, and the methods for analysis have become more sophisticated. This volume, *School Choice and School Improvement,* disseminates the latest research on school choice from the National Center on School Choice (www.vanderbilt.edu/schoolchoice/).

Current research on private schools, charter schools, and voucher and tuition tax credit programs, as well as on intra- and interdistrict choice, adds depth and perspective to the debates about school choice options. In the coming years, we expect to see many more studies on these forms of choice and other evolving forms of choice: homeschooling, Internet-delivered schooling, schooling provided by for-profit educational management organizations and charter management organizations, and supplementary educational services. As time passes, the education alternatives to traditional public schools will continue to grow for educators, parents, and students.

As with *Charter School Outcomes* (2008) and *Handbook of Research on School Choice* (2009), the previous books sponsored by Vanderbilt University's National Center on School Choice (NCSC), our goal with *School Choice and School Improvement* is to offer the most recent, scientifically rigorous studies available on the effects of choice options on communities and on the schools, leaders, students, and families within them. The preface of the first volume outlines our vision for these books:

> The series will examine . . . school choice from multiple perspectives—economic, political, sociological, psychological, historical, and legal. It will also include work on the governance, structure, process, effectiveness, and costs of choice schools. It will feature much domestic research but also draw upon international and comparative studies of choice in foreign countries . . . [T]he work included will report on the methodology of research, substantive findings, and the policy and practice implications.

We intend to solicit the best research on school choice for the series wherever it is done.

Led by the editors of this volume, the NCSC is one of several such centers supported by the U.S. Department of Education's Institute of Education Sciences (IES). NCSC partners are the University of Notre Dame, the Brookings Institution, Brown University, Harvard University, Indiana University's Center for Evaluation and Education Policy, the National Bureau of Economic Research, Northwest Evaluation Association, and Stanford University.

As editors, we are grateful and fortunate that many of the nation's leading scholars of school choice accepted our invitation to participate in the national conference "School Choice and School Improvement" at Vanderbilt University in the fall of 2009. We applaud the hard work of Genevieve Zottola, Kit Lively, and Janet Roberts, who helped bring that conference to life and thus assemble the diverse research represented in this book. (These chapters represent the views of the authors and do not necessarily reflect those of the National Center on School Choice, its partner institutions, or sponsoring agencies.)

We gratefully acknowledge Ann Primus, managing editor of this volume, whose good cheer, organization, and dedication made this volume possible. We are also indebted to Caroline Chauncey, our editor at Harvard Education Press, who was encouraging and enthusiastic throughout the process of developing this book.

Mark Berends
Marisa Cannata
Ellen B. Goldring

PART I

Introduction and Overview

1

School Choice Debates, Research, and Context

Toward Systematic Understanding and Better Educational Policy

Mark Berends, Marisa Cannata, and Ellen B. Goldring

The notion of school choice is becoming embedded in the public discourse. The public may not understand the meaning of the many forms of school choice (e.g., charter schools, private schools, magnet schools, vouchers, tuition tax credits, homeschooling), but the notion that parents should have some choice in the education of their children is deeply engrained in U.S. culture.

School choice also is taking root in the education field, in part because of federal efforts over the past decade. For instance, the No Child Left Behind Act promoted choice for families if schools failed to make adequate progress over time. More recently, the Obama administration has called for an expansion of charter schools as part of the $4 billion Race to the Top program, which allocates funding to states. As choice options expand, public debate continues. Politicians scrutinize voucher programs in cities—such as Washington, D.C., and Milwaukee—while policy makers reexamine the role of school choice in post-desegregation school districts. The rigorous study of issues related to school choice is both timely and important for policy makers, practitioners, scholars, and families.

The chapters in this volume bring together exemplary, policy-relevant research on school choice options—vouchers and private schools; charter and traditional public schools; and intradistrict transfer options—as they are defined and limited by policy and geographical boundaries. The authors examine how communities, districts, and states use choice as a strategy for therefore did not receive vouchers.[8] Peterson found that vouchers were beneficial to students in mathematics and reading achievement after they spent several years in the program.

The competing findings about the effects of vouchers on student outcomes in Milwaukee resulted in tetchy exchanges, some of which were aired in the *Wall Street Journal*. Probably the most balanced analysis of the Milwaukee data is in a paper by Cecilia Rouse, an economist at Princeton currently serving on the Council of Economic Advisers. Relying on multiple methods to analyze the Milwaukee voucher data, Rouse found gains for voucher students in math but not in reading.[9] Although the Rouse paper tamped down the controversy in Milwaukee, other findings as well as research studies from other locations furthered the ongoing debate about whether vouchers were beneficial to students and worthy of public investment.

In the past decade, research on charter schools has also provided fodder for lively exchanges among researchers, politicians, and policy makers. As public schools, charter schools are funded by public monies and run by parents, educators, community groups, or private organizations to encourage school autonomy and innovation. In exchange for this autonomy, charter schools are held accountable for their results.

Although the research on the effects of charter schools on achievement is mixed—some charters outperform traditional public schools, others underperform, and still others perform similarly—in several instances the findings have resulted in public debates in major news outlets.[10] In 2004, for example, a front-page article in the *New York Times* described the results of a report by the American Federation of Teachers (AFT) that compared the test score results of students in charter schools compared with those in traditional public schools.[11] The article began by stating that national comparisons of charter and traditional public schools show that students in charter schools often do worse than comparable students in traditional public schools.

In response, several researchers—some of whom had reputations for supporting market-based reforms, and others who were known for producing objective, rigorous research on charter schools—signed a paid advertisement.[12] They criticized the article for relying on one year's test scores as reported by the so-called Nation's Report Card (the National Assessment of Educational Progress, published by the National Center for Education Statistics of the U.S. Department of Education). This publication is helpful for providing nationally representative snapshots of student achievement but not helpful for understanding the effects of schools on student achievement, such as a study of charter schools. Moreover, the advertisement criticized the AFT report—the source of the original article—for limited family background measures, unsophisticated analyses, a lack of journalistic responsibility, and the need for higher-quality research.

The AFT report and subsequent criticism sparked another round of heated debate concerning appropriate methodologies for choice research and the use of that research, much of it playing out on the public stage of the national media and outlets such as the *New York Times*. As a researcher who has examined school choice for many years, Jeffrey Henig of Teachers College, Columbia University, writes about this particular debate: "My interviews make it apparent to me that many of the researchers active in this arena are personally wrestling with the tension between wanting to be relevant and helpful in meeting social needs, on the one hand, and being wary, on the other hand, of the distortions, simplifications, and misuses of evidence that seem at times to be endemic to interactions in the political sphere."[13]

Thus research can—and should—contribute to the policy discourse about charter schools, vouchers, and other forms of school choice, but the political import of this research often results in high-profile attention given to individual studies rather than systematic understanding gleaned from the larger research base.

ACCUMULATING RESEARCH AND A SYSTEMATIC UNDERSTANDING OF SCHOOL CHOICE

One positive consequence of these debates—whether about private or Catholic schools, vouchers, or charters—is that researchers have increased the use of sophisticated, robust, and rigorous methodologies. With the growth in higher-quality school choice research, researchers have contributed in significant ways to the amount of evidence available and are beginning to shed light on such questions as, What are the conditions under which school choice options are effective?

Because of the growth of school choice programs and the amount of research examining them, knowledge is increasing. Borrowing from what David Cohen has suggested about educational research on other school reforms, knowledge about school choice options has certainly accumulated; but the issue is not about accumulation per se but about "*cumulation*, the systematic knowledge-building, including revision, within a scholarly community, such that one can—looking backward—see the growth in systematic understanding."[14] Researchers have made significant contributions during the past decade to the vigorous debates that have helped push the field forward, and the research on school choice and its many forms continues to grow toward systematic understanding.

The chapters in this volume reflect this understanding and provide examples of the directions in which research is developing. As a group, these authors use sophisticated methods to disentangle the effects of school choice from other influences on student outcomes. Furthermore, there is a growing need to understand the effects of the various school choice options (e.g., charter schools, private schools, vouchers, tuition tax credits) and learn the ways they operate in specific settings—the districts, cities, or states in which they are located.

Settings are important, because what school choice means and how it operates often depend on local context. Although the effects of school choice may not be generalizable from one setting to the next, there may be common lessons about how to implement and sustain school choice options effectively. Thus, the chapters in this volume also explore the mechanisms by which school choice is hypothesized to influence parents and students. In short, this volume brings together rigorous, objective research from national experts to examine how school choice operates in local contexts to improve schools and student outcomes.

FOCUS AND ORGANIZATION OF THIS BOOK

The chapters in this volume highlight three important aspects of school choice in local contexts. First, they examine various choice options (e.g., voucher, private, charter, intradistrict transfers) and discuss how these options are related to student outcomes (academic achievement, social outcomes, and psychological outcomes). Second, the chapters examine parental preferences and describe the process of choosing schools. Finally, the chapters analyze the impact of school choice on the community, including the presence of competitive effects and the extent of segregation of student groups. The examination of these issues is significant for policy makers, practitioners, researchers, and families and will contribute to their ongoing discussions of school choice.

Effects of Choice on Student Outcomes

Using state-of-the-art methodological approaches, the chapters examining student outcomes (Part I) address types of school choice in various locales. The chapters examine the effects of vouchers, charter schools, Catholic schools, and intradistrict transfers on student outcomes. These chapters include experimental as well as quasi-experimental designs and explain in detail how the robustness of the findings was checked.

In chapter 2, Patrick J. Wolf, Brian Kisida, Babette Gutmann, Michael Puma, Lou Rizzo, and Nada Eissa systematically examine the District of

Columbia School Choice Incentive Act of 2003, passed by the U.S. Congress in January 2004. This act established the Opportunity Scholarship Program (OSP), the first federally funded private school voucher program in the United States. The use of lotteries to determine which students would receive scholarships permitted the evaluation team to use a highly rigorous randomized control trial design to evaluate the impacts of the OSP.

The authors report that four years after random assignment, the members of the experimental treatment group offered scholarships performed about 3.9 scale scores higher than their regular public school peers in reading, a statistically significant difference that equates to a gain of about three months of learning. No differences between the treatment and control groups were detected in math achievement. In addition, the offer of an OSP scholarship raised students' probability of graduating from high school by 12 percentage points (82 percent of those offered scholarships graduated, compared with 70 percent of those not offered scholarships). For students coming from public schools in need of improvement, there was also a positive impact on high school graduation. The parents of students offered scholarships were more satisfied with their children's schools after four years than were the parents of students in the control group, and voucher parents viewed their children's schools as safer than did control parents. The chapter reveals that, in contrast, students, whether they were in the scholarship group or the randomized control group, were similar in their views of school satisfaction and safety.

In chapter 3, Anna Nicotera, Maria Mendiburo, and Mark Berends discuss the effects of charter schools on student achievement in Indianapolis from 2002–2003 to 2005–2006. Using student fixed-effects models and both fall-to-spring gains during the school year and spring-to-spring gains common across most studies analyzing student test scores, Nicotera et al. estimate the effect of switching to a charter school on student achievement. Although they find that students who switch to charter schools in Indianapolis experience positive gains in both math and reading compared with their gain trajectories in traditional public schools, the authors caution against generalizing these findings because of the small sample size and the possibility of upward bias in the results. Despite these caveats and the mixed set of charter school findings in the current literature, the positive findings in this study underscore the need to better understand the policy context of charter schools in Indianapolis.

The mayor of Indianapolis is the only mayor in the nation who has the power to authorize charter schools. Although this fact alone makes Indianapolis unique in the landscape of charter school policy, Nicotera et al. argue that there are likely several factors that came together in the mayor's initiative to explain the positive effects on achievement; these factors include local capacity building, the independence of the authorizer of charter schools from the local school district, and the organizational and instructional designs implemented in the charter schools. Although the authors cannot verify that these factors explain the positive effects of charter schools on student achievement, they encourage further research on these factors.

In chapter 4, Paul E. Peterson and Martina G. Viarengo turn their attention to students' cognitive outcomes in the Catholic and public school sectors. Moving the discussion beyond test scores, the authors analyze a nationally representative longitudinal study of students in the United States in grades K–8. Drawing on James Coleman's social capital theory to explain the importance of the Catholic sector and its peer groups, the authors examine several outcome measures. They consider topics related to students' conformity to social norms (tardiness, absenteeism, homework completion, disruptive behavior, class attendance, and academic engagement) and to self-reported psychological traits (self-esteem, locus of control, and internalization of problems). Their analyses rely on propensity score matching, a statistical technique, to match Catholic school students with their public school peers, matching the students according to their social backgrounds and school demographic characteristics.

The authors find general support for social capital theory as indicated by the positive associations between the Catholic sector and students' conformity to social norms. They do not find positive relationships between the Catholic sector and students' psychological well-being. In fact, they find that Catholic school students have lower self-esteem compared with their public school peers.

One aspect of school choice that has been understudied is the area of intradistrict transfers. In chapter 5, Kristie J. R. Phillips, Charles S. Hausman, and Elisabeth S. Larsen examine school choice in a district that does not have many of the shortcomings of other school choice programs, such as limited access to information, lack of transportation, and the ability to obtain one's first-choice option. Not only does the district context provide a best-case scenario for limiting the barriers to choice, but also the district is in a state (located in the Intermountain West) that has a long history of choice legislation, including policies for inter- and intradistrict transfers. Thus, the context is important for examining transfers that are consistent and are promoted by federal policy such as No Child Left Behind.

Phillips et al. examine the effects of intradistrict transfers on student achievement in elementary schools in one urban school district. This district provides a unique context, because all students receive admittance to their first-choice schools, and thus the researchers are able to better understand the effects of intradistrict transfers in a natural setting. Using propensity score matching, they estimate the relationship between intradistrict transfers and student achievement. They find that intra-district transfer in itself does not affect student achievement. However, when students use intra-district transfer options to move from low performing schools to higher-performing schools, their achievement increases in both language arts and mathematics. The authors emphasize that a more nuanced approach—one that would examine particular contexts of choice and more refined measures of the choice options (e.g., transfers from low performing to higher-performing schools)—would further our understanding of the effects of choice and would improve educational policy.

Parent Choice

Not only is it important to understand the effects of school choice on student outcomes, but also it is important to understand another issue of critical relevance: the mechanisms and processes of how parents choose schools. Part III of this volume picks up where Phillips et al. leave off. It turns out that giving parents the option to choose a school does not necessarily mean that parents will transfer their children to higher-performing schools.

Why and how do parents choose schools? In previous studies parents reported that academics was one of the main drivers of their choice of charter public schools for their children. However, in chapter 6, Marc L. Stein, Ellen Goldring, and Xiu Cravens theorize that surveys may be biased because of the social desirability of response, method bias, and the difficulty of asking pointed questions on matters of race, ethnicity, and social class. Therefore, using a unique data set of charter schools authorized by the Indianapolis mayor, the authors compare parents' stated reasons for choosing a charter school with their revealed preferences as evidenced by the schools they actually chose. The chapter shows that although a majority of parents indicated academics as a top priority, in fact there was little evidence of this in actual switching patterns when academic achievement and Adequate Yearly Progress ratings of the sending and receiving schools were considered.

In chapter 7, W. David Stevens, Marisa de la Torre, and David Johnson point out that access to high-quality schools under choice initiatives may be compromised in several ways. For instance, parents may lack information about the quality of schools and may tend to consider nonacademic factors when making decisions, and thus families may select schools that actually limit their children's educational opportunities. In addition, institutional constraints, such as a low number of open slots in highly desired schools, may prevent some students from leaving neighborhood schools.

Drawing on a mixed-method study of the choice system in Chicago, the authors examine how these factors shape students' access to high schools. Contrary to their expectations, their analysis shows that when students leave neighborhood schools, they tend to go to schools having higher graduation rates and test scores. But many students do not leave their assigned high schools in the first place because of concerns about managing the logistics of traveling outside their neighborhoods. In addition, the chapter reveals that students' poor application strategies severely limited their chances of being accepted at other institutions. When students receive support from adults and schools, however, their application behaviors improve.

Although many studies have asked whether students participating in school choice programs differ in social background from those who do not, the interaction between immigrant status and school choice has been largely overlooked in the research literature. Thus, in chapter 8, Carolyn Sattin-Bajaj draws on ethnographic data from research in three middle schools in Queens, New York, and analyzes school choice publications created and distributed by the New York City Department of Education (NYCDOE) to answer this question: how do the district- and school-level communication strategies and materials facilitate or complicate Latin American immigrant families' understanding of the choice process?

Sattin-Bajaj discusses four key findings. First, in virtually none of the NYCDOE publications and at few of the informational events was school quality mentioned as important for parents to consider when selecting schools. Next, there was considerable variation in the availability and quality of translation and interpretation services at the middle school events. Similarly, even when translation and interpretation services were provided, verbatim linguistic translation was often insufficient to convey the meaning of a complicated or unfamiliar concept to immigrant parents. Finally, the NYCDOE relied heavily on Web-based resources and the Internet as a means of disseminating information, creating obstacles for people having restricted access to computers or limited computer literacy.

Competition and Segregation Effects of Choice

Part IV considers the effects of choice on the local context, in potentially both positive and negative ways. One of the arguments for school choice is that as the types of choice increase, there will be competitive pressures on the traditional public schools to improve. Although the research to date is far from conclusive, a significant policy issue is whether increased choice has a substantial effect on traditional public education by applying competitive pressure for public schools to improve.

Although there is some research on the effects of competition on achievement, few studies examine the mechanism by which competition is thought to influence achievement—that is, how principals in noncharter public schools perceive and respond to competition from charter schools by changing their leadership behavior. In chapter 9, Marisa Cannata explores these issues. She discusses the overall finding that principals perceived little competition from charter schools affecting either their financial resources or recruitment of teachers and students. Cannata also shows that there is no evidence that principals' perceptions of charter school competition, or actual charter competition, is related to how they spend their time.

Chapter 10, by David Arsen and Yongmei Ni, examines two questions. First, how does resource allocation change in districts experiencing sustained charter school competition? Second, are there differences in the resource allocation adjustments between districts that do and do not succeed in stemming further enrollment loss to charters? The empirical work focuses on Michigan, where charter schools have been in effect since 1994 and where many local areas have high levels of charter competition.

The authors consider several dimensions of resource allocation, including average class size, teacher salaries, and shares of spending devoted to a variety of disaggregated instructional and noninstructional functions. Charter competition is measured through two dimensions: the magnitude and the duration of the competition. The authors do not find many strong or consistent impacts by charter competition on school district resource allocation. The chapter reveals that, overall, Michigan school districts respond to charter competition by devoting a smaller share of their spending to instructional services and a larger share to noninstructional support services. In addition, higher levels of charter competition, once they persist beyond the short term, clearly generate fiscal stress in districts.

Another area of controversy is the effect of charter schools on the sorting of students across the system of public education as a whole. Critics of charter schools worry that they might skim the cream—enrolling high-ability students at the expense of lower achievers left in traditional public schools—and that charter schools may further stratify an already racially stratified system.

In chapter 11, Ron Zimmer, Brian Gill, Kevin Booker, Stéphane Lavertu, and John Witte ask whether this belief is true. To provide an answer, they examine student-level data from seven locations across the United States. They follow students moving between traditional public schools and charter schools to examine the effect of charter schools on the distribution of students both by race (or ethnicity) and by ability. The authors do not find that charter schools are systematically skimming high-achieving students or dramatically affecting the racial mix of schools.

The Netherlands has a long history of parental choice and school autonomy. In chapter 12, Helen F. Ladd, Edward B. Fiske, and Nienke Ruijs examine why segregation by educational disadvantage has only recently emerged as a policy issue in the Netherlands. In addition, the authors document the levels and trends of school segregation in Dutch cities, finding segregation levels that are high both absolutely and relative to those in U.S. cities. Current efforts to limit segregation in Dutch cities inevitably confront the deeply held Dutch value of freedom of education.

Although much research remains to be done and debates about school choice are far from over, the chapters in this volume add to the body of research that informs research and policy about school choice within different contexts. Additional research with improved data and methods awaits further systematic knowledge building. Yet the authors in the following chapters provide significant guidance in understanding various types of school choice and school improvement within local contexts. They also provide direction for future research and policy.

PART II

Effects of Choice on Student Outcomes

2

School Vouchers in the Nation's Capital

Summary of Experimental Impacts

Patrick J. Wolf, Brian Kisida, Babette Gutmann, Michael Puma, Louis Rizzo, and Nada Eissa

In January 2004 President George W. Bush signed into law the District of Columbia School Choice Incentive Act, establishing the first federally funded, private school voucher program in the United States.[1] It passed by a single vote in the U.S. House of Representatives and cleared the U.S. Senate only after being attached to a "must pass" emergency appropriations bill. The School Choice Incentive Act was packaged as a three-sector strategy to improve education in the nation's capital; the $40 million annual appropriation attached to the bill included an extra $13 million for educational improvements in the District of Columbia Public Schools (DCPS), $13 million to increase the availability of facilities appropriate for public charter schools in the district, $13 million for the Opportunity Scholarship Program (OSP), and $1 million for implementation and evaluation of the OSP.[2] Since that time nearly eighty-five hundred students have applied for this parental school choice program, and a rigorous evaluation of the initiative has been conducted.

Like the other thirteen school voucher programs in the United States that are directly financed by the government, the D.C. OSP is targeted to disadvantaged students. To be eligible to receive a voucher of up to $7,500 annually, students must live in the District of Columbia and have a family income at or below 185 percent of the federal poverty level—about $36,000 for a family of four.[3] Because the program is oversubscribed, vouchers are awarded by lottery, but preference in the lottery is given to public school students attending schools that have been designated "in need of improvement" under the federal government's No Child Left Behind accountability system. Students awarded vouchers can use them at any of more than fifty participating private schools.

Since the spring of 2009, lawmakers have taken steps to end the OSP. The first effort involved Senator Dick Durbin (D-IL) inserting language in an appropriations bill in March 2009 that directed the government to close the voucher program in 2010 unless it was endorsed by a majority of the D.C. City Council and reauthorized for an additional five years by the U.S. Congress, actions that were widely viewed as politically unlikely.[4] That congressional action prompted U.S. Department of Education Secretary Arne Duncan to rescind two hundred vouchers that recently had been awarded to new participants.[5] These events sparked a series of public protests by voucher recipients and supporters, condemnation from the editorial pages of major newspapers, and a quick letter to Congress signed by a majority of D.C. City Council members endorsing continuation of the voucher program.[6]

As the controversy over the future of the OSP reached a head in May 2009, President Obama proposed a compromise that included continuing funding for students currently in the voucher program until they graduate from high school but closing the program to new applicants.[7] Senator Joseph Lieberman, an Independent aligned with the Democratic Party, chaired a Senate committee hearing on the OSP and subsequently introduced legislation supported by several prominent Senate Democrats and Republicans. The bill would have reauthorized the voucher program for five more years and provided some program enhancements, such as a higher-value voucher of $11,000 for high school students.[8]

Lieberman's reauthorization bill ultimately failed to garner enough legislative support. Instead, the federal appropriations law that was enacted in December 2009 effectively codifies in law President Obama's stated position regarding the OSP. The statute closes the voucher program to new applicants, funds existing students through their graduation from high school, and imposes new government regulations on participating private schools.[9] President Obama's fiscal year (FY) 2011 budget proposal includes a request for $9 million in funding for continuing OSP students to remain in their private schools through high school graduation. The budget narrative states that no additional funding beyond FY 2011 is expected as the program winds down.[10]

MANDATED EVALUATION OF THE OSP

When Congress established the OSP, it also mandated that independent researchers evaluate the new program and provide annual reports on the progress of the study. The legislation indicated that the evaluation should analyze the effects of the program on various academic and nonacademic outcomes of concern to policy makers and use "the strongest possible research design for determining the effectiveness" of the program.[11] The results of that evaluation, summarized here, were developed to be responsive to these requirements.

The foundation of the evaluation is a randomized controlled trial (RCT) that compares the outcomes of eligible applicants randomly assigned to receive (treatment group) or not receive (control group) an Opportunity Scholarship voucher. The decision to use this research design was based on the mandate to use rigorous evaluation methods, the expectation that there would be more applicants than funds and private school spaces available, and the requirement that random selection be the vehicle for determining who received a scholarship whenever the program was oversubscribed. An RCT design is widely viewed as the best method for identifying the independent causal effect of programs on subsequent outcomes.[12] Random assignment has been used by researchers conducting impact evaluations of other scholarship programs in Charlotte, North Carolina; New York City; Dayton, Ohio; and Washington, D.C.[13]

The recruitment, application, and lottery process conducted by the program implementer with guidance from the evaluation team created the foundation for the evaluation's RCT and determined the group of students for whom impacts of the program were analyzed in this chapter. Because the goal of the evaluation was to assess both the short-term and the longer-term impacts of the program, it was necessary to focus the study on early applicants to the program (cohorts 1 and 2) whose outcomes could be tracked for at least four years during the evaluation period.

During the first two years of recruitment, the program implementer received applications from 5,818 students, 70 percent of whom were deemed eligible. Of that total pool of eligible applicants those first two years, 2,308 students who were rising kindergarteners or currently attending public schools entered scholarship lotteries (492 in cohort 1, and 1,816 in cohort 2). The lotteries produced 1,387 students assigned to the treatment condition and 921 students assigned to the control condition.[14] These students constituted the impact analysis sample and represented three-quarters of all students in cohorts 1 and 2 who were not already attending a private school when they applied to the OSP.[15]

Data regarding student test score performance and parent and student views of school safety and satisfaction were collected at the time of program application as well as one, two, three, and four or more years after students were randomly assigned to the treatment or control group. We use the phrase "four or more years" to characterize the period over which we evaluated the program's impacts. The 14 percent of the study sample in cohort 1 provided final information about their educational outcomes five years after random assignment, whereas the 86 percent of the sample in cohort 2 provided final outcome data four years after randomization.

Because random assignment approximately equalizes the treatment and control groups regarding measured and unmeasured characteristics, evaluators can determine the impact of the program simply by subtracting the average outcomes for the control group of students from the average outcomes for the treatment group. The difference, by definition, is the impact of the OSP. For the government evaluation, we estimated the impact statistically using a regression model that controls for important characteristics of students at the point of application, such as test scores, disability, family income, mother's education, and race. Controlling for baseline characteristics is not necessary in an RCT, but doing so provides precise statistical estimates of the program's impact.

The effective response rates to outcome data collection were approximately 70 percent each year. Importantly, the rates were similar between the treatment and the control group. To ensure that the equivalence of the two experimental groups persisted over time, we applied nonresponse weights to the data before analysis to eliminate any differences between the treatment and control groups that might have emerged as a result of nonresponse to data collection.

The initial program impact that we provide in the evaluation is the impact of the mere offer of an Opportunity Scholarship, called the *intent to treat* (ITT) estimate. Scholarship programs cannot compel families to use a voucher to attend a private school, and members of the control group are free to enroll in private schools outside the program if they can access the resources to do so. Therefore, we derive the experimental impacts of the scholarship offer by comparing the outcomes for students randomly offered the scholarship opportunity—27 percent of whom were attending traditional public schools and 18 percent of whom were in public charter schools in the final outcome year of 2008–2009—with the outcomes for students randomly assigned to the control group, 12 percent of whom were enrolled in private schools in 2008–2009. To generate an experimental estimate of the impact of actually using an Opportunity Scholarship to attend a private school, called the *impact of treatment* (IOT) estimate, we apply a common statistical adjustment called a *Bloom adjustment*.[16] This adjustment nets out students in the treatment group who never used their scholarships and therefore could not have experienced a program impact.[17]

PROGRAM IMPLEMENTATION AND
PARTICIPATION IN THE OSP

As background, here we examine basic features of the program's implementation, the participating private schools, and the extent to which students offered scholarships moved into and out of them.

The OSP was operated by the Washington Scholarship Fund (WSF), a 501(c)(3) organization based in the District of Columbia, under contract to the Office for Innovation and Improvement (OII) of the U.S. Department of Education. The WSF has operated a privately funded, partial-tuition K–12 scholarship program since 1993.[18] The organization won a grant competition staged by the OII in March 2004 to operate the program for the expected pilot period of five years.[19] Given the timing of program launch (late in the spring of 2004, after private school enrollments for the fall semester are usually established), the WSF and the U.S. Department of Education decided to award a portion of the available scholarships in the summer of 2004 and complete the full implementation of the program the following year.[20]

By the fall of 2009, there had been six rounds of applications to the OSP. Applicants in spring 2004 (cohort 1) and spring 2005 (cohort 2) numbered 5,818 students and represented the majority of program applicants over the five-year period. The evaluation sample was drawn from these two groups.[21] There were smaller numbers of applicants in spring 2006 (cohort 3), spring 2007 (cohort 4), spring 2008 (cohort 5), and spring 2009 (cohort 6), collectively numbering 2,662, who were recruited and enrolled by WSF in order to keep the program operating at capacity each year.

In the initial year of partial program implementation (2004), a total of 1,027 students used Opportunity Scholarships. The program enrolled 1,716 students in 2005, followed by 1,805 students in 2006, 1,930 in 2007, 1,714 in 2008, and 1,322 in 2009 (see figure 2.1). All the scholarship users in 2004 were first-time users. The population of students enrolled in the program from 2005 through 2009 included a mix of continuing students and first-time users. Only continuing students were allowed to use scholarships in 2009. During the scheduled five years of the pilot project, an average of 77 percent of students who were offered scholarships used them to attend a participating private school in the fall immediately after receiving the offer.

Students' reasons for not using the scholarship—either initially or consistently across all years—varied. The most common reasons cited by parents whose children never used their scholarships and who completed surveys are shown in figure 2.2. The three chief reasons were as follows:

FIGURE 2.1 **OSP enrollments**

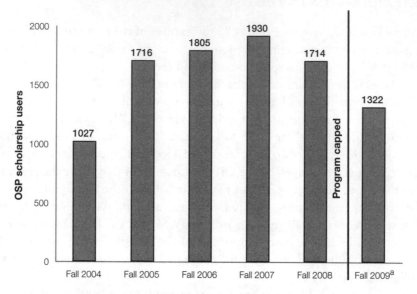

a. The program was closed to new applicants in 2009.

- Lack of available space in the desired private school (31 percent of these parents)
- Participating schools did not offer services for the child's learning or physical disability or other special needs (22 percent)
- Child was accepted into a public charter school (16 percent)

The private schools participating in the OSP represented the choice set available to parents whose children received scholarships. Approximately two-thirds of the eighty-eight general service private schools that existed in Washington, D.C., in 2004 participated in the OSP at some point.[22] Fifty-seven private schools agreed to accept scholarship students in the program's initial year, and fifty-two schools participated in the program in 2008–2009.

The schools that offered the most slots to OSP students, and in which OSP students and the impact sample's treatment group were clustered, have characteristics that differed somewhat from those of the average participating OSP school. Although 54 percent of all participating schools in 2008–2009 were faith based (29 percent were part of the Catholic Archdiocese of Washington), 80 percent of the treatment group attended a faith-based school, with 53 percent of them attending the fifteen participating Catholic

FIGURE 2.2   **Reasons for never using an OSP scholarship**

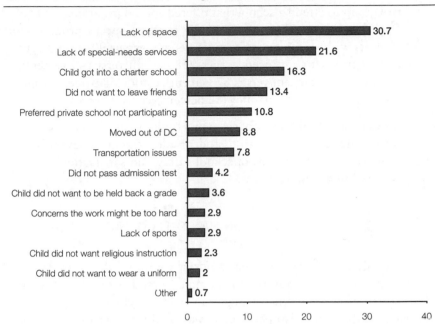

parochial schools.[23] Fourteen percent of treatment group students attended a school that charged tuition higher than the statutory cap of $7,500, even though half of participating schools charged tuition above that cap in 2008–2009.

The characteristics of the participating private schools are important considerations for parents, but in many respects it is how the schools differ from the available public school options that matters most from an educational perspective. In 2008–2009, students in the treatment and control groups did not differ significantly regarding the proportion attending schools that offered a separate library (77 percent versus 79 percent), gym (68 percent and 71 percent), and music program (93 percent and 91 percent). The following differences in school characteristics were experienced by the treatment and control groups at least four years after they applied to the OSP and were statistically significant at the 0.01 (i.e., 99 percent confidence) level:

- Students in the treatment group were less likely than those in the control group to attend a school with a cafeteria facility (76 percent versus 91 percent) or a nurse's office (50 percent versus 82 percent).

- Students in the treatment group were less likely than those in the control group to attend a school that offered special programs for non-English speakers (32 percent versus 57 percent), special programs for students with learning problems (75 percent versus 90 percent), special programs for advanced learners (38 percent versus 49 percent), counselors (77 percent versus 87 percent), tutors (58 percent versus 63 percent), and art programs (84 percent versus 92 percent).

What was the actual impact of the opportunity to attend private schools on student educational attainment, student educational achievement, and parent and student perceptions of school safety and satisfaction? We now turn to those important questions.

IMPACT OF THE PROGRAM ON KEY OUTCOMES AFTER AT LEAST FOUR YEARS

In previously issued congressional reports, we found that after two and three years in the program, the full sample of students awarded scholarships scored at least marginally higher in reading achievement.[24] Students awarded scholarships also performed marginally higher in mathematics after one year but scored at similar levels to the control group in math after two and three years. During the first three years, parents consistently rated their child's school as safer and gave it a higher satisfaction grade if their child was offered or used a scholarship. There was no conclusive evidence of impacts on students' own views of school safety and satisfaction during the first three years.

The analyses in this chapter were conducted using data collected on students at the end of the 2008–2009 school year, at least four years after they applied to the OSP.[25] By the end of the 2008–2009 school year, 22 percent of the impact sample (approximately five hundred students) had aged to the point that they could have completed twelfth grade and graduated from high school. This means that for the first time in the evaluation we were able to estimate the program's impacts on educational attainment in the form of high school graduation rates. This study represents the first time that random assignment has been used to estimate the causal relationship between a school voucher program (or private schooling) and educational attainment in the United States, thus providing a more rigorous estimate than previous observational studies that have addressed this issue.

The main focus of this study was on the impacts of the OSP on the overall group of students that were randomly assigned. The study provides additional consideration of the programmatic impacts on policy-relevant subgroups of students. The subgroups were designated before data collection and include students who were attending "schools in need of improvement" (SINI) versus non-SINI schools at application, those performing relatively higher or lower at baseline, and girls or boys. Earlier reports also considered elementary versus high school students, and those from application cohort 1 or cohort 2.[26]

Impacts on Student Attainment

The attainment analysis focused on students in the impact sample who were forecast to have been seniors in high school during or before the 2008–2009 school year and therefore had the opportunity to graduate before the summer of 2009. A follow-up survey asked parents a series of factual questions about their child's educational and vocational status, yielding answers that permitted us to determine whether each student had received a high school diploma by the end of the 2008–2009 school year. Differences in parental reports of student educational attainment between the treatment and control groups were then measured via the evaluation's standard regression method of analysis. The results, shown in table 2.1, are summarized here:

The offer of an OSP scholarship raised students' probability of graduating by 12 percentage points. The high school graduation rate was 82 percent for the treatment group compared with 70 percent for the control group. Actual use of an Opportunity Scholarship increased the graduation rate by 21 percentage points.

- There was a positive impact (13 percentage points) on the high school graduation rate for students who came from SINI 2003–2005 schools, the subgroup of students for whom the statute gave top priority. The graduation rate was 79 percent for the SINI members of the treatment group compared with 66 percent for the SINI members of the control group. Actual use of a voucher increased the graduation rate for SINI students by 20 percentage points.[27]
- The offer of an OSP scholarship led to a positive impact for students who applied to the program with relatively higher levels of academic performance (14 percentage points) and female students (20 percentage points). Using a scholarship to attend a participating private school increased the graduation rate by 25 and 28 percentage points, respectively, for these two subgroups of participants.
- There was no conclusive evidence of impacts on graduation rates for students who applied to the program from non-SINI schools, those with relatively lower levels of academic performance, and male students as distinctive subgroups.[28]

TABLE 2.1 Impact estimates of the offer and use of a scholarship: Percent with high school diploma

	IMPACT OF THE SCHOLARSHIP OFFER (ITT)				IMPACT OF SCHOLARSHIP USE (IOT)		
	Treatment group mean	Control group mean	Difference (estimated impact)	Effect size	Adjusted impact estimate	Effect size	p-value of estimates
Full sample	0.82	0.70	0.12**	0.26	0.21**	0.46	0.01
SINI 2003–2005	0.79	0.66	0.13*	0.28	0.20*	0.43	0.01
Not SINI 2003–2005	0.89	0.82	0.07	0.19	0.21	0.54	0.46
Difference	−0.10	−0.16	0.06	0.13			0.59
Lower performance	0.60	0.49	0.12	0.23	0.20	0.40	0.12
Higher performance	0.93	0.79	0.14*	0.35	0.25*	0.61	0.02
Difference	−0.33	−0.30	−0.03	−0.06			0.80
Male	0.71	0.66	0.07	0.14	0.14	0.30	0.26
Female	0.95	0.75	0.20**	0.46	0.28**	0.65	0.01
Difference	−0.24	−0.08	−0.15	−0.34			0.18

*Statistically significant at the 95 percent confidence level.

**Statistically significant at the 99 percent confidence level.

Means are regression adjusted using a consistent set of baseline covariates. Impact estimates are reported as marginal effects. Effect sizes are in terms of standard deviations. Valid N = 316. Sample weights used. Robust regression calculations generated by clustering at the family level.

Impacts on Reading Achievement After at Least Four Years

In the full sample, there was a marginally statistically significant impact of the program on reading achievement after at least four years. That is, the average reading test scores of the treatment group as a whole were significantly higher than those of the control group as a whole, with at least 90 percent confidence. Students scored an average of 3.9 scale score points higher (2.8 months of additional learning) in reading than did students in the control group. The calculated impact of using a scholarship was 4.8 scale score points (3.4 months of additional learning) (see table 2.2).[29] Figure 2.3 shows these reading achievement impacts of the voucher program at least four years after random assignment and places the impact in the context of impacts estimated in prior years.

TABLE 2.2   Impact estimates of the offer and use of a scholarship: Reading achievement

	IMPACT OF THE SCHOLARSHIP OFFER (ITT)				IMPACT OF SCHOLARSHIP USE (IOT)		
	Treatment group mean	Control group mean	Difference (estimated impact)	Effect size	Adjusted impact estimate	Effect size	p-value of estimates
Full sample	649.15	645.24	3.90#	0.11	4.75#	0.13	0.06
SINI 2003–2005	657.49	656.41	1.08	0.03	1.33	0.04	0.76
Not SINI 2003–2005	643.25	637.45	5.80*	0.16	6.99*	0.19	0.02
Difference	14.24	18.96	−4.72	−0.13			0.27
Lower performance	629.45	628.27	1.18	0.04	1.54	0.05	0.74
Higher performance	657.79	652.61	5.18*	0.15	6.08*	0.18	0.04
Difference	−28.34	−24.34	−4.00	−0.11			0.35
Male	642.78	640.33	2.45	0.07	3.07	0.09	0.44
Female	654.64	649.38	5.27*	0.15	6.24*	0.18	0.05
Difference	−11.86	−9.05	−2.81	−0.08			0.50

\# Statistically significant at the 90 percent confidence level.

*Statistically significant at the 95 percent confidence level.

Results are for cohort 1 five years after random assignment, and cohort 2 four years after random assignment. Means are regression adjusted using a consistent set of baseline covariates. Impacts are displayed in terms of scale scores. Effect sizes are in terms of standard deviations. Valid *N* for reading = 1,328. Sample weights used. Robust regression calculations generated by clustering at the family level.

FIGURE 2.3   OSP impact on reading

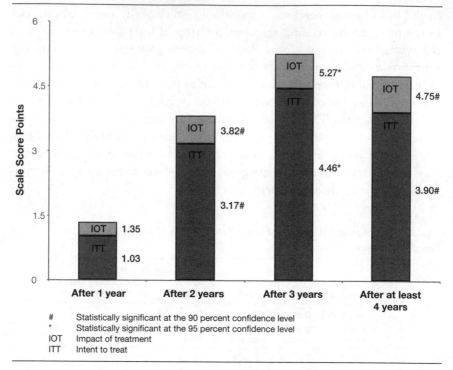

#	Statistically significant at the 90 percent confidence level
*	Statistically significant at the 95 percent confidence level
IOT	Impact of treatment
ITT	Intent to treat

After at least four years, the offer of a scholarship had a statistically significant positive impact on reading achievement at the subgroup level (with 95 percent confidence) for half of the student subgroups (see table 2.2). The subgroups with positive reading impacts included the following:

- *Students in the treatment group who had not attended a SINI school before the program.* These students scored an average of 5.8 scale score points higher (3.5 months of additional learning) in reading than did students in the control group from non-SINI schools (the impact of the offer of a scholarship); the calculated impact of using a scholarship for this group was 7.0 scale score points (4.2 months of additional learning).

- *Students in the treatment group who entered the program in the higher two-thirds of the applicant test score performance distribution.* These students scored an average of 5.2 scale score points higher in reading (3.9 months of additional learning) than did similar students in the control group; the impact of using a scholarship for this group was 6.1 scale score points (4.6 months of additional learning).

TABLE 2.3   Impact estimates of the offer and use of a scholarship: Math achievement

	IMPACT OF THE SCHOLARSHIP OFFER (ITT)				IMPACT OF SCHOLARSHIP USE (IOT)		
	Treatment group mean	Control group mean	Difference (estimated impact)	Effect size	Adjusted impact estimate	Effect size	p-value of estimates
Full sample	644.06	643.36	0.70	0.02	0.85	0.03	0.71
SINI 2003–05	656.67	657.05	−0.38	−0.01	−0.47	−0.02	0.90
Not SINI 2003–05	635.31	633.89	1.42	0.04	1.71	0.05	0.56
Difference	21.36	23.16	−1.80	−0.05			0.65
Lower performance	632.39	631.16	1.24	0.04	1.61	0.05	0.71
Higher performance	649.08	648.59	0.49	0.01	0.58	0.02	0.83
Difference	−16.69	−17.44	0.75	0.02			0.85
Male	639.59	640.70	−1.11	−0.04	−1.38	−0.04	0.68
Female	648.04	645.64	2.40	0.07	2.84	0.08	0.37
Difference	−8.44	−4.94	−3.50	−0.10			0.35

Results are for cohort 1 five years after random assignment, and cohort 2 four years after random assignment. Means are regression adjusted using a consistent set of baseline covariates. Impacts are displayed in terms of scale scores. Effect sizes are in terms of standard deviations. Valid *N* for math = 1,330. Sample weights used. Robust regression calculations generated by clustering at the family level.

- *Female students in the treatment group.* These students scored an average of 5.3 scale score points higher in reading (3.4 months of additional learning) than did female students in the control group; the impact of using a scholarship for females was a gain of 6.2 scale score points (4.0 months of additional learning).

There was no evidence of a subgroup impact in reading for students who applied from a SINI school, students who entered the program in the lower one-third of the applicant test score performance distribution, or for male students as separate subgroups.[30]

Impacts on Math Achievement After at Least Four Years

The offer of a scholarship had no statistically significant impact on math achievement overall, nor was there evidence of significant impacts on math achievement for any of the six subgroups examined (see table 2.3).[31]

FIGURE 2.4   OSP impact on math

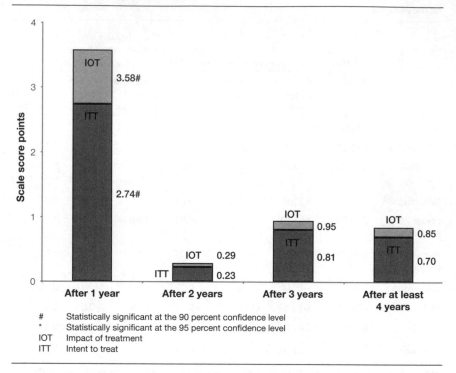

#	Statistically significant at the 90 percent confidence level
*	Statistically significant at the 95 percent confidence level
IOT	Impact of treatment
ITT	Intent to treat

Figure 2.4 shows the math achievement impacts at least four years after random assignment and places the impacts in the context of impacts estimated in prior years.

Impacts on Reported Safety and an Orderly School Climate After at Least Four Years

School safety is a valued feature of schools for the families who applied to the OSP. A total of 17 percent of cohort 1 parents at baseline listed school safety as their most important reason for seeking to exercise school choice, second only to academic quality (48 percent) among the available reasons.[32] A separate study of why and how OSP parents chose schools—a study that relied on focus group discussions with participating parents—found that school safety was among their most important educational concerns.[33]

In contrast to student achievement, there are no specific tests to evaluate the safety of a school. There are various indicators of the relative orderliness of the school environment, such as the presence or absence of property destruction, cheating, bullying, and drug distribution. Students and parents can be surveyed regarding the extent to which such indicators of disorder are or are not a problem at school. The responses can be consolidated into an index of safety and an orderly school climate and then analyzed, as we do here.

Overall, the parents of students offered an Opportunity Scholarship subsequently reported their child's school to be safer and more orderly than did the parents of students in the control group. The impact of the offer of a scholarship on parental perceptions of safety and an orderly school climate was 0.48 on a 10-point index of indicators of school safety and orderliness, an effect size of 0.14 standard deviations. The impact of using a scholarship was 0.58 on the index, with an effect size of 0.17 standard deviations.

This impact was observed for three of the subgroups examined: parents of students from non-SINI schools experienced a positive increase of 0.22 standard deviations; parents of students who entered the program in the higher two-thirds of the applicant test score performance distribution experienced a positive increase of 0.15 standard deviations; and parents of female students experienced a positive increase of 0.17 standard deviations. There was no evidence of an impact on these parental perceptions for the subgroups of students from SINI schools, students who entered the program with relatively lower levels of academic achievement, and parents of male students.

The students in grades 4–12 who completed surveys painted a different picture of safety at their school than did their parents. The student index of school climate and safety asked students whether they personally had been a victim of theft, drug dealing, assaults, threats, bullying, or taunting or had observed weapons at school. On average, reports of school climate and safety by students offered scholarships through the lottery were not statistically different from those of the control group. Additionally, none of the six subgroups demonstrated statistically significant impacts of the OSP on student perceptions of the safety of their school at the subgroup level.

Impacts on School Satisfaction

Economists have long used customer satisfaction as a proxy measure for product or service quality.[34] Although not specifically identified as an outcome to be studied in this evaluation, satisfaction is an indicator of the "success of the Program in expanding options for parents," which Congress asked us to consider.[35] Satisfaction is also an outcome studied in the previous evaluations of K–12 scholarship programs, all of which concluded that parents tend to be significantly more satisfied with their child's school if they have had the opportunity to select it.[36] Satisfaction of parents and students was measured by the percentage who assigned a grade of A or B to their child's or their school.

At least four years after random assignment, parents overall were more satisfied with their child's school if they had been offered a voucher and if their child used a voucher to attend a participating private school. A total of 76 percent of treatment parents assigned their child's school a grade of A or B in 2009 compared with 68 percent of control parents, a difference of 8 percentage points (showing the impact of the offer of a scholarship); the impact of using a scholarship was a difference of 10 percentage points in parents' likelihood of giving their child's school a grade of A or B. The effect sizes of these impacts were 0.18 and 0.22, respectively.

For each of the six subgroups of parents, those in the treatment group were more satisfied than their counterparts in the control group. These differences, however, were not statistically significant at the subgroup level for parents of scholarship students from SINI schools. Parents of students from non-SINI schools, parents of students who had higher and lower test score performance at baseline, and parents of male and female students as distinct subgroups all were significantly more likely to give their child's school a grade of A or B if they were in the treatment group. The effect sizes ranged from 0.17 to 0.27 standard deviations for the offer of, and from 0.20 to 0.32 standard deviations for the use of, an Opportunity Scholarship.

As was true with the school safety and climate measures, students had a different view of their schools than did their parents. At least four years after random assignment, there were no significant differences between the treatment group and the control group in their likelihood of assigning their schools a grade of A or B, either for the full sample or for the various subgroups.[37]

CONCLUSIONS

The results of this analysis of a school choice program emerged from an evaluation structured as a randomized controlled trial at least four years after random assignment to the treatment (offer of a scholarship) or control (not offered) group. Because chance determined whether eligible applicants received the treatment of a scholarship offer or a place in the control group, any subsequent differences between the outcomes of the two groups that are statistically significant can be attributed to the program.

The nation's first and only federally funded school voucher program had a significant positive impact on parent-reported high school graduation rates. Overall, 82 percent of those offered scholarships graduated, compared with 70 percent of those who were not offered scholarships, a difference of 12 percentage points. The impact on the likelihood of graduation from actual use of a scholarship to attend a private school was a gain of 21 percentage points. Similar benefits extended to the high-priority SINI students; those who were higher performing academically when they entered the program; and female participants. These results support prior research suggesting that private schools give students an educational climate that encourages school completion; students are affected either by the faculty and school environment or by having similarly motivated and achieving peers.[38]

On average, District of Columbia low-income students performed higher in reading if offered an Opportunity Scholarship. However, the impact of the OSP on student test scores in math was not significantly different from zero. Parents were much more satisfied with their child's school and viewed it as safer as a result of the scholarship offer. Their children, however, did not appear to share their parents' greater enthusiasm for the private school environments they experienced through the program.

Note that these findings regarding the impacts of the OSP reflect the particular program elements that evolved from the law passed by Congress and the characteristics of students, families, and schools public and private in the nation's capital. The same program implemented in another city could yield different results, and a differently designed voucher program in Washington, D.C., might also produce different outcomes.

School vouchers remain a contested educational intervention. Given the strong positions held by many policy makers in favor of or opposed to means-tested voucher initiatives such as the Opportunity Scholarship Program, the best contribution that we can make to the debate is to inform it with reliable results from this rigorous study. Meanwhile, controversy undoubtedly will continue to swirl around our nation's only federally sponsored school voucher program, as program attrition through graduation and student mobility annually depletes the ranks of Opportunity Scholars. If a new Congress decides to revisit the question of reauthorizing the school voucher program, we sincerely hope that the evidentiary record painstakingly built through our government-sponsored program evaluation will help to inform and guide its decision. The people of the United States, and especially the low-income children of its capital city, deserve no less.

Charter School Effects in Indianapolis

An Analysis of Student Achievement Gains

Anna Nicotera, Maria Mendiburo, and Mark Berends

Since their arrival in the early 1990s, charter public schools have experienced increasing popularity as a school reform effort, having expanded to nearly five thousand schools and 1.6 million students.[1] As public schools, charters are publicly funded. Unlike most traditional public schools, however, charter schools are granted autonomy to operate outside typical school district control under a charter by parents, educators, community groups, or private organizations. The idea is to encourage school innovation and improvements in student performance.

As the popularity of charter schools increased and the number of charter schools grew throughout the past decade, the number of rigorous research studies of charter schools burgeoned. Several examined individual states, such as Arizona, California, Florida, Idaho, North Carolina, Texas, and Wisconsin.[2] Other studies examined multiple states.[3] In addition, researchers studied the effects of charters on student outcomes in major cities, such as Boston, Chicago, Denver, Los Angeles, New York, Philadelphia, and San Diego.[4]

The wide range of locations resulted in a great deal of variability in findings, reflecting differences in state policies and authorizing practices, the age of charter schools, and diverse instructional and governance structures at the school level. Unfortunately, this variability makes it difficult for researchers to systematically study student achievement outcomes in a large number of charter schools.[5] It also points to the importance of understanding the policy context of charter schools in a given location.

In this study, we add to the discussion about the effects of charter schools in a given location by examining student achievement in a unique policy context: Indianapolis. Unlike other states—in which the local school district, a state agency, or not-for-profit agencies authorized the existing charter schools—Indiana passed a special charter school initiative sponsored by the Indianapolis mayor's office during Bart Peterson's tenure, and the majority of charter schools in the city were authorized under this initiative by the mayor's office. Each of these schools received its charter after completing a rigorous and competitive application process, and charter schools risk losing their charter if they fail to meet any of the requirements of the mayor's comprehensive accountability system. This system uses a combination of standardized testing; site visits by an expert team; surveys of parents, students, and staff; and an outside review of school finances to evaluate each of the charter schools annually.[6] Even as the mayoral office transferred from Bart Peterson to Gregory Ballard, the office continued the expansion of charter schools within the city. The mayor's charter school initiative received national recognition for its innovations, entrepreneurial leaders, and capacity to build local support.[7] But despite such accolades, little systematic evidence exists that the charter schools in Indianapolis positively impact student achievement.

To better understand the charter school effect on student achievement in Indianapolis, we used student fixed-effects models to compare gains between charter public school and traditional public school (TPS) students. Specifically, we examined the following research questions:

- What impact do the Indianapolis mayor's office charter schools have on student achievement gains?
- What policy lessons can be learned from these schools?

We addressed these questions using data from 2002 through 2006, the time of Bart Peterson's tenure as mayor.

In this chapter we first review the policy context of charter schools in Indianapolis. Second, we take a close look at the background research of charter school effects on achievement to consider how previous research influences our research approach. We then describe the data and the specific models used to test our research question before discussing the results of our analyses. Finally, we suggest directions for future research and make policy recommendations based on our findings.

INDIANAPOLIS CHARTER SCHOOLS

In 2001, Indiana passed a law that granted the mayor of Indianapolis permission to authorize charter schools.[8] With only 17 percent of African American sixth graders achieving proficiency in language arts and only 25 percent achieving proficiency in math, Mayor Peterson looked to charter schools to increase the number of high-quality school options for students in Indianapolis.[9] The first three opened in fall 2002 and enrolled 479 students. As of the 2008–2009 school year, there were 5,323 students enrolled in seventeen schools that were part of the mayor's charter school initiative.[10]

The Indianapolis charter schools are considered an innovative part of the school choice movement.[11] These charters, many of which have been founded by the most distinguished leaders and organizations, social service agencies, philanthropists, corporate representatives, and government leaders in Indianapolis, operate autonomously as separate legal and financial institutions.[12] The charter schools vary in their educational programs. Some provide project-based learning, and others emphasize direct instruction and back-to-basics approaches. Some rely on external providers of school designs, such as the Knowledge Is Power Program (KIPP), but many are based on locally developed models. A number of the charter schools were developed by local philanthropists with a particular emphasis, such as serving students who have limited English, infusing technology in the school, or serving high-risk populations.

A state law mandates that the mayor's office authorize no more than five new charter schools per year, and rather than attempt to open large numbers of new charter schools, the mayor's office focused on developing strong selection criteria for charter school applicants and implementing rigorous oversight processes for operating schools. All the Indianapolis charter schools went through a competitive application process. In its first five years of authorizing, the mayor's office received applications and prospectuses for forty-five charter schools, approved sixteen schools, and revoked the charter of one school. The approval rate for applications was 36 percent in 2004, 43 percent in 2005, and 14 percent in 2006.[13]

In addition to implementing a rigorous, competitive application process, the mayor's office holds each charter school responsible via a comprehensive annual accountability system. The system includes school performance measures in the form of state assessments, fall and spring administration of the Northwest Evaluation Association (NWEA), visits and school audits by external experts, financial and governance reviews, and results from teacher, parent, and student surveys.[14] In 2006, the Indianapolis accountability system received Harvard's Innovations in American Government Award in recognition of its unique contribution to the U.S. school reform movement.[15] The authorizing practices used by the mayor's office also reflect the high-quality principles and standards recommended by the National Association of Charter School Authorizers.[16]

CHARTER SCHOOL EFFECTS ON ACHIEVEMENT

When student achievement is considered, research on charter schools reveals some positive, some negative, and some neutral effects. In a review of forty-one studies focusing on student test scores, Betts and Tang found that research on charter schools shows that the overall difference in student achievement outcomes between charter schools and public schools is null.[17] However, the authors report that charter schools appear to outperform traditional public schools in two areas: elementary school reading and middle school math. As in most efforts to examine school effects, this line of research faces the challenge of addressing varying policy contexts, differences in school missions, governance, and instruction, along with issues of selection bias.

One set of charter school studies—lottery-in/lottery-out studies—used a methodological design with strong internal validity in order to diminish concerns about selection bias when achievement effects are assessed. Selection bias concerns researchers who study schools of choice, because students who select into charter schools may not be typical of the larger population of traditional public school students in ways that may influence achievement. If selection bias is not controlled for statistically, the charter school effect may reflect the unobservable reasons that a student selected a charter school rather than the true effect of attending a charter school. In the lottery-in/lottery-out studies, researchers take advantage of oversubscribed charter schools (schools whose number of applicants exceeds capacity) that must use random lotteries to admit students. The studies compare students who win the lottery and attend charter schools to students who lose the lottery and attend traditional public schools. Because both sets of students applied to attend the charter schools, the lottery serves as a mechanism to eliminate the unobservable differences that may influence student achievement. With selection bias eliminated, the only difference between the student groups is whether or not they won the lottery.

A number of studies of charter school student achievement use the lottery-in/lottery-out research design.[18] In general, these studies show positive results. Unfortunately, a major problem with lottery studies is that they often lack external validity. In other words, the findings cannot be generalized beyond the students who apply to attend an oversubscribed charter school, and the oversubscribed charter schools may be quite different from the average charter school.

When lottery data are not available, researchers often turn to longitudinal data and alternative model specifications to limit selection bias in the estimation of charter school achievement effects. One option involves matching students who attend charter schools with students who attend traditional public schools on observable student characteristics.[19] This strategy relies on the assumption that the measured student characteristics used to match students adequately control for any unobservable differences between students. This assumption can be significant, especially when the number and quality of student-level variables are limited.

Our study relies on a second methodological option for controlling for section bias: the student fixed-effects model. This strategy estimates the effect of attending a charter school by holding constant the characteristics of the student and comparing the gains a student experienced when attending a traditional public school with the gains the same student experienced in a charter school. Because the model estimates the charter effect for students who attend both kinds of schools, the student fixed-effects model diminishes selection bias.

Nevertheless, other limitations exist.[20] Because the charter effect is based on students who switch between charter and traditional public schools, the switchers, especially students who switch later in their academic careers, may not be representative of the entire charter school population. In effect, results from student fixed-effects models may generalize only to students who switch between school types and not to students who enter a charter school in the entry grade level and stay in the charter school until the final grade offered. Moreover, this model relies on the assumption that past gain trajectories predict future gain trajectories. Students who experience a dip in achievement before making the switch to a charter school violate this assumption, and the subsequent gain experienced in the charter school could overestimate the true impact. Although these concerns are valid, we consider the student fixed-effects model a better strategy for estimating charter school effects than matching techniques.

The conflicting research evidence and theories about what to expect concerning charter school effectiveness make it difficult to state a specific hypothesis about the overall achievement effect of charter schools.[21] However, we believe that the Indianapolis charter school initiative produced greater achievement gains for students than traditional public schools because of the support received by charter schools and because of the underlying theory that charter school autonomy in exchange for accountability leads to educational innovation.[22] Given this belief, we hypothesize that charter school students in Indianapolis made greater gains in mathematics and reading achievement when they attended charter schools than when they attended traditional public schools, but when the students initially switched from a traditional public school to a charter school, the switch possibly resulted in a temporary decrease in student achievement.[23] Thus, we hypothesize that although charter school students may experience an initial loss in achievement levels when transitioning to a charter school, over time they experience greater achievement gains than those they experienced while attending traditional public schools.

DATA

For the analyses that follow, we rely on student-level data from the Northwest Evaluation Association. NWEA contracts with districts like Indianapolis to provide interim assessment data to schools and teachers in mathematics, reading, and language arts. Roughly 4,200 districts in 12,300 schools in forty-nine states and the District of Columbia currently partner with NWEA. The group administers computerized adaptive assessments in the fall and spring of each academic year, but these tests are not used as high-stakes assessments for state or federal accountability.

Charter and traditional public schools in Indianapolis partnered with NWEA for four school years between 2002–2003 and 2005–2006, providing two test points of data per academic year for students in grades 2 through 10 for the charter schools, and grades 2 through 9 for the traditional public schools.[24] The longitudinal data allowed us to follow individual students for the four years as long as they attended an Indianapolis charter or traditional public school. To present consistent results with other charter schools studies, we calculated achievement gains across academic years from spring to spring, as well as within-academic-year gains from fall to spring. Moreover, we report effect sizes as standard deviations to allow for easy comparison with other charter school studies.

Table 3.1 presents enrollment and grade configuration data for the charter schools in operation during the period of this study. In the 2002–2003 school year, the mayor's office authorized three charter schools, enrolling a total of 479 students. By the fourth year of this study, the mayor's office had authorized twelve schools, enrolling 2,768 students. Approximately 1.2 percent of public school students attended mayor's office charter schools in 2002–2003. The proportion of public school students attending mayor's office charter schools grew to 2.4 percent in 2003–2004, to 4.3 percent in 2004–2005, and to 7.4 percent in 2005–2006.

Table 3.2 presents descriptive statistics for the two math samples: spring to spring and fall to spring. The spring-to-spring sample includes 40,263 student-year records, and the fall-to-spring sample includes 52,648 student-year records. Table 3.3 presents descriptive statistics for the two reading samples. For reading, the spring-to-spring sample includes 39,748 student-year records, and the fall-to-spring sample includes 52,315 student-year records. Note that compared with the number of students who attend only public

TABLE 3.1 Indianapolis mayor's office charter schools

	2002–2003		2003–2004		2004–2005		2005–2006	
	Grades	Enrollment	Grades	Enrollment	Grades	Enrollment	Grades	Enrollment
21st Century Charter School	K–6	117	K–7	159	K–8	187	K–9	301
Christel House Academy	K–4	230	K–5	273	K–6	340	K–7	358
Flanner House Elementary	K–4	132	K–5	165	K–6	202	K–7	223
Andrew J. Brown Academy			K–5	389	K–6	490	K–7	572
Charles A. Tindley Accelerated					8–9	138	7–10	241
KIPP Indianapolis College Preparatory					5	83	5–6	167
Indianapolis Metropolitan Career Academy 1					9	49	9–10	88
Indianapolis Metropolitan Career Academy 2					9	51	9–10	86
Southeast Neighborhood School of Excellence					K–3	115	K–4	178
21st Century Charter School—Fountain Square							6–10	160
Decatur Discovery Academy							9–11	97
Indianapolis Lighthouse Charter School							PK–5	297
Charter schools as percentage of total public enrollment in Indianapolis	1.2%		2.5%		4.3%		7.4%	

TABLE 3.2 Sample descriptive statistics, math

	SPRING–SPRING SAMPLE						FALL–SPRING SAMPLE			
	TPS-CPS	CPS-TPS	CPS only	TPS only	TPS-CPS	CPS-TPS	CPS only	TPS only		
Number of students	669	64	982	38,548	931	89	1,774	49,854		
% black	70.0	75.0	74.9	56.4	71.3	73.3	69.2	57.8		
% Hispanic	5.1	3.1	4.3	9.6	3.5	3.4	4.4	9.3		
% white	23.3	18.7	16.9	30.2	22.8	19.1	21.6	29.1		
% other race	1.9	3.1	3.9	3.8	2.4	4.5	4.7	3.8		
% grade 2	2.4	1.6	2.6	2.0	4.9	18.0	23.4	4.3		
% grade 3	18.5	28.1	30.4	16.2	16.0	18.0	19.1	14.5		
% grade 4	20.3	18.7	22.5	15.9	19.9	21.3	13.5	15.3		
% grade 5	18.1	25.0	16.6	16.3	17.3	22.5	14.1	15.9		
% grade 6	14.0	18.7	11.3	13.6	12.1	12.4	7.2	13.3		
% grade 7	8.2	4.7	6.4	12.9	10.3	5.6	4.7	14.3		
% grade 8	7.6	1.6	1.7	12.8	7.9	1.1	4.3	12.0		
% grade 9	7.5	1.6	2.9	10.2	7.9	1.1	8.2	10.5		
% grade 10	3.3	0	5.4	0	3.5	0	5.4	0		
% mobility	44	42	0.8	10	40	41	0.6	10.9		
% first year in a charter	45	0	NA	NA	44	0	NA	NA		
% attend a first-year charter	24	0	0.4	NA	20	10	20	NA		
% TPS test scores	25	69	0	100	35	66	0	100		
Average yearly gain (SD)	0.135 (0.786)	0.146 (0.602)	0.188 (0.713)	−0.006 (0.722)	0.230 (0.700)	0.052 (0.548)	0.329 (0.721)	0.005 (0.653)		

TABLE 3.3 Sample descriptive statistics, reading

	SPRING–SPRING SAMPLE				FALL–SPRING SAMPLE			
	TPS-CPS	CPS-TPS	CPS only	TPS only	TPS-CPS	CPS-TPS	CPS only	TPS only
Number of students	645	60	800	37,973	916	90	1,730	49,579
% black	70.0	75.0	71.4	56.6	71.7	72.2	69.4	58.1
% Hispanic	4.7	0	5.0	9.1	3.7	2.2	4.4	8.9
% white	22.9	21.7	19.4	30.5	22.3	22.2	21.5	29.2
% other race	2.5	3.3	4.2	3.8	2.3	3.3	4.7	3.8
% grade 2	2.0	1.7	3.6	2.2	4.3	18.9	23.5	4.2
% grade 3	18.4	31.7	32.7	16.1	16.8	18.9	19.3	14.7
% grade 4	21.2	20.0	21.6	15.9	20.0	18.9	12.7	15.6
% grade 5	17.5	21.7	14.9	16.5	16.7	22.2	14.2	16.1
% grade 6	13.2	16.7	9.6	14.0	12.2	13.3	7.5	13.5
% grade 7	9.5	5.0	6.1	12.9	11.0	5.6	4.8	13.8
% grade 8	7.4	1.7	1.9	12.2	8.0	1.1	4.6	11.5
% grade 9	7.3	1.7	4.0	10.0	7.3	1.1	8.1	10.6
% grade 10	3.4	0	5.5	0	3.7	0	5.4	0
% mobility	43	43	1	11	39	42	0.7	11
% first year in a charter	45	0	NA	NA	43	0	NA	NA
% attend a first-year charter	24	0	0.7	NA	19	11	NA	NA
% TPS test scores	26	73	0	100	36	65	19	100
Average yearly gain (SD)	0.089 (0.782)	0.116 (0.616)	0.172 (0.662)	−0.001 (0.715)	0.218 (0.810)	0.145 (0.721)	0.312 (0.804)	−0.003 (0.669)

schools, the number of students who attend only charter schools or who move between charter schools and traditional public schools was small. For example, the spring-to-spring sample includes 669 records from students who switched from traditional public schools to charters, 64 records from students who switched from charter schools to traditional public schools, 982 records from students who attended only charter schools, and 38,548 records from students who attended only traditional public schools. In some cases, a student moved between school types midway through the school year, and in these cases we excluded records for that student for that school year.

Overall, the descriptive statistics for both math and reading in each type of sample indicate that the sets of students who switched between charter schools and traditional public schools and students who attended only charter schools contain a higher percentage of black students than the group of students who attended only traditional public schools in Indianapolis.[25] The data also suggest that students in Indianapolis are highly mobile: some 10 percent of records among students in traditional public schools occur after the student made a nonstructural move (a move that did not occur at the transition point between elementary and middle school or between middle and high school). Nearly half of the student-year records for students who switched between charter schools and traditional public schools came from the year after the move occurred, indicated by the data showing that 45 percent of the student records for students who switched to charters are from the first year that the student attended a charter. Moreover, 24 percent of student-year records for students attending charter schools are from the first year of the charter school's operation.

When we look at the mean achievement gains in the descriptive statistics for both the spring-to-spring samples and the fall-to-spring samples, it appears that students who attended charter schools at some point during the four years of the study experienced greater average achievement gains than students who attended only traditional public schools. For example, in the math spring-to-spring sample, students who always attended charter schools experienced average annual achievement gains of 0.188 standard deviations. Students who switched to charter schools experienced average annual achievement gains of 0.135 standard deviations. Students who switched from charter schools to traditional public schools gained an average of 0.146 standard deviations. Finally, the traditional public school students experienced average annual achievement gains of −0.006 standard deviations. Although these descriptive statistics represent only the mean gains for students, they suggest that students who attended charter schools in Indianapolis experienced greater gains than students in traditional public schools.

METHODS

To examine the overall effect of attending a charter school in Indianapolis, we specified a model that included achievement gains as a function of whether a student attended a charter school. The model controlled for nonstructural moves, individual student fixed effects, and grade-by-year fixed effects.[26]

We also adapted the general model by excluding the overall charter variable and including charter variables that estimate charter effects for students by the year they enrolled in a charter school (first year attending a charter, second or more years attending a charter, and unknown year in charter for students who did not switch into charters during the study period), the charter school's year of operation (first year in operation or second or more years in operation), and charter school interacted with student race or ethnicity.

RESULTS

Table 3.4 presents results from our four achievement models for spring-to-spring gains and fall-to-spring gains. The first section presents the overall charter school effect estimates. In the spring-to-spring math sample, charter school switchers in Indianapolis experience positive and statistically significant annual gains of 0.221 standard deviations compared with the gains they experienced while attending traditional public schools. Compared with findings from previous studies of charter schools, these effect sizes are relatively large in magnitude.[27] The spring-to-spring reading sample showed positive but not statistically significant results, suggesting that Indianapolis charter school students experience similar achievement gains in reading compared to gains the same students experienced in the traditional public schools. The results from the overall model for spring-to-spring gains align with findings from several of the previous studies of charter schools that find mixed results for math and reading.[28]

The second section of table 3.4 examines the charter school effect by the year that students enrolled in charter schools. The findings for the spring-to-spring sample suggest that charter school switchers made similar achievement gains in both math and reading in their first year at the charter school compared to the achievement gains they made while enrolled in traditional public schools. By the second year or more of attendance in a charter school, however, students experienced positive and statistically significant gains in math. The achievement gains in reading for the second year or more remained insignificant.

The third section of table 3.4 presents the charter school impact by year of charter school operation. Previous research found that it may take time

TABLE 3.4   **Charter school effect on achievement in Indianapolis**

	SPRING–SPRING		FALL–SPRING	
	Math	Reading	Math	Reading
Overall charter school effect				
Charter	0.221*	0.047	0.305***	0.304**
	(0.124)	(0.100)	(0.078)	(0.101)
Charter by student year enrolled				
First year in charter	0.095	0.028	0.314***	0.319***
	(0.227)	(0.306)	(0.078)	(0.093)
Two or more years in charter	0.215*	0.024	0.356*	0.371
	(0.114)	(0.099)	(0.180)	(0.239)
Unknown year in charter	0.307	0.224	0.043	−0.073
	(0.345)	(0.267)	(0.148)	(0.168)
Charter by year of operation				
First year in operation	−0.015	−0.178*	0.261**	0.198**
	(0.129)	(0.093)	(0.090)	(0.087)
Two or more years in operation	0.354*	0.182	0.335***	0.374**
	(0.193)	(0.125)	(0.074)	(0.131)
Charter by student race or ethnicity				
Charter* black	0.242*	0.125	0.292**	0.407***
	(0.139)	(0.114)	(0.100)	(0.118)
Charter* Hispanic	0.444	0.883*	0.512	0.265
	(0.310)	(0.446)	(0.341)	(0.261)
Charter* white	0.115	−0.239	0.297**	0.062
	(0.229)	(0.146)	(0.115)	(0.090)
Charter* other race	0.443	−0.255	0.563*	−0.290
	(0.373)	(0.193)	(0.280)	(0.209)

*p<.10 **p<.05 ***p<.01

Each model includes year and grade-level dummies, year-by-grade indicators, an overall mobility dummy, and a constant term. Robust standard errors, adjusted for the clustering of students within schools, are in parentheses.

for charter schools to show improvements in student performance.[29] Our results are consistent with this research. In both the math and the reading spring-to-spring samples, the coefficients are negative for charter school switchers who attend a charter school in its first year, and in reading the coefficient is statistically significant. However, students who attend a charter in its second year or more of operation see positive achievement gains in math (0.354 standard deviations) and achievement gains in reading similar to the gains students experienced when attending traditional public schools. The findings confirm the theory that charter schools may need an academic year or longer to put in place the instructional practices that positively impact student performance.

The final section of data in table 3.4 presents results from the models that examine the impact of attending charter schools based on a student's race or ethnicity. For the spring-to-spring sample, it appears that black students make greater gains in math, and Hispanic students make greater gains in reading, compared with the gains they experienced in traditional public schools. Again, it should be noted that the magnitude of the findings—0.242 standard deviations for black students in math, and 0.883 standard deviations in reading for Hispanic students—are quite large when compared with findings from other charter school studies. White students, students of other races or ethnicities, black students in reading, and Hispanic students in math experience similar gains in charter schools to those they experienced in traditional public schools.

The fall-to-spring models provide somewhat different findings. Overall, the fall-to-spring models suggest that charter school switchers experience positive gains: 0.305 and 0.304 standard deviations in math and reading, respectively. Moreover, the findings are positive and statistically significant in the first year at a charter school (0.314 and 0.319 standard deviations in math and reading, respectively); this result is somewhat surprising given that previous research typically found negative impacts on student achievement during the year that students move to a new school.[30]

The fall-to-spring model measures the gain in achievement during one academic year. If students experience a negative bump in achievement in the fall right after the move and then experience normal gains for the spring test, then the difference between these scores could bias the charter school gains upward when compared with the gain trajectory experienced in the traditional public schools. The results for students in their second or later year in a charter school for the fall-to-spring model provide some evidence of positive bias in the first-year gains.[31] The fall-to-spring gain for math in the second year or more remains positive and statistically significant, but the reading gain is not statistically significant. This result suggests that following an initial negative bump in achievement after moving to a charter school, students make reading gains similar to the gains they experienced while in traditional public schools. The findings from the second year or more in a charter school for the fall-to-spring sample align with the overall findings from the spring-to-spring sample.

DISCUSSION

Indianapolis presents a unique case to study the effects of charter schools on student achievement. The Indianapolis mayor's office continues to approve new charter schools, and they enroll a growing percentage of the public school student population. Using data from the time of Bart Peterson's tenure as mayor, we examined the impact of attending charter schools on students who switched from traditional public schools to one of the mayor's charter schools. The findings suggest that students who switched from a traditional public school to a charter school made a good decision in that they were better off after the switch. The students who switched to a charter school and stayed in a charter school for longer than one year experienced greater annual gains in math than if they had stayed in the traditional public schools, but their gains in reading were similar to the gains they experienced while attending traditional public schools.

Our data and analyses include several limitations. First, only small samples of students switch to and attend charter schools, and our longitudinal panel includes only four years' worth of data. Second, a possible explanation for the positive findings in the early years of the initiative is that the students who made the first moves to attend charter schools stood to benefit most from attending the charter schools. Similarly, the first charter schools to open under the mayor's initiative may have been the strongest in terms of vision, support, and instructional design. Finally, the assessments used for the outcome variable in our models were used as accountability measures for the mayor's charter schools, but it is not clear that the traditional public schools were using the assessments in the same way. In other words, the assessments were high stakes for the charter schools but not necessarily for the traditional public schools. This difference becomes especially relevant when one considers that the district stopped using NWEA after the 2005–2006 school year. The mayor's office charter school effort needs further research to confirm the impact on student achievement of attending these schools.

The mayor's charter school initiative received national recognition, and the findings in this study suggest that the accolades the mayor's office received for developing a strong charter school authorizing process are warranted. However, what may explain the effects observed in our analyses? In what follows we provide some avenues not only for further research but also for reflection when charter school policy is framed in local settings.

Several factors came together in the mayor's initiative that may explain the positive effects on achievement. First, as Smrekar argues, there was a long-term effort to build local capacity to make the Indianapolis context ripe for charter school reform.[32] In the late 1990s, local and state politicians, the Chamber of Commerce, local philanthropy, and local and national advocacy organizations played key roles in setting the stage for the Indianapolis charter reform.

Second, as an independent authorizer outside the local school district, the mayor's office probably played a key role in providing conditions for positive student achievement gains. Authorizers are critical to the process of approving high-quality charter school applications and to the process of holding charter schools accountable, especially if, like those in Indianapolis, they emphasize rigor, transparency, and positive outcomes. Focusing on the quality (rather than the quantity) of charter schools also seems to be a positive attribute of the Indianapolis charter schools.[33] The mayor's office approved strong charter school applications that met specific educational needs and increased the range of educational choices in Indianapolis. Charter school operators as well as charter school authorizers can draw on these lessons when creating charter schools that target the specific needs of students and schools that are located in neighborhoods that need high-quality options.

Third, the organization and instructional designs of the schools may further explain the achievement results we observed. Several researchers argue that those conditions closest to the students (teaching, instruction, and curriculum) have the greatest impact on student learning.[34] For example, the instructional designs supplied by local or national providers, such as KIPP, may offer students opportunities that link more closely to mathematics achievement than reading achievement, something that would explain the effects in our analyses. In the case of Indianapolis, some evidence exists that the charter schools differ in instructional conditions when compared with traditional public schools.[35] Specifically, Berends et al. found that charter school teachers went into more depth in their instruction of mathematics than did traditional public school teachers.[36] However, the charter school teachers in the study were more likely to teach basic tasks than higher-order thinking tasks in mathematics. It may be that the focus on back to basics in mathematics in the charter schools helped students on the NWEA assessment, even though higher-order thinking skills are more desirable for long-term learning.

Finally, the role of parents in selecting a school may impact how students perform. Stein et al. found that the majority of parents who selected Indianapolis charter schools cited academics as their top priority when choosing a school.[37] Nearly 65 percent of the parents in this study removed their children from traditional public schools that were failing to make Adequate Yearly Progress (AYP). However, despite the high numbers of parents who cited academics as a priority and also cited the low achievement levels of their children's former schools, only one-third of the parents moved their children to charter schools meeting AYP. Although many of the charter schools failed to meet AYP (and it should be noted that AYP is a blunt indicator of school performance), the families that selected charter schools believed that they chose schools for academic reasons. As a result, the act of choosing may have provided a positive bump to students who switched to charter schools.

All these conditions are worthy of serious reflection for researchers and policy makers. Researchers need to further study achievement effects to explain the social context in which charter school effects occur, whether positive, negative, or neutral. In addition, with the continuing expansion of charter schools, policy makers need to further reflect on those cases, such as Indianapolis, in which some positive conditions seem to exist in local capacity, strength of authorizer, school organizational and instructional conditions, and parental choice.

Eighth Graders and Compliance

Social Capital and School Sector Impacts on the
Noncognitive Skills of Early Adolescents

Paul E. Peterson and Martina G. Viarengo[1]

In his seminal book *The Adolescent Society,* James S. Coleman identifies a disjunction between the high school's manifest educational function, which is under the direction of adults, and its latent social function, quite inimical to educational purposes, which is under peer group control. For adolescents, the focus at school is on the sports stars, cheerleaders, and other members of the leading crowd, known more for smart dressing than for smarts per se. Those who study hard and get good grades are edged to the social sidelines. For those who succeed scholastically, it must appear to have been "gained without special efforts, without doing anything beyond the required work." Otherwise, one is socially isolated by "the crowd."[2]

It is the way in which the schools are organized that is the problem, said Coleman.[3] Like jails, the military, and factories, schools are run by "an administrative corps" that makes demands upon a larger group (students, prisoners, soldiers, workers). In response, the larger group develops a set of norms that governs the choices individuals make: "The same process which occurs among prisoners in a jail and among workers in a factory is found among students in a school. The institution is different, but the demands are there, and the students develop a collective response to these demands. This response takes a similar form to that of workers in industry—holding down effort to a level which can be maintained by all. The students' name for the rate-buster is the 'curve-raiser,'. . . and their methods of enforcing the work-restricting norms are similar to those of workers—ridicule, kidding, exclusion from the group."[4]

A student's psychological sense of self is shaped less by the teachers and administrators at the school than by the peer group culture. Sports stars and members of the leading crowd are much less likely than other students to say, "If I could trade, I would be someone different from myself."[5] Self-esteem and a sense of social isolation are driven less by academic failure than by the inability to negotiate successfully the peer group culture.

More recent studies have echoed Coleman's insights into the way schools function in adolescent society. To maintain order a political bargain is struck, report Powell and colleagues in their book *The Shopping Mall High School*.[6] Students and teachers alike agree to comport themselves properly as long as expectations are minimal.

> Students chose courses that are easy, met at convenient times, and enrolled their friends. They did homework, as long as it was not too much . . . A boy said he deliberately constructed his schedule to avoid homework, so he would have time to "work, play and be with my friends." They never complain when little is expected of them. "Why should we? We just want to get out." They thought their teachers probably felt the same way. They are as much "goof-offs" as the students, as much anxious for the end of school so they too could begin their second jobs. Avoidance treaties were mutually advantageous—like had found like.[7]

"No more important finding has emerged from the inquiries of our study," wrote Theodore Sizer, "than that the American high school student, *as student,* is all too often docile, compliant, and without initiative."[8]

In his later work, Coleman developed a "social capital" theory that enabled him to distinguish between adult capacities to control the functions of Catholic compared with public high schools. Even though the latent social function continued to be controlled by the peer group, Coleman and Hoffer theorized that the social capital available at Catholic schools gave them a greater capacity to offset that culture, something that resulted in higher test score performance of students in Catholic than in public schools.[9] In their view, conversations among regularly interacting Catholic parents, teachers, and parishioners create an adult framework that reinforces a set of social norms that support the schools' educational mission, an intangible resource they dubbed social capital. They speak of "intergenerational closure," a space where parents know their children's friends' parents, and a "communal organization" that develops a great sense of community that is conducive to high levels of engagement on the part of students and teachers. Offsetting the ordinary demands of peer group culture is "the importance of the embeddedness of young persons in the enclaves of adults most proximate to them, first and most prominently the family and second, a surrounding community of adults."[10] In short, social capital theory was applied to education to explain student readiness to comply with educationally productive social norms, such as homework completion, lower absenteeism rates, and greater levels of academic engagement.[11]

Intergenerational closure—conversations among parents of students and the teachers of students—could prevent political bargains of the kind Powell and his colleagues observed. Communication among the adults who sustained the Catholic school altered incentives for teachers and students. Teachers were expected to hold students accountable, and students were expected to be engaged in their studies. Absenteeism was corralled, and homework assignments had to be completed.

The enforcement of public social norms is more easily controlled by the adult community, however, than is the psychological state of the individual adolescent. Whether adolescents have a strong sense of self-esteem or a feeling that their destiny is under their own control is very much shaped by peer group influences, according to Coleman in his early study of adolescent society. Even if intergenerational closure was achieved in Catholic settings, that did not necessarily mean that it could prevent the peer group culture from shaping the students' subjective psychological states. Coleman and his colleagues found no difference in the impact of Catholic versus public schools on student "self-esteem" or "fate control."[12] When it came to an adolescent's internal feelings, the peer group culture appeared as all pervasive in Catholic as in public schools.

Social capital theory has since been applied in numerous ways, most notably by Robert Putnam as an explanation for declines in civic trust in the United States.[13] An anthropological study of the inner workings of Catholic schools by Bryk, Lee, and Holland found a culture and set of practices within Catholic schools that were consistent with Coleman's expectations.[14] Mokan and Tekin found that students at Catholic high schools show less propensity to bad and risky behavior as well as drug consumption.[15] Figlio and Ludwig found that such students exhibit lower rates of arrest and use of hard drugs.[16] Also, Belfield, by examining data from the National Household Education Survey of 1999, showed that the community service participation rate of students in Catholic high schools was higher, as were their civic skills and their political tolerance.[17]

However, all such applications of social capital theory in the study of sector impacts have focused on high school students. Virtually no attention has been given to students in their middle school years, even though the adolescent peer group culture is known to be well established by the time young people reach the age of fourteen, the typical age of an eighth-grade student. With the release of the results from the eighth-grade wave of the Early Childhood Longitudinal Study, Kindergarten Class of 1998–1999 (ECLS-K), it is now possible to see whether social capital theory also applies to early adolescence, that is, whether information from a nationally representative sample of eighth graders provides evidence that those in Catholic schools are more ready than those in public schools to comply with educationally productive social norms.

Sponsored by the National Center for Education Statistics (NCES) of the U.S. Department of Education, the ECLS-K, beginning in 1998, tracked a panel of students from kindergarten through eighth grade in public and private schools. In addition to information on student test score performance, the survey meticulously collected not only a host of family background characteristics from parents but also information about an array of noncognitive attributes from teachers, students, and parents during each wave of the survey. This practice allowed, for the first time, the opportunity for analysts to look at the impact of the Catholic and public school sectors on a variety of outcomes that social capital theory was designed to explain.

PRIOR RESEARCH

We do not review here the rich and diverse literature that has estimated sector impacts on educational achievement and attainment. It is sufficient to say that the quality of that research has greatly improved since the initial Coleman study, but no consensus has yet to be achieved as to whether students learn more in private schools in general, or in Catholic schools in particular, than in public schools. The evidence for a positive Catholic school impact seems to us to be stronger for longer-term outcomes—such as high school graduation, college attendance, and earnings some years later—than on test scores per se, suggesting perhaps that the social capital available to Catholic schools gives them a greater capacity than public schools to impart noncongitive skills that have beneficial long-term consequencs. Positive Catholic high school impacts have been found on educational attainment, on the probability of completing high school, and on the probability of going to college.[18] In many of the studies, positive effects have been reported especially for ethnic minorities and students from disadvantaged socioeconomic backgrounds.[19] But the topic remains so controversial that two reviews of the literature published back to back in the same journal reached substantially different conclusions concerning the benefits of school vouchers that widen the door to private schooling. Neal discusses the possible gains in the productivity of the U.S. K–12 education system arising from the introduction of a large-scale voucher program.[20] Ladd, on the other hand, casts doubts on the likelihood of these programs to generate substantial gains in student achievement.[21]

One fact is clear: more information is available on sector impacts on high school performance than on elementary and middle school performance.

The only elementary school studies of sector impacts that use data from a nationally representative longitudinal survey rely on information available from the fifth-grade wave of the same survey for which we now have data through eighth grade. In one of these studies, Reardon et al. found no sector impact in reading, and a negative private sector impact in mathematics.[22] Peterson and Llaudet, performing a similar analysis, identified positive private sector impacts in the reading performance of those who had had low test score performance in first grade.[23] However, they found no significant impact in math for this group. Among those with high test performance in first grade, these authors found beneficial public school impacts in math, but no differences between the two sectors in reading. Blacks and Hispanics benefited in reading by attending a private school, whereas whites and Asians benefited in math from attending a public school. No sector impacts have yet been reported by either team—or any other investigator—for the eighth-grade wave of the ECLS-K. On the other hand, Carbonaro did not find any consistent advantage of private schools in providing learning opportunities at the kindergarten level.[24]

Despite these studies of sector impacts on the cognitive performance of students, as measured by test scores, no one has used information from ECLS-K or any other nationally representative longitudinal survey to estimate sector impacts on noncongitive skills. That is unfortunate, because a growing number of classical and behavioral economists, to say nothing of sociologists, policy analysts, and educators, have come to believe that the acquisition of noncongitive skills is at least as important for life outcomes as is student test score performance.[25]

THE ECLS-K SURVEY

As part of ECLS-K, NCES conducted seven waves of data collection: fall 1998 (beginning of kindergarten), spring 1998 (end of kindergarten), fall 1999 (beginning of first grade), spring 2000 (end of first grade), spring 2002 (third grade), spring 2004 (fifth grade), and spring 2007 (eighth grade). Attrition from one wave to the next was substantial; students could not easily be tracked as they moved from one school to another, and some parents withdrew their consent, which had to be obtained at each wave of the study. Initially, data were collected from 22,670 students in 1,280 schools. That number fell to 17,760 students in 2,010 schools in first grade, an especially high rate of attrition that was probably due to the especially heterogeneous arrangements for kindergarten instruction. By third grade, the number had fallen to 15,310 students; in fifth grade, the number was 11,820, and in eighth grade the number was 9,730. See table 4.1 for more detail.

TABLE 4.1   **Number of students and schools participating in the Early Child-hood Longitudinal Study—Kindergarten Class of 1998–1999 (ECLS-K) waves in first grade, third grade, fifth grade, and eighth grade, by school sector**

			SCHOOL SECTOR			
	Public	Catholic	Private, other religious	Private secular	School sector unknown	Total
Kindergarten						
Students	17,780	2,510	1,450	930		22,670
Schools	910	120	150	90		1,280
First grade						
Students	13,540	1,980	950	420	880	17,760
Schools	1,650	170	130	70		2,010
Third grade						
Students	11,960	1,680	760	220	680	15,310
Schools	2,250	230	140	60		2,670
5th grade						
Students	9,330	1,320	580	180	420	11,820
Schools	1,180	130	80	20		1,400
8th grade						
Students	7,810	980	450	170	320	9,730
Schools	2,270	240	150	100		2,750

In order to comply with the requirements of the U.S. Department of Education, all unweighted sample size numbers presented are rounded to the nearest 10'. Totals therefore do not add up correctly due to rounding.

There was substantial attrition across the waves, but attrition rates do not introduce bias here if they are consistent across school sectors on observed as well as unobserved characteristics. Table 4.2 provides descriptive statistics, separately, for students in the public and Catholic sectors observed in first and eighth grades, as well as for those observed in first grade but not again in eighth. In the column labeled "(e)" we report the statistical significance of differences in the attrition rates from the public and Catholic samples by background characteristic. For most characteristics, sector differentials in attrition rates are not statistically significant. For example, attrition rates in the two sectors are similar for those having below-average math scores; for those from lower socioeconomic backgrounds; for blacks, whites, and Hispanics; and for those not living with their parents. However, attrition in the public sector was greater for those having lower reading scores, for those who were Asian, for those whose mothers did not finish high school, and for those from large towns and cities. As discussed later, the use of propensity score matching reduces the likelihood of selection bias from differential attrition rates, but if attrition on unobserved characteristics is not well correlated with observed ones, estimates may be biased.

Certain kinds of students are excluded from our analysis. All those who attended non-Catholic private schools are excluded on the grounds that the number of such schools participating in ECLS-K was small, the number of participating students in later waves became very small, and the category is so heterogeneous that it is difficult to interpret results. We also exluded the students who changed sectors on the grounds that we could not estimate sector impact for this group without making strong assumptions. We also excluded the students whose geographic location changed dramatically—from one of the four regions of the country to another, or from one type of community to another (urban, suburban, rural)—because we could not assign location without making strong assumptions. To check whether the exclusion of students who moved affected the results, we separately estimated impacts that included those who had changed location or sector (or both), assigning them to the sector and location reported in first grade. Sector impacts do not differ significantly from those reported in the main analysis, although impacts attenuate slightly, as one would expect given the student migration from one sector or location to another.[26]

After exclusions, the number of eighth graders remaining in the analytic sample consists of a maximum of 7,810 students in 2,270 public schools, and 980 students in 240 Catholic schools. Numbers vary slightly from one estimation to the next, depending on response rates to specific items. Table 4.2 provides the summary statistics for the full sample and the analytic sample used for the ordered probit model. As shown in the table, the characteristics of those included in the analytic sample resemble closely those of the entire sample. Table 4.2 also identifies the characteristics of students included in the propensity score matching models. As is to be expected, differences in the background characteristics of the students in the Catholic and public sectors are much smaller in the matched comparison than those in the analytic sample, and for that reason we place greatest weight on the results from the matched comparison analysis.

For baseline information and for initial sector assignment, we rely on the data collected at the end of first grade, because test score information of the kind collected in a national survey is generally thought to be more reliable by that age. Also, in many parts of the country, sector arrangements for those in kindergarten are strikingly different from those that emerge beginning in the first grade of school, because many private schools offer preschool education through kindergarten but not beyond.

TABLE 4.2 Characteristics of students observed in first grade who were and were not observed in eighth grade

Background	Students in public school in first grade		Students in Catholic school in first grade		Difference (a–b) and (c–d) is statistically significant (e)
	Observed in eighth grade (a)	Not observed in eighth grade (b)	Observed in eighth grade (c)	Not observed in eighth grade (d)	
Math first grade	55.0 (15.88)[a]	51.8 (15.82)	60.6 (14.27)	57.4 (15.08)	No
Reading first grade	68.0 (20.13)	64.6 (20.31)	75.4 (18.79)	71.6 (20.84)	Yes
Male	0.50	0.53	0.50	0.50	No
Female	0.50	0.47	0.50	0.50	No
White	0.58	0.47	0.74	0.69	No
African American	0.12	0.21	0.03	0.09	No
Hispanic	0.18	0.19	0.13	0.13	No
Asian	0.06	0.08	0.06	0.05	Yes
Other	0.05	0.06	0.04	0.04	Yes
Disability	0.15	0.15	0.09	0.13	No
Non-English-speaking home	0.81	0.73	0.91	0.85	No
SES	−0.08 (0.97)	−0.25 (0.96)	0.64 (0.83)	0.41 (0.87)	Yes
Mother did not finish high school	0.13	0.16	0.01	0.02	Yes
Mother finished high school	0.28	0.27	0.17	0.21	No
Mother finished college	0.14	0.10	0.32	0.22	No
Mother with more than college	0.12	0.19	0.15	0.19	No
Poverty	0.20	0.27	0.02	0.05	No
Number of siblings	1.54	1.56	1.48	1.45	No
Living with parents	0.75	0.58	0.88	0.77	No

School characteristics

Midwest	0.27	0.21	0.35	0.34	No
Northeast	0.19	0.17	0.24	0.27	No
South	0.33	0.37	0.23	0.24	No
West	0.21	0.25	0.19	0.16	No
Large town	0.15	0.17	0.27	0.23	Yes
City	0.14	0.21	0.26	0.23	Yes
Small town or rural area	0.28	0.29	0.27	0.27	No
Observations	7,050	6,500	870	1,110	

a. Standard deviations in parentheses. Math, reading, and SES have been standardized: mean = 0, std. dev. = 1. Weighted using ECLS-K sampling weights; only those respondent students who were in the sample in first grade are included. In order to comply with the requirements of the U.S. Department of Education, all unweighted sample size numbers presented are rounded to the nearest 10'.

Dependent Variables: Noncognitive Outcomes

Inasmuch as the study of noncognitive outcomes is still in its infancy in the research on Catholic school effects, no standard classification system or set of rubrics has evolved. In the early waves of the ECLS-K, the teacher questionnaires focus on students' psychological characteristics rather than on their compliance with social norms. It is not until the eighth-grade wave that the survey solicits from teachers the information needed for a solid test of social capital theory, and only in the eighth-grade wave are students asked an extended battery of questions about their own pyschological well-being. The items used to construct the self-esteem and locus of control indexes are the same as those used in the National Educational Longitudinal Study of the Class of 1988 (NELS:88), a previous U.S. Department of Education longitudinal survey that followed a cohort beginning in eighth grade. Our analysis thus focuses on results from the eighth grade wave, the wave that has the best set of indicators of both social compliance and of students' perception of their own self-worth. However, we include in Appendix A estimates of sector impacts on outcomes for fifth-grade students. Appendixes for this chapter can be found online at http://www.vanderbilt.edu/schoolchoice/.

Consistent with social capital theory, we distinguish between two sets of noncognitive outcomes: (1) conformity with social norms and (2) self-perceived psychological traits. The first set—social conformity—refers to actions easily observed by others. It is those types of outcomes that are most susceptible to control by a community of adults such as the parents and parishoners Coleman deemed critical to Catholic school success. Variables in this category include tardiness, absenteeism, homework completion, disruptive behavior, classroom attentiveness, and academic engagement. All indicators come from the teacher questionnaire except the last one, which is an index of the students' own assessment of the strength of their educational commitments and performance at school.

The second set—self-perceived psychological traits—are matters internal to the students: self-esteem, sense of control over their own destinies, and propensity to internalize the problems they face.

All variables either are single indicators or are measured by scales constructed by those responsible for the ECLS-K survey and are used by us without modification. Except to conduct a sensitivity test, we ignore data from the parent questionnaire on the grounds that parents do not have the same comparative framework teachers have when assessing compliance with social norms, nor are parents a direct source of information about a child's psychological well-being.

We do not claim that our bipartite scheme is the only way to classify non-cognitive outcomes. For example, a number of behavioral economists have suggested a "Big Five" taxonomy: agreeableness, conscientiousness, extroversion, neuroticism, and openness to experience.[27]

Our dependent variables thus consist of the following five teacher-generated indicators of student conformity to social norms, one student-generated indicator of academic engagement, and three student-generated indicators of psychological well-being. Reliability reported for these noncognitive variables is high.[28] The content of each variable is as follows:

- Conformity to social norms (the first five taken from teacher questionnaire, the sixth from the student questionnaire).
  - *Tardiness.* The teacher is asked to rate how often the student is tardy. The following five-point scale is used: "never," "rarely," "some of the time," "most of the time," "all of the time." (The scale has been reversed so that positive coefficients indicate low levels of tardiness.)
  - *Absenteeism.* The teacher is asked to rate how often the student is absent. The following five-point scale is used: "never," "rarely," "some of the time," "most of the time," "all of the time." (The scale has been reversed so that positive coefficients indicate low absenteeism.)
  - *Homework completion.* The teacher is asked to rate how often the student completes homework when assigned. The following five-point scale is used: "all of the time," "most of the time," "some of the time," "rarely," "never."
  - *Disruptive behavior.* The teacher is asked to rate how often the student is disruptive in class. The following five-point scale is used: "never," "rarely," "some of the time," "most of the time," "all of the time." (The scale has been reversed so that positive coefficients indicate nondisruptive behavior.)
  - *Attention in class.* The teacher is asked to rate the frequency with which the student pays attention. The following five-point scale is used: "all of the time," "most of the time," "some of the time," "rarely," "never."
  - *Academic engagement.* The student is asked about grades in English and perceived competence, interest in, and enjoyment of reading.
- Self-perceived psychological traits (scales constructed from items in student questionnaire)

- *Self-esteem.* A scale was constructed from student responses to seven questions about their perceptions of their own self-worth. The items included in the scale, drawn from the NELS:88 student questionnaire, were as follows: (a) I feel good about myself; (b) I feel I am a person of worth, the equal of other people; (c) I am able to do things as well as most other people; (d) On the whole, I am satisfied with myself; (e) I certainly feel useless at times; (f) At times I feel I am no good at all; and (g) I feel I do not have much to be proud of.
- *Locus of control.* A six-item index scale was constructed from responses to questions about the amount of control students had over their own lives. Items were drawn from the NELS:88 student questionnaire. The items were as follows: (a) I don't have enough control over the direction my life is taking; (b) In my life, good luck is more important than hard work for success; (c) Every time I try to get ahead, something or somebody stops me; (d) My plans hardly ever work out, so planning only makes me unhappy; (e) When I make plans, I am almost certain I can make them work; (f) Chance and luck are very important for what happens in my life.
- *Internalizing problems.* An eight-item scale was constructed from responses to the following items: (a) I feel angry when I have trouble learning; (b) I worry about taking tests; (c) I often feel lonely; (d) I feel sad a lot of the time; (e) I worry about doing well in school; (f) I worry about finishing my work; (g) I worry about having someone to hang out with at school; (h) I feel ashamed when I make mistakes at school.

All but two of these indicators are positively correlated with one another as well as with reading and math test score performance. But the indicators of social compliance have only weak relationships with the indicators of psychological well-being (see table 4.3). The six indicators of compliance with social norms have an average intercorrelation of 0.32, and the intercorrelation among the three scales measuring student self-perception of their psychological well-being is no less than 0.44. But there is only a 0.12 average intercorrelation between social-norm and psychological-trait indicators, suggesting that the two dimensions are almost completely orthogonal to one another.[29]

For indicators derived from the teacher questionnaire, most assessments are made by teachers of English because every student in the survey was assessed by that teacher and English teachers were asked the full battery of questions. But we also include observations of science and math teachers on those aspects of student behavior about which these teachers were

TABLE 4.3 Correlations among test score and noncognitive variables of eighth-grade students participating in ECLS-K

	Math eighth	Reading eighth	Academic engagement	Attention in class	Homework completion	Disruptive behavior[a]	Tardiness	Absenteeism	Self-esteem scale	Locus of control	Internalizing problem behavior
Math eighth	1.00										
Reading eighth	0.71	1.00									
Conformity to social norms											
Academic engagement	0.19	0.35	1.00								
Attention in class	0.31	0.37	0.33	1.00							
Homework completion	0.34	0.38	0.33	0.60	1.00						
Disruptive behavior	0.20	0.25	0.21	0.52	0.39	1.00					
Tardiness	0.20	0.23	0.17	0.38	0.36	0.40	1.00				
Absenteeism	0.17	0.16	0.13	0.27	0.29	0.12	0.34	1.00			
Self-perceived psychological traits											
Self-esteem scale	0.23	0.24	0.24	0.20	0.20	0.07	0.08	0.12	1.00		
Locus of control	0.31	0.35	0.26	0.25	0.27	0.14	0.15	0.13	0.59	1.00	
Internalizing problem behavior	0.15	0.13	-0.06	0.03	0.04	-0.02	0.01	0.06	0.40	0.33	1.00

a. The variables "disruptive behavior," "tardiness," "absenteeism," and "internalizing problem behavior" have been reverse scaled.

questioned. The sample of students was split randomly between the math and science teachers, leaving a smaller number of math and science teacher observations.

Independent and Control Variables

The primary independent variable of interest is school sector—whether or not a student was educated within the Catholic or the public school sector. Also included in the analysis are controls for gender, ethnic group, an indicator of disability, socioeconomic status (an index that jointly measures parental education, income, and occupational prestige), status with respect to the poverty threshold, mother's age at the birth of the first child, number of siblings, region of the country, type of community, and first-grade test scores in mathematics and reading. Socioeconomic status and first-grade mathematics and reading test scores have been standardized with a mean set to equal zero and a standard deviation set to equal 1.0. Table 4.4 provides descriptive statistics for all variables.[30]

ANALYTIC STRATEGY

An ordered probit model is used to estimate sector impacts on all students included in the analytic sample. The model is preferred over an ordinary least squares regression because many variables are not continuous.[31] However, an ordered probit model that includes all students must make strong assumptions about the comparability of the students in the two sectors, because the social composition of the two sectors differs sharply (see table 4.2). For this reason estimates are also made from matched comparison models.[32] A propensity score matching model matches control students to treated students having similar observable pretreatment characteristics.[33] The model assumes that treated and untreated groups, if similar on observable characteristics, differ only with respect to the treatment. If so, it is possible to establish the causal effect of school sector on student outcomes.

The propensity score matching estimator is implemented in two steps. First, the propensity score is estimated by using a binary choice model that estimates the propensity score as a function of the control variables measured before treatment. To improve the quality of the matches used to estimate the average effects of treatment on the treated, we restrict the analysis to those observations where the propensity score belongs to the intersection of the supports of the propensity score of treatment and control units.[34] We use nearest neighbor matching for this estimation, because it appears to be the method that minimizes group differences among many items.[35] To verify that the results of the match satisfy the balancing property hypothesis, one

TABLE 4.4 Descriptive statistics for background and dependent variables for the entire eighth-grade sample, the analytic sample, and the sample used for the matched comparison models

	ENTIRE SAMPLE			ANALYTIC SAMPLE[a]			MATCHED COMPARISON SAMPLE[b]		
	All	Public	Catholic	All	Public	Catholic	All	Public	Catholic
School sector									
Catholic	0.11	0.00	1.00	0.14	0.00	1.00	0.50	0.00	1.00
Background									
Math first grade	-0.02 (0.99)[c]	-0.05 (0.99)	0.26 (0.92)	-0.02 (1.00)	-0.08 (1.01)	0.30 (0.91)	0.30 (0.97)	0.30 (1.02)	0.30 (0.91)
Reading first grade	-0.02 (0.99)	-0.06 (0.99)	0.29 (0.88)	-0.04 (0.98)	-0.09 (0.99)	0.30 (0.88)	0.31 (0.92)	0.33 (0.96)	0.30 (0.88)
Male	0.50	0.50	0.51	0.50	0.50	0.51	0.50	0.49	0.51
Female	0.50	0.50	0.49	0.50	0.50	0.49	0.50	0.51	0.49
White	0.60	0.59	0.72	0.61	0.58	0.75	0.75	0.75	0.75
African American	0.11	0.12	0.04	0.11	0.12	0.03	0.03	0.05	0.03
Hispanic	0.18	0.18	0.14	0.18	0.18	0.13	0.13	0.13	0.12
Asian	0.06	0.06	0.06	0.06	0.05	0.06	0.06	0.07	0.06
Other	0.05	0.06	0.04	0.05	0.06	0.04	0.04	0.03	0.03
Disability	0.14	0.14	0.10	0.13	0.14	0.09	0.10	0.05	0.05
Non-English-speaking home	0.15	0.16	0.08	0.15	0.17	0.07	0.06	0.07	0.07
SES	-0.09 (1.01)	-0.17 (1.00)	0.52 (0.87)	-0.12 (1.02)	-0.22 (1.00)	0.54 (0.86)	0.53 (0.91)	0.52 (0.95)	0.54 (0.86)
Mother did not finish high school	0.084	0.09	0.01	0.09	0.10	0.01	0.02	0.02	0.01
Mother finished high school	0.21	0.22	0.12	0.21	0.22	0.12	0.13	0.14	0.12
Mother finished college	0.17	0.15	0.31	0.17	0.15	0.33	0.29	0.25	0.33

continued

TABLE 4.4 *continued*

	ENTIRE SAMPLE			ANALYTIC SAMPLE[a]			MATCHED COMPARISON SAMPLE[b]		
	All	Public	Catholic	All	Public	Catholic	All	Public	Catholic
Mother with more than college	0.21	0.20	0.24	0.08	0.06	0.14	0.12	0.11	0.14
Mother's age at first child birth	23.40	22.51	23.60	24.40	23.35	25.52	24.60	23.55	25.52
Poverty	0.19	0.21	0.04	0.20	0.23	0.03	0.03	0.03	0.03
Number of siblings	1.48	1.48	1.45	1.49	1.49	1.44	1.41	1.38	1.44
Living with parents	0.70	0.68	0.82	0.70	0.68	0.83	0.82	0.80	0.83
School characteristics									
Midwest	0.28	0.27	0.33	0.28	0.27	0.33	0.34	0.34	0.33
Northeast	0.19	0.18	0.23	0.21	0.21	0.25	0.24	0.23	0.25
South	0.33	0.34	0.23	0.29	0.30	0.21	0.21	0.21	0.22
West	0.21	0.21	0.21	0.22	0.22	0.22	0.21	0.21	0.22
Large town	0.38	0.38	0.37	0.36	0.36	0.37	0.38	0.39	0.37
City	0.29	0.26	0.52	0.31	0.28	0.54	0.53	0.51	0.54
Small town or rural area	0.33	0.36	0.12	0.32	0.36	0.09	0.09	0.10	0.09
Conformity to social norms									
Tardiness	4.52 (0.70)	4.49 (0.71)	4.72 (0.53)	4.53 (0.69)	4.48 (0.71)	4.72 (0.54)	4.64 (0.61)	4.56 (0.66)	4.72 (0.54)
Absenteeism	3.90 (0.62)	3.88 (0.62)	4.10 (0.58)	3.91 (0.62)	3.87 (0.62)	4.10 (0.58)	4.01 (0.57)	3.91 (0.55)	4.10 (0.58)
Homework completion	4.90 (1.16)	4.84 (1.18)	5.39 (0.74)	4.91 (1.17)	4.82 (1.21)	5.42 (0.73)	5.24 (0.95)	5.07 (1.11)	5.42 (0.73)
Disruptive behavior	4.26 (0.88)	4.25 (0.89)	4.33 (0.79)	4.26 (0.88)	4.25 (0.89)	4.31 (0.80)	4.35 (0.81)	4.39 (0.81)	4.31 (0.81)

Perceived interest/competence	2.54 (0.74)	2.52 (0.75)	2.70 (0.69)	2.54 (0.74)	2.51 (0.75)	2.71 (0.70)	2.69 (0.72)	2.68 (0.75)	2.71 (0.70)
Attention in class	3.99 (0.80)	3.97 (0.81)	4.15 (0.72)	3.99 (0.81)	3.96 (0.82)	4.16 (0.72)	4.17 (0.73)	4.17 (0.75)	4.16 (0.72)

Psychological traits

Self-esteem scale	−0.004 (0.69)	−0.02 (0.70)	0.10 (0.63)	−0.01 (0.69)	−0.03 (0.70)	0.11 (0.63)	0.09 (0.65)	0.07 (0.68)	0.11 (0.63)
Locus of control	−0.01 (0.63)	−0.03 (0.63)	0.14 (0.56)	−0.02 (0.62)	−0.05 (0.63)	0.15 (0.56)	0.12 (0.57)	0.09 (0.58)	0.15 (0.56)
Internalizing problem behavior	2.89 (0.62)	2.88 (0.62)	2.93 (0.58)	2.90 (0.62)	2.89 (0.62)	2.95 (0.57)	2.94 (0.56)	2.93 (0.57)	2.95 (0.57)
Number of observations	8,780	7,810	980	5,800	4,990	810	1,620	810	810

a. Analytic sample includes eighth-grade students who did not change region, location, or school sector during the four waves.

b. Attention in class, homework completion, disruptive behavior, tardiness, absenteeism, and class behavior for students in their English class. The four variables "disruptive behavior," "tardiness," "absenteeism," and "internalizing problem behavior" have been reverse scaled.

c. Standard deviations in parentheses. Math, reading, and SES standardized so that mean = 0, std. dev. = 1 for the entire sample. Weighted using ECLS-K sampling weights.

may compare the characteristics of the treatment and control groups after matching.[36] As shown in table 4.2, differences in covariates have been significantly reduced.

Second, we ran an ordered probit regression to estimate the average effects of treatment on the treated. Following Abadie et al.'s methodology, we correct the standard errors to make matching estimators consistent.[37] We also take into account the fact that we are using an ordered probit model on a previously matched sample.

Propensity score matching limits the number of observations to the subset that can be matched. But because every Catholic student in the analytic sample is matched to its closest neighbor in the public sample, the matched comparison is representative of the relative impact of the private sector, if it can be assumed that there are no biases introduced by attrition or by differences in unobserved characteristics not captured by observables.

Exclusion of observations where values are missing for specific characteristics introduces bias whenever nonresponses are not randomly distributed. To retain those observations, missing values are estimated by means of a multiple imputation technique that follows King et al.[38] This technique is known as multivariate imputation by chained equations (MICE).[39] It relies on the imputation of missing variables by using switching regressions, an iterative multivariable regression technique. Five imputed data sets have been created, and the regression estimates have been averaged over the five sets of results. We use this technique to estimate values for the missing independent variables.

Because observations of students are clustered within schools, hierarchical linear modeling is used for the ordered probit estimations.[40]

RESULTS

Results lend credence to Coleman's social capital theory. As can be seen by examining the results from the matched comparison models in table 4.5, most estimates show positive Catholic sector impacts on several indicators of student readiness to comply with educationally productive social norms.[41] According to the assessments made by English teachers, attendance at a Catholic school reduces tardiness and absenteeism and enhances homework completion and academic engagement in eighth grade. However, no significant impact on attentiveness in class and nondisruptive behavior is observed. A similar pattern is reported by science teachers. In math, a positive Catholic sector impact is detected for all six indicators of social compliance. Results from the ordered probit models resemble closely those obtained from the matched comparison models. In sum, a robust set of positive Catholic sector impacts on student compliance with social norms is observed, just as Coleman hypothesized.

TABLE 4.5 Estimated Catholic sector impacts on conformity to social norms in English, math, and science classes and self-perceived psychological well-being of eighth-grade students from ordered probit models for all students and matched comparison models

Conformity to social norms in English class

	TARDINESS		ABSENTEEISM		HOMEWORK COMPLETION		DISRUPTIVE BEHAVIOR		ACADEMIC ENGAGEMENT[a]		ATTENTION IN CLASS	
	All students	Matched comparison models	All students	Matched comparison models	All students	Matched comparison models	All students	Matched comparison models	All students	Matched comparison models	All students	Matched comparison models
Catholic												
Without controls[b]	0.447***[c] (0.051)		0.461*** (0.046)		0.619*** (0.041)		0.082* (0.042)		0.102*** (0.023)		0.290*** (0.040)	
With controls	0.294*** (0.057)	0.279*** (0.070)	0.371*** (0.052)	0.363*** (0.078)	0.278*** (0.048)	0.296*** (0.064)	-0.084* (0.049)	-0.089 (0.072)	0.051** (0.026)	0.077** (0.039)	0.041 (0.046)	0.029 (0.063)
Observations	5,800	1,540	5,800	1,540	5,800	1,540	5,800	1,540	5,800	1,540	5,800	1,540

Conformity to social norms in math class

	TARDINESS		ABSENTEEISM		HOMEWORK COMPLETION		DISRUPTIVE BEHAVIOR		ATTENTION IN CLASS	
	All students	Matched comparison models	All students	Matched comparison models	All students	Matched comparison models	All students	Matched comparison models	All students	Matched comparison models
Catholic											
Without controls	0.421*** (0.070)		0.429*** (0.065)		0.724*** (0.062)		0.375*** (0.063)		0.519*** (0.058)	
With controls	0.275*** (0.078)	0.234** (0.113)	0.282*** (0.074)	0.313*** (0.091)	0.467*** (0.072)	0.529*** (0.089)	0.204*** (0.072)	0.228** (0.094)	0.342*** (0.068)	0.369*** (0.089)
Observations	2,730	730	2,730	730	2,730	730	2,730	730	2,730	730

continued

TABLE 4.5 *continued*

Conformity to social norms in science class

Catholic	TARDINESS		ABSENTEEISM		HOMEWORK COMPLETION		DISRUPTIVE BEHAVIOR		ATTENTION IN CLASS	
	All students	Matched comparison models	All students	Matched comparison models	All students	Matched comparison models	All students	Matched comparison models	All students	Matched comparison models
Without controls	0.402*** (0.070)		0.442*** (0.065)		0.627*** (0.058)		0.139** (0.061)		0.289*** (0.058)	
With controls	0.307*** (0.079)	0.332*** (0.099)	0.349*** (0.074)	0.364 (0.088)	0.285*** (0.071)	0.350*** (0.104)	0.009 (0.071)	0.012 (0.099)	0.096 (0.069)	0.013 (0.091)
Observations	2,730	730	2,730	730	2,730	730	2,730	730	2,730	730

Self-perceived psychological traits

Catholic	SELF-ESTEEM SCALE		LOCUS OF CONTROL		INTERNALIZING PROBLEM BEHAVIOR	
	All students	Matched comparison models	All students	Matched comparison models	All students	Matched comparison models
Without controls	0.011 (0.010)		0.137*** (0.026)		0.085*** (0.024)	
With controls	-0.021** (0.010)	-0.053 (0.035)	0.038 (0.027)	0.032 (0.032)	0.017 (0.027)	0.016 (0.034)
Observations	5,800	1,540	5,800	1,540	5,800	1,540

a. In reading.

b. Controls include prior math and reading test scores (first grade), prior noncognitive variable (first grade), gender, ethnicity (black, Asian, Hispanic, and other race), presence of a disability, language spoken at home, whether or not the student comes from a home whose income was below the poverty line, number of siblings, whether or not the student lives with both parents, mother's age at birth of first child, region (Northeast, Midwest, West, South), community type (city, large town, or small town/rural), and a socioeconomic status (SES) index, a composite that jointly measures parental education, income, and occupational prestige. Models estimating homework completion as dependent variable also include as controls the frequency with which homework is assigned and the time teachers expect students to devote to the homework.

c. Significance level: *** $p<.01$, ** $p<.05$, * $p<.1$

In order to comply with the requirements of the U.S. Department of Education, all unweighted sample size numbers presented are rounded to the nearest 10'.

Although Catholic sector impacts on student compliance with social norms are generally positive, sector impacts on student self-reports of their psychological well-being are not. Sector impacts on student self-control and tendency to internalize problems are statistically insignificant. A negative Catholic sector impact on students' self-esteem is suggested by the ordered probit model. The sign in the propensity matching model is also negative, but the coefficient fails to reach the standard level of statistical significance. All in all, the most cautious interpretation is that no consistent impacts on student self-perceived psychological well-being can be detected. Nor should one expect any other result from Coleman's social capital theory, inasmuch as it identifies the peer culture as the primary source of student self-esteem.

To see whether impacts on noncognitive outcomes varied by minority status, socioeconomic status, and initial test score performance (measured in first grade), we estimated ordered models with interaction terms for outcomes in English classes. This was the context in which the number of observations was large enough to estimate interaction terms with a fair degree of precision.

In the probit analysis for all students, four of the six estimates of Catholic impacts on social-norm outcomes revealed smaller Catholic impacts on minority students. However, only two of the matched comparison estimates showed those smaller impacts, whereas another indicated that the impact for minorities was larger. No significant impacts of the interaction term on student psychological traits were observed. In sum, there is some—though hardly conclusive—evidence that Coleman's social capital theory is more tenuous for minority group students.

Results for students having lower socioeconomic status (SES) and those having lower test scores showed no consistent pattern of results; twenty of the twenty-four estimates were statistically insignificant. Nor were impacts on psychological traits any less erratic; nine of twelve estimates were statistically insignificant, two had larger impacts for those of lower SES, and one had a smaller impact for the latter.

We also examined results only for those math and science teachers who were not also the student's English teacher. In a few cases—fewer than 5 percent of the total—the English teacher served as the student's math or science teacher (or both), so in these instances observations in math and science are not separate and independent of those made in English classes. In table 4.6, we isolate the Catholic sector impacts in math and science classes for only those classes taught by a teacher other than the English teacher. We provide probit estimates for impacts on all students in the analytic sample for all outcomes measured in math and science classes: tardiness, absenteeism, homework completion, disruptive behavior, and attention in class.[42] The estimates do not change significantly from the main results reported in table 4.5. In math, sector impacts on two outcomes—homework and class attentiveness—remain positive. In science, Catholic sector impacts on homework remain positive, and impacts on attention in class continue to be insignificant. In other words, the identification of consistent impacts across subject areas is not dependent on the assessments of the small number of English teachers who also taught the same students in math or science (or both).

Interpretation of Estimates

For outcomes that were significantly impacted by the Catholic sector in the matched sample estimations, we used Clarify software developed by King et al. to simulate those impacts for the representative student.[43] For all estimates in which the Catholic sector variable was found to be statistically

TABLE 4.6 **Estimated Catholic sector impacts on conformity to social norms in math and science classes from ordered probit models for all students and for those in classes where teacher is not the same as the student's English teacher**

	MATH CLASSES		SCIENCE CLASSES	
	All classes	Classes with different teacher	All classes	Classes with different teacher
		TARDINESS		
Catholic	0.275***a (0.078)	0.256*** (0.080)	0.307*** (0.079)	0.319*** (0.083)
Observations	2,730	2,620	2,730	2,620
		ABSENTEEISM		
Catholic	0.282*** (0.074)	0.270*** (0.075)	0.349*** (0.074)	0.344*** (0.079)
Observations	2,730	2,620	2,730	2,620
		HOMEWORK COMPLETION		
Catholic	0.467*** (0.072)	0.448*** (0.073)	0.285*** (0.071)	0.259*** (0.075)
Observations	2,730	2,620	2,730	2,620
		DISRUPTIVE BEHAVIOR		
Catholic	0.204*** (0.072)	0.190*** (0.074)	0.009 (0.071)	0.009 (0.073)
Observations	2,730	2,620	2,730	2,620
		ATTENTION IN CLASS		
Catholic	0.342*** (0.068)	0.320*** (0.069)	0.096 (0.069)	0.259*** (0.075)
Observations	2,730	2,620	2,730	2,620

a. See notes to table 4.5. Estimates from matched comparison models not provided because they contain too few observations to estimate impacts precisely. Only half the sample was asked about math and science classes.

In order to comply with the requirements of the U.S. Department of Education, all unweighted sample size numbers presented are rounded to the nearest 10'.

significant in the matched comparison model, we simulated that impact by estimating the change in the predicted probability of school sector on outcomes for the average student, holding constant all the control variables in the analytic sample model, as reported earlier in table 4.5.[44] The method is discussed in appendix B, including an illustration in table B.1. (Appendixes for this chapter are online at http://www.vanderbilt.edu/schoolchoice/.) In the right column (matched students) we present this point estimate of the Catholic school impact, whereas in the left column (simulated probability) we present the simulated probabilities that an observation will take on any of the values of the dependent variable specified.[45]

Based on these calculations, one can see that impacts were not only statistically significant but also substantively meaningful. Attending a Catholic school increases the predicted probability for the representative student of always completing homework by 12 percentage points, an increase of 23 percent over the benchmark simulated probability. Similarly, attending Catholic school increases the predicted probability of never being tardy by 10.5 percentage points, an increase of 14 percent. The impact on the probability of never being absent increases by 9.3 percentage points, which represents an improvement of nearly 51 percent. The impact on the probability of being the most academically engaged increases by 0.04 percentage points, a gain of 19 percent. Greater sector effects are observed for the noncognitive skills more easily monitored by teachers (for example, absence and homework completion).

The impact of school sector on noncognitive skills demonstrated in math and science classes is similar. In mathematics the increase in the probability of never being tardy is 7.9 percentage points, an increase of 11 percent. The increase in the probability of never being absent is 8.2 percentage points, an increase of 42 percent. The probability of always completing homework goes up by 20.8 percentage points, an increase of 35 percent. The increase in the probability of paying attention all of the time climbs by 13.3 percentage points, a jump of 36 percent. In science, estimates show an 11.4 percentage point increase in the probability of never being tardy, an increase of 15 percent. The probability of always completing homework increases by 13.9 percentage points if one is in the Catholic sector, an increase of 25 percent.

DISCUSSION

In this chapter we provide the first rigorous test of social capital theory as developed by James Coleman. We draw on data from a nationally representative longitudinal survey of students in eighth grade, a time in the life cycle when compliance with educationally productive social norms is most problematic. Results are quite robust to a range of indicators of social compliance: reductions in student tardiness, absenteeism, and disruptive behavior as well as positive impacts on academic engagement, homework completion, and class attentiveness in English, math, and science classes. However, in some cases—class attention and student disruption in English and science classes—null findings are obtained. The results from the analytic sample models are very consistent with those generated by the preferred matched comparison models.

At the same time, no consistent impacts on a student's self-perceptions of psychological well-being are identified, a finding not necessarily inconsistent with Coleman's social capital theory. That theory focused explicitly on compliance with adult expectations and did not address the consequences for a student's sense of self-worth.

We obtained these results after controlling for a broad range of characteristics, including family background and student test scores in first grade, and the results are based on estimates that retain as many observations as possible by imputing values for missing data. For the analytic sample model for all students, we use hierarchical linear modeling to take into account multiple observations at a single school site. Results do not change when all those who change sectors are assigned to the sector in which they first began. Results are generally, if not entirely, robust to independent observations by English, math, and science teachers.

Although our test of social capital theory has been rigorous, it is nonetheless subject to several limitations. The observations available from the ECLS-K decline steadily with each wave, and the eighth-grade wave consists of only 9,730 of the 17,760 observations available in first grade. Attrition rates from the public and private sectors differ with respect to a number of observable characteristics, and it is possible that the unobservable characteristics of those who disappear from the sample could also have varied by sector. Of special concern is the possibility that a higher proportion of noncompliant students in the private compared with the public sector may have been among those who are missing from the eighth-grade wave. For that reason, we place the greatest weight on the findings from the matched comparison sample, in which every remaining student in Catholic school is matched to a public student who comes nearest to resembling the Catholic school student on observable characteristics. We nonetheless recommend that randomized experiments seeking to estimate sector impacts obtain information on students' compliance with social norms as well as their test scores and self-perceptions of personal well-being.

No less interesting is the minimal Catholic sector impact on students' sense of self-worth and other indicators of psychological well-being, as reported by students themselves. Coleman probably would not have been surprised to hear of this finding, because his theory of adolescent society identified the primary sources of self-esteem as coming from the student's place in the peer group status hierarchy. Left for further research is the determination of the independent significance of learned social compliance behavior and a student's sense of self-worth for such long-term outcomes as educational attainment and labor market participation. However that question is resolved, it seems clear that the study of human capital acquisition could benefit substantially from the exploration of school impacts on noncognitive as well as cognitive outcomes, as measured by test score performance.

5

Does Intradistrict Transfer Make the Grade?

A Case Study of the Effects of School Choice on Achievement

Kristie J. R. Phillips, Charles S. Hausman, and Elisabeth S. Larsen

As the accountability movement has progressed, schools, districts, states, and federal government departments of education have placed an increased emphasis on student achievement. In support of this increased emphasis, a variety of educational policies and programs has emerged aimed at increasing student test scores. One such program expressly outlined in the federal No Child Left Behind Act of 2001 (NCLB) involves increasing parental school choice as a mechanism to raise student achievement. Under NCLB, students who are assigned to Title I schools that do not meet Adequate Yearly Progress (AYP) goals for two consecutive years are given the option of attending another school.[1] Furthermore, the Voluntary Public School Choice Program uses federal dollars to fund efforts that establish or expand public school choice options such as open enrollment, interdistrict transfer options, and intradistrict transfer programs.[2] These policy trends make it important to examine public school choice options and assess their effects on student achievement.

Existing literature on school choice has focused largely on the impact of specialized programs such as vouchers, charter schools, and magnet schools. Little research has examined the link between increased student achievement and student participation in intradistrict transfer—a type of school choice prescribed under NCLB for students attending Title I schools that have been identified as needing improvement. In addition to playing a major role in federal education policy, intradistrict transfer policies are increasingly adopted across the United States. As of 2008, programs facilitating this type of choice had been enacted in thirty-four states.[3] Because of their widespread adoption and political relevance, intradistrict transfer policies deserve a careful examination of their ability to raise student achievement; however, such policies are currently understudied in the school choice literature.

Because school choice is a politically complex issue, the school choice literature covers a broad array of topics. Some research focuses on the opportunity to choose a school and whether or not choice is equally accessible to all students.[4] Other studies evaluate specific programs.[5] Still other studies examine the role of school choice in achieving social goals such as desegregation.[6] Although all these aspects of school choice are important, research focusing on the link between students' and parents' school choices and subsequent student achievement is critical in the current climate of high-stakes accountability. Furthermore, the effects of the specific types of public school choice recommended and funded by the federal government warrant further attention by researchers and policy makers alike. To accomplish this, we examine the effects of one district's intradistrict transfer program on student achievement.

We find that intradistrict transfers do not raise students' test scores in language arts or mathematics. However, when students use the intradistrict transfer option to leave an academically lower-performing school and attend a higher-performing school, they experience large increases in both language arts and mathematics achievement. Nevertheless, relatively few students use intradistrict transfer options as a way to leave a lower-performing school. Most parents choose schools for their children that are academically similar to the schools they are zoned to attend. These results highlight the importance of using school choice in coordination with other policies to ensure that students who face the most educational disadvantages are most able to choose schools having good academic records. To inform our study, we first highlight the research on school choice and its influence on student achievement, and we then describe the context of our study, outline our methodology, and report the results of our study. We then draw conclusions based on our findings and discuss relevant policy recommendations that might enhance the use of school choice to improve achievement outcomes for students.

RESEARCH ON SCHOOL CHOICE AND ACHIEVEMENT

Despite the prevalence and growing popularity of intra-district transfers, very little research has addressed their effects on student achievement. Extensive research has attempted to assess the influence of a variety of other types of school choice programs on student achievement. These studies, however, have not reached consensus on the nature of this relationship. Our review of the school choice literature focuses first on the varying results found in studies of school choice programs. We then identify and discuss three major factors that facilitate this lack of consensus: the effects of socially motivated behavior, the complications involved in choosing appropriate methodological tools, and the importance of context in determining the effects of school choice.

Lack of Consensus About the Effects of School Choice

Determining the effectiveness of school choice policies in improving student achievement requires extensive research, which, to date, has not led to a preponderance of evidence supporting a decisive conclusion. Perhaps this lack of consensus is not surprising given the differences in the school choice options and policies that have been studied. However, even within studies of magnet schools, charter schools, voucher programs, and intradistrict transfer programs, the effects of each type of choice on achievement are debated. Even though the focus of this chapter is to determine the effects of intradistrict transfers on student achievement, this type of choice is underrepresented in the choice literature. Thus, to provide a context and foundation for our study of intradistrict transfers, we discuss a range of school choice options and their influence on student outcomes.

Magnet Schools. Studies of the impact of magnet schools on student achievement offer a wide range of conclusions. In a national study of urban high schools, Gamoran found that magnet schools were more effective than urban public schools in raising student proficiency in science, reading, and social studies.[7] Further statistical analysis addressing selectivity and independence raised questions about the positive effect on science scores but upheld the positive effect on the other two subjects. In contrast, a study of elementary-level magnet schools in Maryland found mild positive effects that varied by type of program.[8] The study examined magnet programs with seven different themes and found that only one program had a positive impact on students' reading and math performance. The remaining six types of programs did not yield meaningful effects. Finally, a national study of career academy magnet schools found no significant effect on student achievement.[9]

Two obstacles limit the degree to which consensus can be reached among studies of magnet schools and student achievement. First, the types of programs and theme-based instructional practices examined in each study vary greatly. Although researchers approach the same type of choice when studying magnet schools, they do so in different contexts. Second, it becomes difficult to disentangle, on the one hand, the effect of exercising choice on achievement and, on the other hand, the impact of specific programs, such as a career academy magnet school or an academically selective magnet program.

Charter Schools. Studies of charter schools also yield mixed results. Some studies indicate that charter schools raise student achievement beginning in the first year of participation, with achievement gains increasing in each additional year.[10] Others have suggested that charter schools are more effective in raising student achievement only after several years of enrollment.[11] On the contrary, other studies indicate that attending a charter school is associated with either an actual decline in achievement relative to public school students or at least a smaller gain than the students would have experienced in public schools.[12]

Whereas these studies examined charter schools broadly, more contextualized studies differentiate the results according to the type and quality of charter schools. After accounting for these characteristics of charter schools, results suggest that higher-quality or classroom-based charter schools significantly improved student performance, and lower-quality or non-classroom-based schools were negatively related to student achievement.[13] Again, as with magnet schools, the differences in program type make it difficult to reach a consensus among charter school studies. Charter school research also points to contextual issues that may impede consensus. The design of charter school attendance policies bars researchers from focusing on single districts, and it results in researchers comparing charter school students to students from the entire state. This comparison may not be meaningful, because it includes schools that operate in a variety of contexts and students who may not have had the opportunity to attend a charter school.[14]

Voucher Programs. The lack of consensus concerning the effects of school choice on achievement has been most apparent in studies of voucher programs. Such studies have reported results that range from vouchers exhibiting significant positive effects on student achievement, to mixed effects, to no effect whatsoever.[15] Other studies have suggested that findings may vary by race.[16] The differences in these findings stem largely from variations in research design.

In a series of studies of the Milwaukee voucher programs, results varied widely based on the choice of control group. One study compared voucher participants with a random sample of Milwaukee public school students and concluded that voucher participation led to no relative achievement gains.[17] In a second study, researchers compared the same voucher participants to the group of students who applied to the program but reenrolled in public schools because they were not accepted. With this comparison group, researchers found significant test score gains in both math and reading after three to four years of program participation.[18] A final study implemented improved methodological techniques in an effort to settle the debate concerning the effectiveness of Milwaukee's voucher program in raising student achievement, finding small yet significant effects for math and no effects for reading.[19]

Studies of vouchers and achievement also highlight the importance of appropriate definition of variables. In Howell and Peterson's study of three large urban voucher programs, the only group with significant positive effects was African American students in the New York City program.[20] However, Krueger and Zhu's follow-up research cast doubt on these findings.[21] First, the authors found that including students having missing baseline scores significantly weakened the effect of being offered a voucher. Additionally, the original study classified students solely on the basis of their mother's race. When father's race was included, the effect size related to race diminished. The voucher research demonstrates that research design plays a major role in the diverging results of school choice studies. Without an appropriate comparison group, researchers cannot make meaningful inferences about the true effects of school choice on achievement. This may be further compounded by inaccurate definition of variables.

Intradistrict Transfer. Although intradistrict transfer policies are widespread, relatively few studies have looked at them. Of the few studies that have examined their impact on student achievement, Ozek's research on intradistrict transfer in Pinellas County, Florida, found that participation in intradistrict transfer produced no significant improvement in student achievement, and student achievement declined after the initial transfer.[22] However, this decline was less for students from disadvantaged backgrounds. In a study focusing on the effects of NCLB transfer options on low-SES (socioeconomic status) students, Hastings and Weinstein concluded that program participation increased achievement only when students switched to higher-performing schools.[23] Students who switched to a similar-performing school did not increase achievement levels. Furthermore, when parents received test score information about schools, it significantly increased their propensity to choose a higher-performing school for their children. This study points to another reason that school choice studies may have divergent results: parents may not always make the optimal choice, either because they lack the information, they are constrained by other factors, or they make choices based on social and not academic factors.

These two studies focus on two types of intradistrict transfer: one developed as a districtwide choice program, and one mandated by NCLB. Both types of transfers resemble the types of school choices encouraged by federal initiatives to increase school choice efforts, and they provide an important backdrop for studying the relationship between intradistrict transfers and student achievement. Because intradistrict transfers do not necessitate specialized schools, studies of such plans can isolate the effects of choice without the need to account for specialized programs and school themes and to explain how these programs and themes might appeal to students differently; therefore, the effects of intradistrict transfers on student achievement that are currently reported in the literature are not confounded by the potential effects of specialized programs. However, both of the aforementioned studies focused on districts having oversubscribed schools, and therefore lotteries were required for student admittance. Thus, the schools children attended did not necessarily represent their first-choice option, and that, in theory, would decrease the likelihood that choice would increase achievement. Under such circumstances, the foundational assumption that choice optimizes the match between school and student and therefore leads to increased student achievement would be violated.[24]

Literature on Non-Optimal School Choices

One reason that existing research fails to reach a consensus about the effects of school choice on student achievement is the possibility that parents make non-optimal school choices when improving achievement is the main goal of a choice policy. Socially motivated behavior, along with barriers to academically optimal choices, may limit the degree to which students end up attending schools that are ideal academic environments for them. Nevertheless, the assertion that school choice can improve achievement rests on the assumption that all students can and will choose schools that optimize the students' abilities to achieve. However, as Hastings and Weinstein suggest, this may not always occur.[25] In their study, student achievement results changed when parents were given easily accessible information about school achievement before exercising choice. This result suggests that a lack of information may prevent parents from choosing the ideal school for their child. Lack of access to information may occur as a result of parents' proficiency levels in English. Non-English speakers often do not have access to translated information about school quality or about the school choice process. Also, lack of Internet access in homes tends to disproportionately affect low-SES and minority families' ability to exercise school choice.[26]

District size and lack of access to transportation may also prevent families from choosing the optimal school. In large, countywide school districts, attending some schools could require a ninety-minute (or longer) commute. Thus, only students whose parents have the time and resources to accommodate this long commute can take advantage of the full spectrum of choices within the district—particularly if school choice is not accompanied by district-sponsored transportation.[27]

The school choice literature also suggests that families base their choices on guidelines of what they consider to be socially acceptable schools for their children.[28] Although these may be valued considerations, they may not actually constitute an ideal *academic* match. Holme's study found that parents moved away from schools with high minority populations without ever obtaining test scores or visiting the campuses of schools they deemed unacceptable.[29] Ancess and Allen found that parents would send their children only to a themed school located in what they believed to be an acceptable neighborhood, regardless of the applicability of the theme to their child's interests.[30] As these studies suggest, an emphasis on social interests can result in parents making choices about their children's schooling that may not benefit the children academically. If these behaviors occur, participation in choice may not have the expected effect of increased academic achievement.

The Importance of Context. Perhaps the most important lesson to be learned from the extant literature is the importance of context when research is conducted on school choice. Context often determines the type of choice that most merits study, the degree to which choice is available to all students, the group to which choosers should be compared, and the most appropriate research design and methods for investigating the relationship between school choice and achievement. Key contextual factors that could significantly contribute to the outcomes of school choice studies include the geographic and demographic characteristics of the schools, districts, or states within which school choice takes place; state and local laws regarding school choice; the presence of court-ordered desegregation mandates; racial or socioeconomic balancing initiatives; resource allocation; and the overarching purpose and design of each school choice plan. Failure to consider such contexts could lead to the misrepresentation of the effects of choice on student outcomes.[31]

Because contexts can vary widely in school choice plans, it is important to focus on a unit of study in which contextual factors can be thoroughly explored. In the case of intradistrict transfers, a single school district provides a meaningful unit of study, because the context of the district can be explained in relation to student participation, as can the role context might play in student outcomes such as academic achievement. Many existing studies focus on single districts; however, they tend to study the same types of districts. For example, for school districts to sustain a magnet school system with a wide variety of instructional programs, such schools must draw from a large student population.[32] Similarly, the presence of a voucher system typically requires a large low-income population and a sufficient number of nearby private schools for these students to attend.[33] A final factor influencing the type of district studied comes from the historical use of school choice policies as a desegregation tool. Thus, many districts using school choice policies have previously been under court-ordered desegregation and are often located in urban settings.[34]

Examining the contexts of school choice policies in districtwide settings demonstrates that research has indeed been conducted in large urban districts having a history of racial balancing programs. Such contexts include the greater Washington, D.C., area; Cleveland; Milwaukee; Charlotte, North Carolina; New York City; Pinellas County, Florida; and Chicago.[35] Although these contexts are important for advancing the research on school choice, the results often represent outcomes associated with non-optimal choices. In these districts, parents' choices traditionally have been constrained by race- or SES-based lotteries and quotas, potentially minimizing the degree to which optimal matches between students and schools could be made.

Similar limitations occur when schools are oversubscribed, a common problem in the large districts that tend to be studied most often.[36] Because of the popularity of certain choice schools, some students cannot attend their first choice due to the lack of available space. When schools are oversubscribed they often employ a lottery to admit students. The lottery winners are able to attend the school, but the losers must enroll in a different school—one that may not be their first choice and therefore may not represent their ideal match. Students who lose a lottery might exercise choice but not gain access to their ideal school, and that may influence the effects of the students' choice on their achievement. These issues demonstrate a need for school choice research that optimizes school–student matches. Ideally, this would take place in a district where all students were able to enroll in their first-choice school.

Although charter, magnet, and voucher programs are typically located in large urban districts, intradistrict transfer policies exist in many districts, regardless of district size, region, and population density. Currently, studies do not examine smaller districts, nor do they look at the way school choice works in a context outside the South, the urban Northeast, or the Midwest. Nevertheless, school districts across the United States of varying sizes and locations use intradistrict transfer policies, and given the similarities between these policies and NCLB's school choice options, such options should be studied in a variety of district contexts. Furthermore, small districts whose choice policies are often not represented in the school choice literature allow for a study of choice that minimizes the barriers posed by access to transportation and distance of travel in large districts. If families can easily travel to any school within the district, then all schools are more accessible, especially when compared with a large countywide district. Intradistrict transfer policies are increasing in popularity, and the federal government is encouraging the expansion of public school choice options.[37] This study aims to provide information about the effectiveness of such school choice policies in raising student achievement in an era of high-stakes accountability.

CONTEXT OF THE STUDY

To study the effects of intradistrict transfers on student achievement, we focus on one small urban school district located in the Intermountain West. This district was selected because it has several characteristics that provide an optimal context for exploring the impacts of school choice on student achievement. These characteristics include small geographic size, which limits the extent to which transportation is a barrier to choice; a stable population of students, which ensures that each school in the district is under-subscribed and therefore able to admit intradistrict transfer students; and a long history of and support for intradistrict transfer choice options at both the state and the district level, which facilitates greater access to information about the school choice process. The unique characteristics of this district limit the extent to which common barriers to school choice—such as lack access to information, lack of transportation, and an inability to secure enrollment in one's first-choice school—interfere with parents' ability to choose the school they believe is best for their children.

The school district analyzed in this study is located in a state with a long history of school choice legislation, including policies for inter- and intradistrict transfers. By state law, schools are open to nonresident students (students living outside the school attendance zone) if the school is at or below 90 percent enrollment capacity. Furthermore, a local school board may allow enrollment of nonresident students in schools operating at greater than 90 percent enrollment capacity. Although the state has supported school choice for more than fifty years, the school districts have maintained varying levels of support for school choice. On one end of the spectrum, some districts notify parents annually of the state policy that permits inter- and intradistrict transfers and then go on to state that such transfers are discouraged. The district analyzed in this study, however, falls at the other end of the spectrum. Not only does the district inform parents of the state transfer policy, but it also provides information about the process and options. Furthermore, this information is translated into multiple languages and made available to all

parents through mailings, Web sites, and formal school and district meetings in which translators are available. As a result, this district has developed
local policies that are consistent with those of the state. Like the state, this
district has a long-standing commitment to school choice.

The district's commitment to school choice is a vital contextual factor
that makes it a good candidate for the study of intradistrict transfers, but
this district also provides a diverse racial setting that mirrors the "minority
majority" patterns common in the western United States.[38] Specifically, this
district serves a student population composed of 47 percent white, 37 percent Hispanic, 5 percent Pacific Islander, 5 percent Asian, 4 percent African
American, and 2 percent Native American students. Approximately two-
thirds of students qualify for free and reduced-price lunch. This indicates
a high level of economic disadvantage within the district, a situation that
is typical of districts that serve students located in urban areas. Therefore,
even though this district is unique in many respects, its student population
is representative of schools in western cities—a region of the United States
where school choice has been understudied.

Although minority and economically disadvantaged students are slightly
underrepresented among intradistrict transfer participants in this district,
approximately 50 percent of all choosers are low-income students and 43
percent belong to racial or ethnic minority groups. Relative to much of the
research done on school choice, this mix represents surprisingly high choice
participation for minority and economically disadvantaged students. The
literature has demonstrated that such students usually face significant barriers to school choice participation, such as lack of access to information
and transportation.[39] Thus, high participation indicates that the district has
reduced at least some of the barriers to choice that have been identified in
the literature as obstacles for some groups of students. This relatively large
population of students who are underrepresented in many school choice
options allows us to assess the types of choices these students make and the
effects of those choices on achievement.

This district context is also particularly pertinent because it is geographically stratified, a pattern that is persistent in much of the United States.
Although the student population is diverse, residential housing patterns in
the district are segregated, with most low-income and minority students
living on one side of the district, and the more affluent Caucasian students
on the other side. Students are zoned to neighborhood schools, and the student populations at these schools reflect these patterns of housing segregation. Furthermore, neighborhood and school segregation are correlated
with school quality, because low-income and minority students are disproportionately zoned to lower-performing schools, and higher-income and

white students are disproportionately zoned to higher-performing schools. According to district records, approximately 80 percent of low-income students and 75 percent of nonwhite students are, on average, zoned to lower-performing schools. As school districts across the country increasingly move toward neighborhood school zoning policies, this district provides an investigation of school choice in a segregated context.

As mentioned, the relatively high intradistrict transfer participation among low-income and minority students may be related to the district's ability to reduce barriers to choice. The unique geographic characteristics of this district minimize certain barriers to choice that may discourage families from choosing the school that would best facilitate an ideal school–student match or even discourage them from participating in choice altogether. The small size of the district (approximately twelve square miles) lessens transportation barriers that are prevalent in larger districts. Coupled with widespread access to choice information, the close proximity of all schools in the district facilitates greater access to all school choice options—even though, like most districts with intradistrict transfer plans, the district does not provide transportation to transfer students' chosen schools.

Two additional characteristics of this district ensure a greater likelihood that participation in intradistrict transfers will result in parents' ability to enroll their children in the schools they believe are best for them. First, this district has never enacted any type of racial or SES balancing strategies in its schools. Thus, the intradistrict transfer program has always operated as an unrestricted choice option in which every opening at every school is equally available to all students in the district. More important, the district is a city-wide district that has experienced very little population growth over the past twenty years. As a result, all the schools in the district operate at less than 90 percent capacity , and each school is eligible to accept intradistrict transfer students. In fact, all schools in the district receive students each year through intradistrict transfer requests. Furthermore, all families who participate in intradistrict transfers are virtually guaranteed attendance at their first-choice school. Because intradistrict transfers in this district occur in a natural setting with limited barriers to choice and very few restrictions on admissions to first-choice schools, its unique conditions allow us to assess the assumption that ideal school–student matches under school choice will result in increased student achievement.

PURPOSE OF THE STUDY

As we have demonstrated, intradistrict transfer policies have been understudied in regard to their effects on student achievement. Studies of magnet, charter, and voucher programs have provided valuable contributions to the understanding of school choice and achievement, but the research has not yet addressed a major avenue of school choice that current federal education policies assume will lead to increased student achievement. In this study, intradistrict transfer is open to all students in the district and provides students the option to attend any school within the district boundaries. In contrast, other choice policies, such as magnets, charters, and vouchers, limit participation to students who qualify for specific choice options (either academically or based on other characteristics such as family income) or whose interests fit with a specialized, school-based program. This lack of specific programs or choice restrictions opens the choice process to all students regardless of background or interests.

Because the district we study is a small urban district located in the Intermountain West, the intradistrict transfer policy also provides a unique contribution to the literature. Only a few studies of intradistrict transfer programs have been done, and they have typically looked at districts where preferred transfer options are oversubscribed, or in formerly segregated districts where lotteries and racial guidelines prevent many parents from receiving their first choice of schools. To better assess the true effects of unrestricted choice on student achievement, we study intradistrict transfer within the context of one district where all choice participants are able to enroll in their first school of choice and where many barriers to choice (such as lack of information and transportation) have been diminished. With this context in mind, we address the following questions:

- Which schools do parents choose for their children when participating in intradistrict transfers?
- In general, does participation in intradistrict transfers predict increases in student achievement?
- More specifically, does participation in intradistrict transfers predict increases in student achievement when students who are zoned to lower-performing schools choose to attend higher-performing schools?

METHODS

Data and Sample

The data used in this study came from the official student records of the school district, which include four years' worth of records for each student collected over four consecutive school years (from the 2003–2004 school year through the 2006–2007 school year). For each year the student attended a school within the district, the data set contained the student's demographic information, English language proficiency, the school the student was zoned to attend, participation in special education or other specialized programs, participation in intradistrict transfer, and the student's state standardized test scores.

For the purposes of this study, we narrowed our focus to elementary school choice, which included kindergarten through sixth grade. Because the district is a small, citywide urban district, there are relatively few middle and high schools; therefore, students had fewer choice options as they progressed through school. In contrast, elementary students chose from among twenty-seven schools that reflected a variety of demographic backgrounds and academic achievement levels. In addition to our focus on elementary students, two types of students were excluded from analyses: students in self-contained special education programs and students in self-contained academic programs. Each of these types of students exercised school choice to attend specialized programs; however, their choices were different from intradistrict transfers in that students had to qualify for each of these programs. Furthermore, even though these programs were housed at specific elementary campuses within the district, they were considered by the district to be "schools within schools." Thus, students who attended these programs rarely interacted with the majority of the student body attending the school.

During the time frame of this study (from fall 2003 to spring 2007), the district enrolled approximately thirteen thousand elementary students per year. This period was selected for four reasons. First, these years did not involve any school openings, closings, or other school zoning changes that might influence families' choice decisions. Second, by the 2003–2004 school year, all elementary schools in the district provided on-site services for English language learners. In previous years, these services had been provided only at certain schools, and that influenced the choices as well as the choice options for English language learners. Third, these years provide the most comprehensive and accurate data on a number of measures such as choice participation, language proficiency, special education classifications, and student achievement. Because a lack of English language proficiency may act as a barrier to choice participation, accurate measures are necessary to account for this. Similarly, parents of students with disabilities often make school choices based on program availability; therefore, it is important to accurately account for student disabilities within the context of the types of choices students made. Finally, during the 2003–2004 school year through the 2006–2007 school year, the required state achievement tests were not significantly revised. During this time, some test items were changed; however, the tests did not undergo significant restructuring or rescaling, and that enables a consistent comparison of student achievement over time.

Measures

To best measure the effect of intradistrict transfers on student achievement, the measures used in our study included variables related to student achievement and prior achievement and indicators of students' participation in intradistrict transfer. We also included other variables, including student background measures, because of their likely relationship with both intradistrict transfer participation and student test scores.

Outcome Variable. Academic achievement was used as the outcome of interest in this study. NCLB specifies that schools must provide adequate instruction to meet achievement requirements measured through Adequate Yearly Progress (AYP). In this district, student achievement was measured by student language arts and mathematics scores on state-administered criterion reference tests (CRTs), which have been used since 2003 to meet the testing requirements mandated in NCLB.

Students in all elementary grades within the district took the language arts as well as the mathematics CRTs in the spring of each academic year. The tests, which were developed and scored based on the state standards at each grade level, were scored on a scale from 130 to 200. At each grade level, students who earned scores of 160 and higher were considered proficient in state and federal accountability calculations. For all grades in our analysis, students were scored within this same 70-point range. Therefore, although a student may earn the same score from year to year, the score would indicate progress in learning because the content of the tests from year to year reflected a student's achievement relative to grade-level-appropriate tests and standards.

Although CRTs are useful in determining what students do and do not know based on grade-level standards, the CRTs used in this district differ by grade and are not vertically scaled, creating problems for our analyses because scores were not directly comparable across years or grades. To enable such comparison of scores, we converted each score into a z-score by subtracting each score from the mean and dividing by the standard deviation, as is typical in research using such scores as outcome measures.[40] Means and standard deviations were computed separately by year, grade, and test content area (language arts and mathematics). Standardizing the test scores in this way placed all scores on a similar scale, with a mean of zero and a standard deviation of 1. Because of high ceiling effects of the CRT scores for first and second graders, which presented significant skew in the distributions of scores, all students who were second graders or younger were excluded from analyses.[41] Test scores in all other grades were normally distributed in both language arts and mathematics.

Treatment Variable. To assess the effect of intradistrict transfers on student achievement in language arts and mathematics as is highlighted in our second research question, we consider intradistrict transfers as "treatments" that are hypothesized to enhance student academic performance. We measure intradistrict transfer participation by using a dichotomous indicator of whether or not a student participated in intradistrict transfer, which was coded 1 for participating students and 0 for students who did not participate. A 1 (participating) indicated that a student applied for, was granted, and then followed through with transfer plans—a process that described the experiences of the vast majority of intradistrict transfer applicants in our study. As noted previously, all schools in the district were underenrolled to the extent that all students who applied for a transfer were granted one, with rare and infrequent exceptions.

Not only does this study investigate the effects of intradistrict transfers on student achievement generally, but also it assesses the extent to which the school selected through the choice process might influence achievement outcomes. More specifically, we asked whether or not a switch from a lower-performing school to a higher-performing school significantly influenced student achievement. Addressing this question is of particular importance because using school choice mechanisms to attend an academically superior school resembles the type of policy-relevant choice that is encouraged under NCLB.

To assess the extent to which the quality of the school chosen through intradistrict transfer affects achievement, we created a series of six dummy variables. Separating these groups is an essential step in the analysis, because past research suggests that the level of performance of the chosen school may affect achievement.[42] For the purposes of this study, schools are classified as "lower performing" or "higher performing" (or, as we refer to them in this study, "lower" schools and "higher" schools). Schools in which the percentage of all students scoring proficient on the CRTs is equal to or higher than the percentage required to achieve AYP are identified as higher performing. Schools in which the percentage of all students scoring proficient fell below these benchmarks are classified as lower performing. For additional details about how we determined school-level proficiencies and whether a school was higher performing or lower performing, see our appendix online at http://www.vanderbilt.edu/schoolchoice/.

The six groups coded in this study include the following: (1) students who did not exercise choice but were zoned to higher-performing schools; (2) students who did not exercise choice but were zoned to lower-performing schools; (3) students who were zoned to higher-performing schools and chose another higher-performing school; (4) students who were zoned to higher-performing schools and chose to attend a lower-performing school; (5) students who were zoned to lower-performing schools and chose another lower-performing school; and (6) students who were zoned to lower-performing schools and chose a higher-performing school by applying for a transfer. This series of variables allowed us to examine specifically how students who were zoned to low performing schools but chose high performing schools compare to students who were zoned to low performing schools and did not exercise choice (the group used as the reference group in our analyses). In this way, we are able to assess the effect of choice when students enact policy-relevant choices by choosing not to attend lower-performing schools.

Control Variables. To accurately predict whether intradistrict transfer increases student achievement, we used several student background measures to account for differences between choosers and nonchoosers and also to account for general differences between students that might also influence achievement. These measures included gender, SES, race or ethnicity, English language proficiency, disability status, guardianship, neighborhood, number of years in the district, grade level, and prior achievement.[43]

To make the best use of accurate test score data, we restricted our use of scores to third through sixth graders in the 2003–2004 to 2006–2007 school years. However, when we used the measures of prior achievement, we were forced to exclude all third graders and all student observations from the 2003–2004 school year. When the test scores of these groups of students were used as prior achievement measures, the test scores were no longer eligible to be considered "outcomes" in our study. Because third grade marks the first point at which reliable test data were collected, we used all third-grade scores solely as measures of prior achievement. Furthermore, all scores from the 2003–2004 school year in grades 3 through 5 were also used solely as prior achievement measures.

In addition to control variables that may be related to student background, we included measures that account for the longitudinal nature of the study. To account for possible growth in achievement over time, we created a continuous variable coded 0 to indicate the first year of the study (2004–2005), 1 for the second year (2005–2006), and 2 for the third and final year (2006–2007). This measure was also multiplied by the treatment variable as an indicator of whether intradistrict transfer predicts achievement growth in addition to end-of-year achievement status.

Analytic Strategy

The decision to participate in any form of school choice is not random and is influenced by a variety of factors, both observed and unobserved. This endogeneity presents difficulties in establishing causation in studies of the effects of school choice on academic achievement. To address issues of endogeneity in the unique context of our study, we employed propensity score matching (PSM). PSM is a method of data organization designed to reduce bias and increase precision in observational studies in which the random assignment of treatments to subjects is absent.[44] It is a statistical procedure that estimates each individual's propensity to receive a binary treatment (which, in this study, means participating or not participating in intradistrict transfer) as a function of observable measures. As a result, members of a treatment group are matched with members of an untreated group who have similar propensity scores.[45]

Analyses

To address our first research question (which schools do parents choose for their children when participating in intradistrict transfer?), we descriptively analyzed the differences between students who do and do not participate in school choice. Furthermore, we examined the degree to which participating students enroll in schools having better academic records. Specifically, we analyzed whether students who were zoned to low performing schools chose high performing schools.

To assess our second question, we determined the effects of intradistrict transfer on student achievement. To accomplish this, we ran two separate sets of linear regression models: one with language arts achievement as the outcome, and another with mathematics achievement as the outcome measure of interest. To minimize the differences on all covariates that were related to both intradistrict transfer and student achievement, we weighted each model using the sampling weights generated by the PSM procedures.[46]

Our third research question seeks to identify the effects of intradistrict transfer on students who chose not to attend lower-performing schools and selected to attend higher-performing schools. We measured this effect by dropping the treatment variable from the aforementioned language arts and mathematics models and replacing it with a series of dummy variables that capture the types of choices parents make for their children. Students were identified as being zoned to a higher-performing school and remaining there, zoned to a higher-performing school and choosing another higher-performing school, zoned to a higher-performing school and choosing a lower-performing school, zoned to a lower-performing school and choosing another lower-performing school, or zoned to a lower-performing school and choosing a higher-performing school. All groups were compared to students who were zoned to lower-performing schools and remained in those schools. Replacing the simple treatment measure with this series of dummy variables provided an opportunity for the comparison of potential achievement differences across different choice options. Specifically, we were interested in how school choice affects the achievement of students who were zoned to lower-performing schools and chose higher-performing schools, when compared to students who remained in their low performing schools.

RESULTS AND DISCUSSION

We present our results as they relate to our three research questions. We first describe intradistrict transfer participants as well as the types of schools participants choose. We then discuss the overall effects of intradistrict transfer on student achievement. And finally, we address the effects of choice on student achievement when parents use intradistrict transfers to remove their children from a lower-performing school and send them to a higher-performing school.

The Schools Parents Choose

In this district, intradistrict transfers are exercised by 15 percent of the elementary school students. Of these choosers, low-SES students, racial or ethnic minority students, and English language learners are slightly less likely to participate in choice when compared to the makeup of elementary schools in the district. Half of choosers receive free or reduced-price lunch, compared with 63 percent of all elementary students in the district. Similarly, 43 percent of choosers belong to a racial or ethnic minority group, whereas 53 percent of all elementary students are racial or ethnic minorities. Additionally, 30 percent of English language learners participate in intradistrict transfers, compared with 39 percent of all elementary students in the district. The characteristics of choosers are nearly identical to those of the full sample of elementary school students for gender, disability status, and guardianship. These trends highlight the fact that even though this district has reduced some barriers to school choice for students who face disadvantages, such barriers still exist at least to some extent.

Student background not only plays a role in determining which students choose but also influences the choices they make. On average, 54 percent of intradistrict transfer students are zoned to lower-performing schools. Of the choosers who were zoned to lower-performing schools, about two-thirds (65 percent) transferred to another lower-performing school. A similar trend emerged for students zoned to higher-performing schools. Nearly all of the choosers who were zoned to higher-performing schools (87 percent) transferred to another higher-performing school. Therefore, students are likely to choose schools that are academically similar to the schools they leave. Nevertheless, 19 percent of the choosers in our sample used intradistrict transfer as a way to leave a lower-performing school and attend a higher-performing school. Of that 19 percent making policy- and theory-relevant choices, the students are demographically similar to all intradistrict transfer participants and to all intradistrict transfer participants who were zoned to lower-performing schools. Therefore, even though parents' choices to remove their children from a lower-performing school and send them to a higher-performing school may be a result of their individual tastes and preferences (which we are unable to assess in this study), parents who make the types of choices that theory suggests would increase student achievement do not differ on the characteristics we measure in this study.

Surprisingly few families who were zoned to low performing schools (about one-third) participate in choice as a way to send their children to schools having better academic records. The reason may be that parents make socially motivated decisions when choosing schools for their children. As discussed earlier, parents may make decisions based on whether they deem the school socially acceptable rather than solely on whether the school is academically successful.[47] Related research in the context of this district demonstrates that parental choice is strongly motivated by social factors rather than academic factors.[48] In other words, because of underenrollment in all schools in the district (including higher-performing schools), intradistrict transfer participants in this district could choose high performing schools; however, our analysis demonstrates that, on average, parents do not rely solely on academic criteria to choose a school for their children.

The Effects of Intradistrict Transfers

To determine the effects of intradistrict transfer on student achievement, we ran two sets of models: one predicting language arts achievement, and one predicting mathematics achievement. The results of both models consistently demonstrate that, in general, intradistrict transfers do not affect student achievement outcomes. Intradistrict transfers are associated with a 2 percent of a standard deviation gain in language arts achievement scores; however, this effect is small and not statistically significant (see table 5.1, model 1). Furthermore, intradistrict transfers do not significantly affect achievement growth.

We found similar results for mathematics achievement. Intradistrict transfers were associated with a 1.5 percent of a standard deviation increase in mathematics test scores, but the effect was neither statistically significant nor large enough to be meaningful (see table 5.2, model 1). Therefore, on average, intradistrict transfers do not influence student test scores in either language arts or mathematics.

TABLE 5.1 **Effects of intradistrict transfers on student achievement in language arts**

	Model 1			Model 2		
Variable list						
Intercept	0.190	−0.04	***	0.066	−0.04	
Time	0.027	−0.01	*	0.031	−0.01	*
Treatment variables						
Student participated in intradistrict transfer	0.022	−0.03		—		
Transfer participation × time	−0.008	−0.02		−0.003	−0.02	
Choice type (ref=student attended a failing zoned school)						
Student did not choose and attended a higher school	—			0.144	−0.03	***
Student zoned to higher school and chose a higher school	—			0.168	−0.04	***
Student zoned to higher school and chose a lower school	—			0.012	−0.06	
Student zoned to lower school and chose a lower school	—			−0.019	−0.04	
Student zoned to lower school and chose a higher school	—			0.141	−0.04	***
Student prior achievement						
Spring achievement for prior year	0.679	−0.01	***	0.667	−0.01	***
Student background measures						
Student gender (ref = male)						
Female	0.050	−0.02	**	0.051	−0.02	**
Student participates in free lunch program	−0.163	−0.02	***	−0.126	−0.03	***
Student race (ref = white)						
Asian	0.053	−0.04		0.065	−0.04	
Black	−0.104	−0.05	*	−0.083	−0.04	
American Indian	−0.149	−0.06	**	−0.119	−0.05	*
Latino	−0.160	−0.03	***	−0.121	−0.03	***
Pacific Islander	−0.090	−0.06		−0.056	−0.06	
Student is an English language learner	−0.045	−0.02	*	−0.006	−0.02	
Student has mild disability	−0.256	−0.03	***	−0.260	−0.03	***
Student guardianship (ref = two parents)						
One parent	−0.010	−0.02		−0.009	−0.02	
Other guardianship	−0.134	−0.05	*	−0.131	−0.05	*
Student grade (ref = fourth grade)						
Fifth	−0.008	−0.02		−0.006	−0.02	
Sixth	−0.010	−0.03		−0.012	−0.03	
Number of years student has attended school in district	−0.004	−0.01				
R^2	0.6409	0.005		0.6451	−0.01	

$***p < .001; **p < .01; *p < .05$

TABLE 5.2 **Effects of intradistrict transfers on student achievement in mathematics**

	Model 1			Model 2		
Variable list						
Intercept	0.242	−0.04	***	0.073	−0.06	
Time	0.018	−0.02		0.040	−0.02	*
Treatment variables						
Student participated in intradistrict transfer	0.016	−0.03		—		
Transfer participation × time	−0.034	−0.02		−0.041	−0.03	
Choice type (ref = student attended a failing zoned school)						
Student did not choose and attended a higher school	—			0.178	−0.04	***
Student zoned to higher school and chose a higher school	—			0.192	−0.05	***
Student zoned to higher school and chose a lower school	—			0.015	−0.06	
Student zoned to lower school and chose a lower school	—			0.034	−0.06	
Student zoned to lower school and chose a higher school	—			0.147	−0.05	**
Student prior achievement						
Spring achievement for prior year	0.634	−0.01	***	0.628	−0.01	***
Student background measures						
Student gender (ref = male)						
Female	0.030	−0.02		0.027	−0.02	
Student participates in free lunch program	−0.140	−0.03	***	−0.109	−0.03	***
Student race (ref = white)						
Asian	0.097	−0.06		0.094	−0.06	
Black	−0.207	−0.06	***	−0.196	−0.06	***
American Indian	−0.166	−0.08	*	−0.129	−0.08	
Latino	−0.182	−0.03	***	−0.148	−0.03	***
Pacific Islander	−0.121	−0.05	*	−0.099	−0.05	*
Student is an English language learner	−0.002	−0.03		0.036	−0.03	
Student has mild disability	−0.293	−0.04	***	−0.291	−0.04	***
Student guardianship (ref = two parents)						
One parent	−0.069	−0.02	**	−0.068	−0.02	**
Other guardianship	−0.117	−0.06		−0.130	−0.06	*
Student grade (ref = fourth grade)						
Fifth	0.028	−0.03		0.029	−0.03	
Sixth	−0.013	−0.03		−0.015	−0.03	
Number of years student has attended school in district	−0.004	−0.01		−0.004	−0.01	
R^2	0.5514			0.5561		

***$p < .001$; **$p < .01$; *$p < .05$

Switching from a Lower-Performing School
to a Higher-Performing School

Even though intradistrict transfers in general do not affect academic achievement, we also test for the possibility that this type of school choice may be effective in raising achievement for students who use intradistrict transfers as a way to move from a lower-performing zoned school to a higher-performing choice school. To examine this possibility, instead of using our dichotomous treatment variable we used a series of dummy variables aimed at addressing the effect of intradistrict transfers for students who were zoned to lower-performing schools but chose to attend higher-performing schools. When compared with students who were zoned to lower-performing schools and remained in those schools, the choices of students who transferred to higher-performing schools positively and significantly affected their level of achievement in language arts and mathematics. When students use choice to leave a lower-performing school and attend a higher-performing school, intradistrict transfer improves their language arts test scores by 14 percent ($p < 0.001$) of a standard deviation (see table 5.1, model 2). A similar trend emerged when we examined the effects of intradistrict transfer on mathematics achievement. Students who left a lower-performing zoned school to attend a higher-performing choice school scored nearly 15 percent ($p < 0.001$) of a standard deviation higher in mathematics than did students who did not exercise choice and remained in a lower-performing zoned school (see table 5.2, model 2).[49] Furthermore, the size of these effects is large. In fact, according to our models, leaving a lower-performing school to attend a higher-performing school can more than make up the achievement difference associated with low-SES students (as measured by student participation in free and reduced-price lunch), after controlling for prior achievement. Thus, we suggest that the effects associated with leaving a lower-performing school to attend a higher-performing school are both large and meaningful.

Although intradistrict transfer does not affect student achievement outcomes in general, it does increase achievement for students who make policy- and theory-relevant choices by using school choice options to leave lower-performing schools and attend higher-performing schools. These results demonstrate that intradistrict transfers do, in fact, increase student achievement in ways hypothesized by theories of school choice and also by current federal education initiatives and policies that promote school choice as an accountability mechanism. However, these findings are tempered by another finding of our study: that very few students actually engage in school choices that facilitate increased achievement.

The context of this district makes these findings particularly important. Given that all students can attend their first choice of school, each student who participated in intradistrict transfers should be attending the school that represents an ideal school match for that student. These results suggest one of two possibilities: first, that parents do not necessarily choose the schools that provide an ideal school–student match (either because they face constraints when exercising choice, because they lack information about schools, or because they do not necessarily know how to best match their children to schools), or, second, that an "ideal match" does not necessarily improve achievement unless such a match involves switching to a school that is of significantly higher quality than the school the student would otherwise be attending. In either case, improved academic achievement as a result of intradistrict transfer participation can be expected only for 19 percent of the students who exercise choice in this district. Furthermore, this group of students represents only about 3 percent of the elementary student body in the district.

CONCLUSIONS AND POLICY RECOMMENDATIONS

This study addresses the relationship between student achievement and intradistrict transfer options within a unique context. Intradistrict transfer options are important forms of school choice that have been increasing in popularity across the United States but have largely remained unstudied. Our study of intradistrict transfers is an important contribution to the literature on school choice and achievement, because it offers a rigorous examination of a rapidly growing form of choice within a specific context. Our study suggests that for the majority of students, intradistrict transfer has no effect on achievement; however, it does have a significant effect for students who choose to leave a low performing school to attend a high performing school. This indicates that a change in school quality may be more influential than simply a change in schools. Furthermore, this study highlights the degree to which consistent effects on achievement for any specific type of school choice (whether it be intradistrict transfers or other choice options) could be masked by differences between the schools that parents choose for their children and the schools these students would have attended if a choice mechanism had not been in place. In other words, school choice must be examined within the context in which such choices are made.

Furthermore, the context in which we study intradistrict transfers is unique in that it limits the extent to which traditional barriers inhibit choice and all students are granted access to their first-choice school. This contextual element is particularly important for two reasons. First, these factors essentially allow all parents the opportunity to send their children to the school they believe would provide the best school–student match. Furthermore, because all choosers were able to enroll in their first-choice school, we know that our findings accurately represent the natural choices people make about their children's schooling. Second, these contextual factors also mean that we can isolate the effects of simply participating in choice. The choice behavior is not confounded by program effects or the inability to attend the first-choice school due to space limitations. Thus, our findings on the relationship between choice and achievement accurately identify the effects of intradistrict transfers as well as the types of choices parents make as they occur in a natural setting.

The results of this study are encouraging in that they demonstrate that certain types of school choices can indeed raise student achievement. Furthermore, unlike voucher programs, charter schools, and magnet schools, intradistrict transfers are easy to implement and relatively inexpensive, because they do not rely on specialized programs or choice options that fall outside the public school system. The unfortunate side of our results is that the vast majority of the intradistrict transfer participants in our study did not make the types of choices necessary to improve student achievement. In fact, parents were likely to choose schools for their children that were similar in achievement levels to the schools they left.[50] As we indicated previously, this may suggest that families make decisions based on criteria other than a school's academic performance.

As is highlighted in this chapter, the type of unrestricted school choice we examine in this study will likely not facilitate widespread improvement in student achievement. However, as we find in this study, intradistrict transfer may result in a general shuffling of students from one school to another school that performs similarly. As such, intradistrict transfers demonstrate little promise for improving student achievement in meaningful, systematic ways. From a policy perspective, this study demonstrates that choice by itself—even in the best of contexts and circumstances—will likely not improve student achievement. However, this study also highlights the fact that certain types of choice are related to increased student achievement. In an effort to maximize the positive results associated with intradistrict transfers as they are highlighted in this study, policy makers may consider a few possibilities. One is that school choice plans may be more effective in raising student achievement if they are targeted toward students who are most likely to face educational disadvantages (including all students who are zoned to lower-performing schools) and if the available choice options are restricted to high-quality schools. Because this district's higher-performing schools consist of mostly white and mostly middle-class students, the schools in the district are segregated. Furthermore, school choice results in even greater segregation of racial (or ethnic) minority and low-SES students. Within this context, controlled choice plans might include an effort to implement SES balancing to decrease stratification in the district and to eliminate disparities between lower- and higher-performing schools.

Another possible consideration for maximizing the positive effects of choice identified in this study is to consider policies aimed at improving schools. Because school intradistrict choice in our analyses does not generally affect achievement, the most important aspect of school choice may be the possibility of choosing a better school. Thus, school quality is a more influential factor in predicting achievement than school choice. Therefore, in conjunction with school choice initiatives, policy makers may be more successful in raising student achievement by focusing on ways to improve schools.

We may expect too much from school choice when we hypothesize that it will—by itself—improve educational outcomes for all students. As this study suggests, even in a context that provides a best-case scenario for reducing barriers to choice, school choice policies face severe limitations in their ability to raise student achievement. We suggest that school choice policies may work best when they operate in coordination with other policies aimed at targeting specific problems in specific contexts.

PART III

Parent Choice

6

Do Parents Do As They Say?

Choosing Indianapolis Charter Schools

Marc L. Stein, Ellen B. Goldring, and Xiu Cravens

Much of the debate surrounding school choice in general and charter schools in particular concerns the types of students who will choose to leave their traditional public school (TPS) for a charter school and the effects these choices may have on the schools they are leaving behind.[1] As Witte and Thorn have noted, one of the most important sets of research questions in this regard is, "Who chooses and why?"[2] This question set is important because it addresses the persistent fear, especially among opponents of public school choice, that expanded public school choice may lead to an increase in school segregation along racial, ethnic, and socioeconomic lines.[3] They also fear it will exacerbate inequities based on special needs.[4] Another concern is that it will lead to "cream skimming," whereby charter schools take higher-performing students from traditional public schools.[5]

"Who chooses and why?" also addresses the role of parents in the school choice process. Advocates argue that parents will make rational decisions and "will opt for a school that can provide the best education for their child."[6] The notion is that parents will leave low performing schools to opt for higher-performing schools and that academics will be the main driver of parents' school choices. If school choice is to be an engine for school improvement through competition and innovation, as hypothesized, then parent choice based on academic performance is key. Given this, it is important to understand why parents make the school choices they do.

The focus of this chapter, then, is to unpack the "who chooses and why" question, with special attention to why parents choose. Getting to the answer is complex. The most straightforward methodology is to simply ask parents and students why they choose to attend a charter school. Much research regarding reasons for school choice follows this approach by using surveys or parent or guardian interviews.[7] However, as discussed later, it is difficult to ascertain the extent to which espoused reasons for choice actually mirror real choices that parents and students make; surveys and interviews can be biased.

Using a unique data set of charter schools authorized by the Indianapolis mayor's office, this chapter compares parents' stated reasons for choosing a charter school versus their revealed preferences as evidenced by their actual school switching behavior. Specifically, we address the following research questions:

- To what extent do public school switchers say they switch to a charter school for academic versus other reasons in a parent survey?
- How do these espoused preferences compare to revealed (actual) preferences based on school switching behavior?

STUDYING PARENT CHOICE PREFERENCES

An educational reform strategy that has gained traction and popularity over the past decade is the idea of public school choice, meaning that parents and students should have more choices in the types of public schools they attend. Charter schools are the most widespread public school choice option; broadly speaking, charter schools are publicly funded schools that are granted some measure of independence from state and district regulations in exchange for accountability to increase student achievement.[8] In part because of this broad definition of charter schools, they have wide appeal across divergent philosophical and ideological sectors of American society.[9]

Embedded within the market metaphor of school choice, charter schooling operates on the notion that parents and students will be active consumers of education, and, as such, they will make school choices that best fit academic and social needs. The underlying assumption of this market metaphor is that when given a wider choice of schools in which to enroll their children, parents will shop around, weighing all available evidence and information on curricula, missions, services, and academic accomplishments and achievements.[10] They will then make informed decisions as to which school best fits their own educational beliefs and needs.

Charter school proponents argue that allowing parents and students to choose their schools will lead to family–school matches in which educational needs and values are closely aligned, and that in turn will increase the likelihood of positive educational outcomes such as higher achievement and graduation. This is both a supply- and a demand-side argument. From the supply side, proponents argue that to remain in business, charter schools must be responsive to the needs and wants of the market and their consumers. On the demand side, parents' and students' choices signal to charter schools and the market their preferences and desires for schools and education, whether in curricula (e.g., "back to basics," Afrocentric) or other tangible and intangible characteristics.

Empirical evidence of parents' school preferences in the context of school choice comes generally from two sources. First, many studies have used surveys of parents to gauge the importance of various school characteristics (e.g., academic quality, racial composition) on parent choices. Most of this survey research indicates that all parents, regardless of race, ethnicity, or socioeconomic status, tend to report that the academic quality of schools is at the top of their list of important characteristics.[11]

A careful review of the surveys and interview protocols used by researchers to study the role of academics in parent preferences, however, reveals confusion regarding the questions that were asked. There are a number of errors pertaining to construct validity, wording ambiguity, cognitive complexity, item priming effects, social desirability, and mood state and temporal influences.[12] In what follows, we discuss these sources of confusion.

Regarding construct validity, it is not clear what the research is measuring when referring to academics as a preference for school choice, because researchers tend to ask different questions, and the wording of the questions varies from study to study. This variability leaves open to interpretation what is meant by "academics." Schneider et al. included such statements as "quality of teachers and staff" and "high math and reading scores."[13] Kleitz et al. asked, "How important was educational quality to you when you chose your child's charter school?"[14] Weiher and Tedin asked parents to identify the most important factor from a list, including "test scores," whereas Teske et al. used the term "academic quality."[15] Lee et al. asked about school qualities in the choice process, including, "The school requires students to take a lot of classes in basic subjects like math, English and science."[16] Goldring and Rowley asked parents to rate each criterion for choosing a school as being a high, medium, or low priority in their thinking about school choice.[17] Then composites were derived from factor analysis: "academic priority" consisted of (alpha reliability = 0.68) items such as the overall reputation of the school, the school's test scores, and the quality of the teachers.

A second source of confusion results from the way the questions on the surveys or in interviews were asked. Some researchers asked, "Which reason is the most important?" whereas others used open-ended questions, rankings, or a Likert scale. Thus, some of these question types are relative to other reasons of choice (ranking), but others are rated on a scale. Still others are quite complex, especially those asked over the telephone. One telephone survey read the following:

> Different parents believe that different things are important. We are interested in knowing which things you think are important. In this next section I will read you a list of some of the things that parents believe are important in a school and I'd like to know what you believe to be most important in your child's education. From the following list of qualities about schools, first tell me which is the most important to you.[18]

The list of eleven items was then repeated four times, each time omitting already named responses, changing the order of the list to control for order effects. A similarly complex question is from Lee et al., also an interview:

> People consider a number of different things when they choose a school for their children. Even if you do not have school-age children, please tell me the three qualities on the list that you would consider to be the most important in choosing a child's school. Which quality would you consider to be the least important?[19]

Ranking in general is a difficult task, and doing it numerous times without having the items in front of the respondent can increase the complexity.

Such long introductions may also bias a respondent because of item priming, that is, "inclusion of an introduction that informs the respondent about what the items are attempting to measure before the respondent views the items, thereby increasing the face validity of the items."[20] Although Schneider and colleagues randomized the order of the choices to control for order effects, this factor may be an influence in other surveys or interviews used to inquire about parents' decisions.

Furthermore, survey research must always consider the threat posed by social desirability: the propensity for respondents to answer in self-serving or socially desirable ways. Social desirability suggests that respondents will want to represent themselves in a favorable way through their survey responses.[21] What parent respondent will readily indicate that his first, most important reason for choosing a school is race or social status? Or what parents would not indicate that some type of academic consideration was a factor in choosing a school? Kleitz et al. acknowledge that parents would be aware that they should say educational quality is an important reason for choosing a school.[22] Weiher and Tedin clearly state the problem with many of these studies: "A common weakness of this research into the ethnic and racial implications of choice for choosers themselves is that the linkage between respondents' stated preferences and actual racial and ethnic patterns in choice schools tend to be tenuous."[23] One obvious reason is the social undesirability of expressing racial or ethnic reasons for choosing a school. Even if it were a response option on a survey, it is highly unlikely that parents would be willing to choose this response, even if racial or ethnic concerns were driving their decisions and choices in school.

Finally, some of the parent responses may suffer from mood state or temporal influences. That is, the person's mood at the time she responds to a survey or interview, or her mood over a period of time, could influence her responses. If a parent had a negative or positive encounter with his previous school over time or during a particular time close to the data collection, it is hard to evaluate the extent to which these external factors or events could influence survey responses. In short, there may be common method bias in surveys and interviews used to evaluate the extent to which academic preferences are important to parents in making school choice decisions.[24]

In an effort to clear the hurdle of these confusions arising from self-report measures, a handful of recent studies (because of the difficulty of obtaining the data) examined parents' decisions by analyzing their actual choices of schools. Using longitudinal student-level data, researchers have tracked students from their initial school of enrollment (before making a switch) to their school of choice to assess the extent to which parents' actual choices indicate their switching from a school having lower academic achievements to a school having higher achievements.[25] For the most part these studies have looked at parental choices to investigate student sorting based on individual achievement and race or ethnicity.

For example, in a study of California and Texas charter school students, Booker et al. found that in both states it appears that charter schools are not skimming the best students, as many opponents of charters fear. Rather, they appear to be targeting lower-achieving or more at-risk students.[26] In a similar investigation of segregation in North Carolina charter schools, Bifulco and Ladd found that African American switchers moved to charter schools whose average achievement in mathematics and reading on North Carolina end-of-grade testing was markedly lower than that of the school from which they came, whereas white students tended to enroll in charter schools that had higher average mathematics and reading achievement than the traditional public schools they left.[27]

In the most recent study to date of this type, Zimmer et al. looked at switching patterns of traditional public school students who had switched to a charter school in seven sites compared to nonswitchers from the same districts and states.[28] In all but one case (reading scores in Chicago), the authors found that charter school switchers had achievement scores that were, on average, lower than those of their nonswitching peers. When disaggregated by race or ethnicity, comparisons showed that African American switchers had lower scores in five of the seven sites and that Hispanic switchers had lower average achievement in four of seven sites (compared with scores of their same-ethnicity nonswitching peers). In contrast, white switchers in four of the seven sites had achievement scores that were higher than those of their nonswitching white peers.

Although the results of these studies do not speak directly to the role of perceptions of schools' academic quality in driving school choices, they do raise questions as to whether parents choose for academic reasons, whether they have sufficient information about the schools they are choosing, and whether they actually know whether their chosen schools have better academic performance than the schools from which they are removing their children. It also raises the possibility that parents switch schools based on reasons beyond academic considerations. Prior research has noted location, discipline, race, and overall "school reputation" as factors that influence parent choices.[29]

In summary, studies of actual switching contrast with the self-report survey findings and demonstrate the need for closer examinations of parents' choices of schools. In this chapter we extend this line of research by comparing actual choices with espoused choices on a parent survey.

METHODOLOGY

Context of the Study

Indiana passed initial legislation authorizing charter schools in 2001, with revisions in 2007. The law provides for multiple authorizers, funding formulas on par with those of traditional public schools, and the presence of automatic waivers from state and district regulations and policies.[30] The charter law is unique in that it gives the mayor of Indianapolis the power to authorize charter schools. Beginning with three charter schools that opened in the fall of 2002, the Indianapolis mayor's office has chartered a total of nineteen schools. (It closed one financially troubled school in the fall of 2009.) At the time of this study, the average time the charter schools had been in operation was approximately three years; the range spanned from start-up to five years. The smallest schools enrolled about one hundred students, and the largest enrolled just over six hundred. Average enrollment was two hundred fifty students.

Parents in Indianapolis who consider enrolling their children in a mayoral charter school have a wide variety of options, ranging from schools that focus on a "back-to-basics" curriculum of math and reading, to those specializing in the arts or technology, to those offering a college preparatory curriculum, to those based on experiential learning. Some charter schools are run by national networks, such as Knowledge Is Power Program (KIPP), or are associated with school reform groups, such as the Big Picture Company; other schools are locally developed. For example, a number of the charter schools were developed by local philanthropists and community groups with particular emphases, such as serving students with limited English or infusing technology in school.

Data and Methods

In spring 2007, the National Center on School Choice administered surveys to parents having children enrolled in mayoral charter schools in operation in Indianapolis. Parents were offered a $15 gift card if they returned the survey, and classes (homerooms) received a $200 gift card if 80 percent of the classroom parents returned the survey. These procedures resulted in 84 percent of parents responding, for a total of 2,493 parents. Of these, 1,587 (63.7 percent) reported that they had switched to their current charter school from another public school—either a traditional public school (N = 1,471) or another charter public school (N = 116). Because of the lack of data availability for private and homeschooled students, these records are excluded from the analysis, and we focus on public school switchers only. We call these parents "charter school switchers." Further, data from one of the mayoral charter schools were removed because it serves a special population of students who are recovering from drug and alcohol addictions (*n* = 15). Finally, we have removed three twelfth-grade parent observations because of low sample size. After these restrictions our sample includes 1,569 parent records of charter school switchers enrolled in an Indianapolis mayoral charter school during the 2006–2007 academic year.

Parent Demographics. From demographic and personal information that we gathered from the parent surveys, we constructed a measure of parents' socioeconomic status (SES) using a combination of reported parent education and family income. Across all parents in the sample, the mean reported income is approximately $31,000, and the mean highest level of education approximates to having gone to college but did not graduate. There is wide variation in mean parental SES across mayoral charter schools in Indianapolis. The school having the highest mean parental SES has an average parental annual income of approximately $42,000, and an average parental education level that is between some college and an undergraduate degree. In comparison, the school with the lowest average parental SES has an average parental annual income of approximately $25,000, and an average parental education level between a high school graduate and some college. There is also considerable variation in parental SES among parents within the same schools.

We asked parents on the survey, "What race or ethnic background do you identify with?" Responses were coded into four groups: white (388, 24.7 percent), black (959, 61.1 percent), Latino (83, 5.3 percent), and other (139, 8.9 percent). These percentages reflect the racial or ethnic composition of the Indianapolis public schools from which the majority of these students come; however, there is also a wide range of variation in ethnic composition between charter schools, which vary from ones that are predominately African American to some that are predominately white.

Variables: Parents' Espoused Preferences. To ascertain parents' emphasis on academics as a reason for choosing their charter school, we created a variable from the parent survey that we have termed *Academics as a Top Priority for School Choice* (ATP). Parents were asked to select the first and second most important reasons for choosing the specific charter school for their children. Parents were categorized as placing an emphasis on academics as a top priority if they selected one of two academic-related responses as the first most important reason for their choice.[31]

To further triangulate parents' espoused preferences, we asked about their perception of the quality of their child's previous school. Parents may exercise school choice options to enroll their children in a charter school if they feel that the academic quality of their currently enrolled school is not high enough or if they perceive it to be of poor academic quality. In a sense, a perception of poor academic quality may operate to "push" parents away from their currently enrolled school and compel them to look for better perceived options through school choice. Each respondent was asked to rate the overall quality of the school that her child went to immediately prior to this school as excellent, very good, good, fair, or poor. Answers of excellent or very good were coded as Above Average (386, 24.3 percent), answers of good and fair were coded as Average (861, 54.9 percent), and answers of poor were coded as Below Average (313, 19.9 percent). Thirteen (0.82 percent) parents did not respond and were treated as missing.

Finally, a third variable is the parents' estimate of the average grade that their child received at the previous school, from A to F. As with a parent's perception of the quality of the child's previous school, we might expect that parents whose child is performing poorly may have an additional reason to enroll the child in a new school. The responses were coded into four grade average levels: D or F (186, 11.9 percent), C (467, 29.8 percent), B (462, 29.5 percent), and A (273, 17.4 percent). Nonresponses and parents who responded "No grades given" at their previous school were coded as missing (181, 11.5 percent).

Parents Revealed (Actual) Preferences. To investigate the actual behavior of parents who switched to charter schools—charter school switchers—we used data from the Northwest Evaluation Association's (NWEA) growth research database (GRD) of student testing records. This database is linked to school demographic data from the National Center for Education Statistics Core of Common Data. NWEA is a nonprofit student achievement testing company that tests students in grades 2 through 10 in mathematics, reading, and language arts. From the 2002–2003 to the 2005–2006 school year, the Indianapolis Public Schools and other metropolitan public school districts located within Marion County, Indiana, contracted with NWEA to provide testing in the fall and spring semesters. Also during this time all of the mayoral charter schools contracted with NWEA for testing.

Of the 2,807 students who were tested in the fifteen mayoral charter schools during the 2006–2007 school year, we were able to locate 1,050 students in their school of enrollment before they switched to a charter school. These students represent approximately 37 percent of the total students enrolled in the fifteen mayoral charter schools in grades 2 through 11 in the 2006–2007 school year.[32] Unfortunately, we cannot link the parent surveys to the student records because the surveys were anonymous. Although we cannot link parent responses to their actual switching behavior at the individual level, we can examine the two data sources to seek general patterns in parents' espoused and actual choices and draw inferences from those patterns about parental choices in the mayoral charter schools. We examine the academic level at students' previous and current schools by comparing students' previous schools to their current charter schools in terms of academic achievement as measured by Adequate Yearly Progress (AYP) status under the state of Indiana's No Child Left Behind plan. We also examine the switching patterns by reviewing academic achievement as measured by NWEA achievement tests in mathematics and reading.

RESULTS

We first ask, To what extent do parents espouse academics as a top priority in their reasons for choosing a charter school? We then compare these results to parents' actual switching behavior to see whether espoused preferences are similar to actual preferences.

Parents' Espoused Reasons for Choosing a Charter School

To what extent do parents espouse academics as a top priority in their reasons for choosing a charter school for their children? We first examine the distribution of parents' responses as captured by our variable ATP from the parent surveys. Overall, a majority of parents (63 percent) state that academics are a top priority in their choice of a charter school.[33]

Although there is little variation across grades in parental rankings of academics as a top priority, with the noted exception between high school and lower levels, there appears to be much more variation in ATP by individual schools (see figure 6.1). For example in school N, which is known for its accelerated learning and college preparatory curriculum, 81 percent of parents rated ATP as the first reason for their choice of school, compared with only 31 percent of parents in school G, where the curriculum is centered on individualized attention in small classes and out-of-school internships. Both of these schools are high schools, indicating that even though, overall, high school parents had lower on average reporting of ATP, there is significant variation not only between all schools but also between schools of the same instructional level. This result may signal differences in mission, organizational structure, academic features, student population, and other school-level characteristics. In a case study of school N we learned that it is known both for its rigorous expectations of students (e.g., all students must take a college-level class as part of a middle college program) and for its assumption that all students and parents understand these expectations upon enrollment.

FIGURE 6.1   Variation in parental ranking of ATP by school

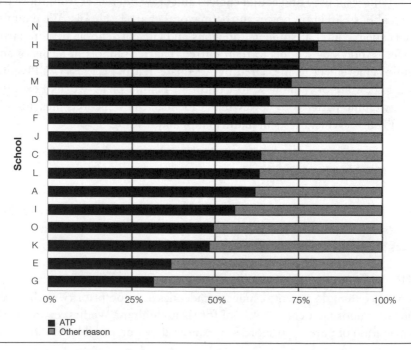

To further investigate parents' espoused preferences we looked at the association between our other two academic factors and the way parents regarded academics as a top priority. To detect whether there is an association between ATP and parent-reported previous academic performance, and between ATP and grades received at the previous schools, we created a contingency table from each of the two sets of factors. The contingency tables allowed us to determine whether the levels of ratings between the two factors in each table are independent of each other.

First, we looked at parents' ratings of the academic quality of their previous school compared to their preference for academics as a top priority for choosing their charter school. From the row labeled "Total" in table 6.1, we see that 20.1 percent of parents rated their previous school as being below average, 55.3 percent rated it as average, and the remaining 24.6 percent rated it as above average. We detect a small association between parents' report of the quality of their previous school and their academic priority.[34] A smaller percentage of parents who rated their previous school as above average reports academics as a top priority (57.3 percent) than parents who rated their previous schools as average or below average (65.0 and 65.8 percent, respectively). Across racial or ethnic and socioeconomic groups of parents we found very similar patterns. We might think of this finding as evidence of a potential push factor for parents who believed that their previous school was unsatisfactory and therefore removed their children from that school for a charter school for academic reasons.

Another factor that might push parents to exercise school choice options and enroll their child in a charter school is a displeasure with the academic performance of their child in the previous school. For example, if a child does poorly in school as measured by parents' reports of average grades received, parents may feel that their child is not being served academically and seek a different educational environment. It may also be that parents of students who are doing well academically (as measured by the grades they

TABLE 6.1   **Academics as a top priority by perceptions of the quality of previous school for all parents**

Academics as top priority	QUALITY OF PREVIOUS SCHOOL			
	Below average	Average	Above average	Total
No	107 (34.2%)	301 (35.0%)	163 (42.7%)	571 (36.7%)
Yes	206 (65.8%)	560 (65.0%)	219 (57.3%)	985 (63.3%)
Total	313 (20.1%)	861 (55.3%)	382 (24.6%)	1,556

Pearson χ^2 (2) = 7.8362 Pr = 0.020, N=1556

received in the previous school) may feel dissatisfied with the academic experiences of their child despite the good grades because the child is not being adequately challenged. Table 6.2 presents the data regarding the relationship between parents' academic priority in school choice (ATP) and average grades received by their child at the previous school. Tests of statistical significance failed to find a significant relationship between the previous grade and whether parents reported academics as the primary reason for choosing a charter school. We also examined these factors across racial and socioeconomic groups and found no significant differences between these groups of parents and the overall pattern of relationship between previous grades received and rating academics as a top priority.

These patterns seem to indicate that for many parents who chose to switch to a mayoral charter school in Indianapolis, the perception of academic quality, but not their child's grades, was an impetus for their decision to switch to charter schools. Further it appears that these perceptions of academics may have acted as both push and pull factors in their decision; perceptions of low academic quality in the previous school may have pushed parents to seek a different school for their children. The high level of ATP suggests that for some parents, there is a pull to charter schools based on perception of academic quality. Together, the patterns suggest that there is considerable support for the notion that academic reasons are a strong component of parents' stated preferences for switching and choosing a charter school.

Revealed (Actual) Parent Preferences

Do Indianapolis parents' actual choices of charter schools reinforce their stated preferences from the survey findings? To inform this question we looked at AYP, a widely available potential indicator of academic quality that could reasonably inform parents' notions of a school's academic quality. AYP status is reported publicly every year for all schools under No Child Left Behind provisions. AYP scores are reported in local news sources as well as

TABLE 6.2   **Academics as a top priority by grades received at previous school, for all parents**

| Academics as top priority | PREVIOUS GRADE | | | | |
	D or F	C	B	A	Total
No	75 (40.3%)	178 (38.1%)	152 (32.9%)	92 (33.7%)	497 (35.8%)
Yes	111 (59.7%)	289 (61.9%)	310 (67.1%)	181 (66.3%)	891 (64.2%)
Total	186 (13.4%)	467 (33.6%)	462 (33.3%)	273 (19.7%)	1,388

Pearson χ^2 (3) = 4.9584   Pr = 0.175, N=1388

on school, district, and state Web sites. If parents are making school choices based on perceived quality (as evidenced in the survey results), then we might expect to see parents making charter school choices that switch their children from schools that failed to make AYP to schools that did make AYP, or at the very least switching horizontally between schools that did make AYP. We investigated actual choices by comparing the AYP status of students' previous schools (the "sending" school) with the AYP status of the charter to which they switched (the "receiving" school) in the year before the switch.

To set the context of the AYP landscape among mayoral charters and traditional public schools in Marion County, table 6.3 presents the total number of schools from each sector that met and did not meet AYP for a given school year from 2002–2003 through 2006–2007. Over time we see a rise in the number of traditional public schools in Marion County failing to make AYP, from a low of 43 percent of schools in 2002–2003 to 60.9 percent of schools in 2006–2007. This pattern may indicate the structure of rising AYP targets within the No Child Left Behind system. The first section of table 6.3 shows the introduction of new mayoral charter schools over time (those that have no AYP rating due to their being new schools). Further, we see that by the end of the section in 2006–2007, 60.0 percent of the mayoral charters did not meet AYP, and that is similar to the trend for traditional public schools in Marion County.

When we look at the patterns of actual choices we see that the vast majority of switchers are switching from schools that failed to make AYP (see table 6.4). We divide the sample of parent switchers into two groups: those who switched to the current charter school from another charter school (charter school switchers), and those who switched to their current charter school

TABLE 6.3   AYP status by year for charter and traditional public schools in Marion County, 2002–2007

School year		2002–2003		2003–2004		2004–2005		2005–2006		2006–2007	
Charter schools	Did not meet AYP	0	0.0%	0	0.0%	0	0.0%	6	46.2%	9	60.0%
	Met AYP	1	33.3%	5	83.3%	4	40.0%	4	30.8%	4	26.7%
	No rating	2	66.7%	1	16.7%	6	60.0%	3	23.1%	2	13.3%
	Total schools	3		6		10		13		15	
Marion County TPS	Did not meet AYP	79	43.4%	93	48.9%	127	63.2%	121	60.5%	120	60.9%
	Met AYP	103	56.6%	97	51.1%	74	36.8%	79	39.5%	77	39.1%
	Total schools	182		190		201		200		197	

TABLE 6.4 Patterns of choice as a function of AYP status of sending school and receiving school

| | | RECEIVING SCHOOL | | | | | | | | | | | |
| | | CPS SWITCHERS | | | | TPS SWITCHERS | | | | TOTAL | | | |
Sending School		Failed AYP	Passed AYP	No AYP	Total	Failed AYP	Passed AYP	No AYP	Total	Failed AYP	Passed AYP	No AYP	Total
Elementary school switchers	Failed AYP	16.1	9.7	25.8	51.6	16.7	16.7	18.5	51.8	16.6	16.0	19.2	51.8
	Passed AYP	9.7	11.3	24.2	45.2	15.2	20.7	12.3	48.2	14.7	19.7	13.5	47.9
	No AYP	0.0	1.6	1.6	3.2	0.0	0.0	0.0	0.0	0.0	0.2	0.2	0.3
	Total	25.8	22.6	51.6	100.0	31.9	37.3	30.8	100.0	31.3	35.8	32.9	100.0
Secondary school switchers	Failed AYP	15.6	6.3	9.4	31.3	42.6	19.1	27.5	89.1	40.6	18.1	26.1	84.9
	Passed AYP	34.4	25.0	9.4	68.8	4.0	1.5	5.4	10.9	6.2	3.2	5.7	15.1
	No AYP	0.0	0.0	0.0	0.0	0.0	0.0	0.0	0.0	0.0	0.0	0.0	0.0
	Total	50.0	31.3	18.8	100.0	46.5	20.5	32.9	100.0	46.8	21.3	31.9	100.0
Total	Failed AYP	16.0	8.5	20.2	44.7	27.6	17.7	22.3	67.6	26.6	16.9	22.1	65.5
	Passed AYP	18.1	16.0	19.1	53.2	10.5	12.6	9.4	32.4	11.1	12.9	10.3	34.3
	No AYP	0.0	1.1	1.1	2.1	0.0	0.0	0.0	0.0	0.0	0.1	0.1	0.2
	Total	40.4	34.0	25.5	100.0	31.7	38.1	30.2	100.0	37.7	29.8	32.5	100.0

from a traditional public school (TPS switchers). Overall 65.5 percent of students in this sample switched from schools that had failed AYP in the school year before their switching to a charter school. When we look by the sector of the sending school ("CPS Switchers" and "TPS Switchers" columns in table 6.4), we see that even though 67.6 percent of TPS switchers are moving from a school that failed to make AYP, only 44.7 percent of charter school switchers left a school that failed to make AYP. Overall these patterns seem to indicate that there may be a push on parents to switch from a poorly performing school to explore other educational options in charter schools.

When we look at the schools that the students switch to (the receiving schools), we see that parents are not choosing in large percentages schools that have passed AYP as expected. Rather, only 29.8 percent (last row, "Total" column, table 6.4) of students are switching to charter schools that have passed AYP, with 37.7 percent choosing charters that failed to make AYP and the remaining choosing charters that are too new to have received an AYP designation. Of particular interest in this pattern, large percentages of students and parents are choosing to switch to new charter schools for which they did not have AYP determinations to potentially assess a school's quality. This result may indicate that parents are using other sources of information to gauge the educational quality of charter schools (visits to the schools, conversations with teachers and administrators). However, this pattern may also suggest that even though parents indicated in their survey responses overwhelmingly that academic quality was most important, there are other considerations and indicators of academic quality, such as the academic focus and overall reputation of a school.

When we further disaggregate the data by school level (the Elementary and Secondary School Switchers sections, table 6.4), we see that the pattern for elementary school switchers is similar across sectors; approximately 52 percent of switchers from charter schools as well as TPSs leave schools that failed AYP. However, for secondary school switchers the vast majority of TPS switchers (89.1 percent) leave schools that failed AYP, whereas the majority of charter school switchers leave schools that passed AYP. This pattern may indicate that an academic push for parents away from poorly performing schools becomes stronger as children grow older and move into and through secondary school. However, this interpretation is tempered by the fact that 40.6 percent of secondary school switchers move from one AYP-failing designated school to another. This finding may indicate that even though there may be a strong push for parents and students to leave poorer-performing schools, they do not largely choose to switch to other schools because they are higher performing (at least as measured by overall AYP status); there is a strong possibility that there are other preferences involved in choosing a new school. For example, school safety may play a more prominent role in parent and student choices among secondary schools. Parents may switch to a school that they perceive as being safer than their previous school even though the new school is performing poorly as measured by AYP status. It is important to also remember from table 6.3 that over time, the percentage of schools failing to meet AYP (both charter schools and TPSs) has grown, and therefore the potential pool of schools to choose from that have met AYP is smaller in later years.

We next examined the switching patterns by reviewing academic achievement as measured by NWEA achievement tests in mathematics and reading. When we look at the average achievement scores of switching students' grade-level peers in both sending and receiving schools, we largely replicate the findings from our investigation of AYP status. For each switcher, a standardized grade-level aggregate average achievement was calculated for the semester immediately before students changed schools.[35] This was done for both the sending and the receiving school. Figures 6.2 and 6.3 present the distribution of standardized differences in mathematics and reading scores between switchers' previous school of enrollment and the charter school to which they switched. If parents and students were choosing to switch from lower- to higher-performing schools, then we would expect to see observations cluster in the upper-left quadrant of the figures. As with our investigation of AYP status, we see that there is no clear indication or pattern of parents and students making school choices based on higher academic achievement scores. Approximately 50 percent of parents and students choose to switch to charter schools that have higher average mathematics and reading scores, and, concomitantly, half of them choose a charter school that is relatively lower performing. The AYP analyses and the student achievement analyses do not support the notion that parents overwhelmingly choose charter schools based on these two indicators of academic quality.

CONCLUSIONS

Why do parents choose charter schools? Overwhelmingly, parents in Indianapolis mayoral charter schools indicate on parent surveys that academics are the main driver of their choice of a charter public school. However, in this study, as well as in previous studies, these results can be attributed to biases in the surveys. Therefore, we compare the revealed choices of parents by examining their switching behavior compared to those choices espoused in a parent survey.

FIGURE 6.2 **Distribution of standardized differences in mathematics scores between switchers' previous school and new charter school**

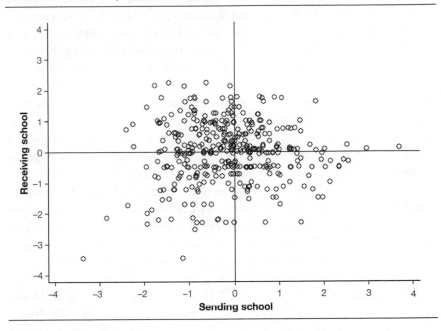

FIGURE 6.3 **Distribution of standardized differences in reading scores between switchers' previous school and new charter school**

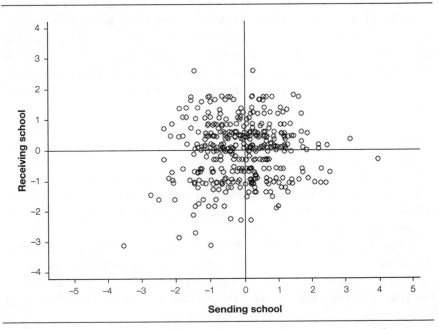

Academics as a reason for choice is less clear when parents' choices are examined in terms of the AYP status—a highly visible and public indicator of quality—of the schools they choose verses the schools the children leave. The majority (65 percent) of parents and students in our sample leave traditional public schools that did not pass AYP in the year before their switch. This choice may indicate parent and student dissatisfaction with the academic quality of the previous school as a possible reason for the decision to switch to a charter public school. However, if school quality, at least as indicated by AYP, is a main driver of choice, then we would expect to see parents choosing charter schools that have passed AYP, indicating a switch to a "higher-quality" school. However, this was not the case. Only one-third of students, on average, chose to enroll in a charter that had passed AYP. Most interesting is the finding that 32.5 percent of parents and students choose to enroll in charter schools that are new and therefore have no AYP designation.

Our findings may indicate that parents base their determination of school quality on indicators other than AYP, such as the overall reputation of a school. In fact, prior research on school choice clearly indicates that parents rely on informal social networks to collect information to make choices regarding their children's education.[36] Parents then share information and make interpretations and judgments about what is considered a "good school" from within their social networks. Thus, some parents may indicate they chose a charter school for academic reasons but have limited objective information regarding the actual academic state of the school they chose. Howell reports that few parents understand test score information and are unaware of their school's AYP status in Massachusetts.[37] Parents, especially those who are isolated and unemployed, may have limited access to AYP or other test score information. Those without the Internet are also at a disadvantage at a time when the Internet is becoming an increasingly important tool in school choice.[38]

The results were similar when we examined average academic achievement of grade-level peers as measured by NWEA achievement test scores in mathematics and reading. Specifically, there was no clear pattern of students switching from lower-performing schools to higher-performing schools. Although some students do switch from a lower- to a higher-performing school, there appears to be an equal number of students who switch from a higher- to a lower-performing school.

Researchers have noted that for parents, choosing a school based on its reputation for being a "good" school may be synonymous with choosing a school for "academic reasons." Academics may be a proxy for good schools, but good schools could include schools that are safe (fewer fights), have smaller class sizes (where the teacher knows the child's name), or are in a neighborhood that is accessible and free from violence.[39]

To better understand what parents mean when they indicate they make school choices based on academic quality, future research can explore what is meant by academic quality. When parents speak of academic quality, are they speaking of students' performance on standardized tests, or are they referring to particular curricula and pedagogies or an overall impression of the school (e.g., "back-to-basics" focus on mathematics and reading, emphasis on the arts, or college preparatory programs)? If the education and policy communities believe that AYP and other achievement indicators are central to parents' choices, then renewed efforts of outreach, information, and explanation are needed. If rational choice is the impetus for school choice, and if rational choices are construed as switching to schools having higher or better academic achievement, then it is important to reconsider how this information is portrayed to parents so that they can and will use it when making enrollment decisions for their children. In contrast, if parent sovereignty in making choices is the yardstick for judging school choice, then there are few criteria for judging what constitutes a good choice, beyond allowing parents to exercise their choice to maximize their own preferences, whatever they may be.

Social desirability of responses, method bias, and the difficulty in asking pointed questions on such matters as race, ethnicity, and social class suggest that alternative ways of studying these important elements of parent choice are needed. Although the choice patterns represented here do not negate the parents' self-report of academic quality as the main reason for choosing to switch to a charter school, they do provide evidence that other processes may be operative in these choices that are yet to be measured.

7

Barriers to Access

*High School Choice Processes
and Outcomes in Chicago*

*W. David Stevens, Marisa de la Torre,
and David Johnson*

O ne of the central debates in school choice policy is whether choice initiatives facilitate access to better educational opportunities for all
students. Proponents contend that low-income children of color are frequently stuck in schools that have few resources, underqualified teachers,
and unsafe learning environments. Whereas affluent families can ensure
that their children receive a quality education by enrolling them in private
schools or moving to better resourced neighborhoods, disadvantaged families generally do not have these options open to them.[1] In this view, school
choice evens the playing field by creating a mechanism that allows students
to leave schools that are not meeting their educational needs, thus giving all
children access to a broad range of school options.

Critics of school choice counter that in practice, access is compromised
in several ways. For instance, they point out that families often lack information about the quality of potential school options.[2] In addition, parents
may make choices that disadvantage their children if they take nonacademic factors into consideration. Finally, institutional constraints such as
school acceptance policies and travel challenges may prevent some students
from leaving assigned high schools. Given these factors, critics contend that
school choice programs may not provide access to high-quality schools
across social groups.

Despite various arguments endorsing or questioning the potential of
school choice initiatives to facilitate access to better educational opportunities, there have been few direct, empirical studies of this question. In this

chapter we address this research gap by assessing students' access to schools under choice systems in a mixed-methods study of high school choice in Chicago. Specifically we examine how families' choice decisions are related to access to better schools, and we identify barriers students face in leaving assigned neighborhood schools.

ACCESS UNDER SCHOOL CHOICE

Several studies suggest that disadvantaged families may be less likely than others to make informed, high-quality decisions about where to send their students. For example, parents in underserved districts often know very little about the performance or demographics of schools in their communities.[3] Additionally, they are more likely than high-income parents to rely on relatives for information about schools.[4] As a result, they may not be aware of school choice options because of their reliance on social networks that circulate lower-quality information.[5]

Disadvantaged families also consider other factors in addition to academic quality when choosing schools.[6] Smrekar and Goldring found that low-income parents were more likely than middle-class parents to consider transportation issues when choosing schools.[7] Social comfort is also an important factor, because many families value sending their children to schools where they have family and friends.[8] Although decisions favoring transportation and social comfort may be understandable, at best they do nothing to further the goal of improving access to high-quality schools, and at worst they may undermine it.[9]

In addition to poor information and decision making, there is another mechanism that might limit access to schools: in many large urban school districts, school choice is a zero sum game, with high quality and open seats in short supply. Thus, many students are at the mercy of chance as they compete in lotteries for a place at coveted schools with limited space. The emphasis on parental preferences and decision making also obscures the fact that not only do families choose schools, but also schools choose students. With selective-choice programs, students must meet minimum test score and grade requirements to be considered for admission. Even schools without formal academic admission requirements can "select" their students through other practices, such as locating in affluent neighborhoods or adopting other admission requirements that effectively weed out "undesirable" students.[10]

Finally, families make choice decisions, not in ideal markets, but in contexts with substantial transaction costs for them.[11] For example, if the supply of high-quality schools is limited and geographically dispersed, families may need to invest a great deal of money, effort, and time to access preferred educational programs. In addition, families may be deterred from removing a child from an unsatisfactory school to attend a better one because the challenge of helping children meet new classmates and adjust to new teachers can be a significant disruption to student learning. Thus, the cost of opting out of neighborhood schools may substantially restrict families' real access to other options.

Given the importance of individual preferences as well as institutional factors, we use two questions to frame our assessment of students' access to schools under choice initiatives: first, do students who leave their assigned neighborhood schools attend "better" schools? and second, why do students stay in their neighborhood schools? To ground our analysis, we examine high school choice in Chicago Public Schools (CPS). Contrary to critics' predictions, our analysis shows that students tend to go to schools having higher graduation rates and test scores than neighborhood schools when they opt out of the latter. We also argue that the primary reasons students stay in neighborhood schools are that concerns about managing the logistics of traveling discourage them from considering other institutions and that poor application strategies severely limit their chances of being accepted at other institutions. Adult support from families and schools, however, can improve students' application behaviors and increase their access to other schools.

CHOICE IN CHICAGO PUBLIC HIGH SCHOOLS

CPS students have a wide array of school options as they prepare to enter their freshman year of high school. As a default, students are assigned to a neighborhood high school with an attendance boundary. If they are not satisfied with their assignment, however, students can apply to any other high school in the city. Their options include charter high schools, career academies, selective-enrollment high schools, military academies, and special magnet programs, as well as other neighborhood high schools having available seats. If they are not accepted to another school, students attend their neighborhood school as a default.

This system of choice has been in place in CPS since 1980, when the district entered into an agreement with the U.S. Department of Justice to desegregate the school system by creating magnet schools open to all qualified students across the city.[12] CPS recently made a second big push for choice as part of the district's new efforts to improve secondary education. A prominent feature of the districts' new high school reform initiative is to create a good fit between students and schools by offering a diverse "portfolio of schools" from which families can choose.[13] Various academic, vocational, and cultural themes—as well as a mix of structures such as small, charter, and contract schools—are being developed to help meet the diverse needs of students and encourage greater buy in from their families. As of the 2009–2010 school year, there were 122 CPS high schools in operation. Thirty-eight percent of the schools have traditional attendance boundaries and serve approximately 58 percent of the students in the district. By 2007, 54 percent of the freshmen cohort attended a school outside their assigned attendance boundary.[14]

In an effort to aid students and families with the application and selection of high schools, CPS publishes an annual directory of all the high schools. This directory contains information, such as graduation rates, attendance rates, special programs, and other activities, about each school. It also contains the common application to neighborhood schools. Neighborhood schools, however, are free to create their own unique applications. In addition, there are separate applications for selective-enrollment schools, charter schools, military academies, and special programs.[15] A study conducted by the Office of School Demographics and Planning in CPS estimated that about seventy different high school applications were in circulation during the 2008–2009 school year.

Acceptance criteria vary across the types of high schools and programs. Selective-enrollment high schools, International Baccalaureate programs, and military academies use test scores, attendance, recommendations, testing, and other factors to determine acceptance. Most other schools and programs use a random lottery to select students when they receive more applications than there are open spots.[16] Schools may also take into account whether applicants have siblings in the school and how close they live to school. The application deadline to join a high school in September is mid-December of the prior school year. By the end of April, students should have been notified which schools they have been accepted to and need to inform schools where they plan to attend. If no school has been selected, students are placed in their neighborhood school.[17]

STUDYING ACCESS

Research showing that family preferences and use of quality information vary across social groups provides little leverage for assessing access to high-quality schools under choice, because it only hints at what may happen in practice. A more exact assessment requires directly examining whether students who participate in choice options attend schools that are academically different from their assigned schools. Such an assessment should not compare the outcomes of disadvantaged and advantaged families but rather those of disadvantaged families and the district. As Brighouse points out,

> Whether a system which extends choice to all parents is worse with respect to equality and segregation does not depend on whether wealthier parents are better choosers than poorer parents, but whether poor parents are better choosers than the state on their behalf in the prochoice era. If the state chose better in the past than poorer parents do now, then we should expect a worsening of inequality; if it chose worse then we should expect an improvement with respect to equality and possible segregation.[18]

Thus, the real question is whether students from underprivileged families go to better schools than the ones they are assigned to by school districts. If most do, it would strongly suggest that families' decisions about where to send their children do not limit students' access to better educational opportunities.

To explore this issue we examine differences between CPS students' chosen high schools and their default neighborhood schools by drawing on CPS administrative data detailing student enrollment information, school-level graduation rates, and the average ACT composite scores. This analysis focuses on the 2007 cohort of freshmen students and the 2005–2006 high school data available to them at the time they submitted their high school applications.

We use qualitative and quantitative data to examine why students stay in their neighborhood schools. Our qualitative data draw on sixty-eight interviews with eighth-grade students in four elementary or middle schools collected during the spring of 2008.[19] Based on family reports and school counselor interviews, all these students were expected to attend neighborhood high schools the following academic year. This purposive sample gives us a unique opportunity to understand how and why students stay in their neighborhood high schools. To uncover these issues, interviews focused on the support students received during the application process and on identifying the factors that affected students' decisions about where to apply and attend high school. For details on the qualitative sample and how the qualitative data were analyzed, see our appendix online at http://www.vanderbilt. edu/schoolchoice/. We also use interviews with the four eighth-grade counselors serving the students in our sample. These interviews were also collected in the spring of 2008 and focus on support the counselors and the schools provided students during the choice process, along with general information about how the high school application process is organized in CPS.

To place the experiences of our sample students in the larger district context, we also rely on data from the biannual districtwide survey of the

Consortium on Chicago School Research. These data allow us to describe students' experiences in choosing high schools and measure their perceptions of adult support.[20] For a technical description of the data sources and analytical methods used, see our appendix online at http://www.vanderbilt.edu/schoolchoice/.

DO STUDENTS ATTEND "BETTER" SCHOOLS?

As discussed earlier, critics of school choice worry that families do not have the information or proper orientation to effectively choose schools for their children, thus limiting the effectiveness of choice initiatives to improve access to quality schools. We empirically tested this claim by examining whether CPS students who choose not to attend their assigned neighborhood school attend another school with better academic characteristics. We restrict our definition of "better" to qualities that are relatively accessible and understandable to families: higher school-level graduation rates and ACT scores. Although this definition does not take into account how much value schools add to student learning, it nonetheless represents a good indicator of whether students choose schools that are academically different from their neighborhood assignment, because this information is readily available to families in the CPS high school directory.

Our analysis shows that when students opt out of their neighborhood high school, they tend to pick schools having higher graduation rates and test scores. For example, on average students choose schools with graduation rates 19 percentage points higher than that of their assigned high school. This pattern holds even when we disaggregate choice decisions across different neighborhood schools. Figure 7.1 shows the five-year graduation rates for each neighborhood high school in Chicago ordered from the lowest to highest. For each school, diamond symbols plot the average graduation rate, whereas squares show the weighted average graduation rate of destination schools attended by students who chose not to go to the assigned neighborhood school. For example, the school on the far left side of the figure, Robeson, has the lowest five-year graduation rate in CPS, at 34 percent. The square above Robeson shows that students assigned to this school, but who choose to go to another school, attend institutions that on average have graduations rates of 57 percent. As a whole, the figure shows that students across the entire range of CPS schools choose alternatives that have higher graduation rates.

Overall, 87 percent of students who choose not to attend their neighborhood school pick a school with a higher graduation rate, and 79 percent choose a school with higher test scores. Even when we disaggregate students

FIGURE 7.1   2007–2008 freshman students opting out of their assigned high schools choose schools with higher graduation rates.

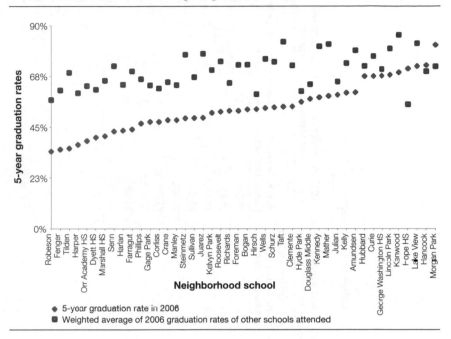

by race and neighborhood poverty status, the majority of students in all subgroups still select better schools (see table 7.1). It is important to note, however, that white and Asian students end up in stronger schools than black and Latino students. In addition, there are substantial differences between students having different test scores. Ninety-five percent of the top-scoring students attended schools with higher graduation rates, and, on average, they went to schools that were 27 percentage points better.[21] At the other end of the spectrum, 73 percent of the lowest-scoring students attended schools having higher graduation rates, but they improved on their neighborhood schools by only 9 percentage points. The differences between the two groups are more stark when one considers test scores: some 94 percent of top-performing students went to schools that, on average, had test scores 5 points higher than their assigned school. Yet only 55 percent of low-performing students went to schools with better test scores. Furthermore, their chosen schools were better by a mere 0.5 point.

In sum, we found that most students choose alternative schools that have higher graduation rates and test scores. This suggests that, at least for students who opt out of their neighborhood schools, family decisions do not

TABLE 7.1 Differences between students' assigned high school and chosen high school

Category	% attending non-assigned high school	GRADUATION RATES FOR THOSE STUDENTS WHO ARE NOT ATTENDING ASSIGNED HS		ACT COMPOSITE FOR THOSE STUDENTS WHO ARE NOT ATTENDING ASSIGNED HS	
		% in schools with higher graduation rates	Average percentage point difference in graduation rates	% in schools with higher ACT scores	Average difference in ACT scores
All students	54.1%	86.8%	19.0	79.2%	2.6
White students	58.9%	91.8%	24.8	95.9%	4.7
African American students	62.4%	82.5%	15.4	71.1%	1.7
Asian students	77.9%	97.4%	30.6	95.0%	5.5
Latino students	40.0%	88.4%	19.0	83.6%	2.8
High concentration of poverty	61.3%	82.5%	15.6	71.1%	1.6
Low concentration of poverty	52.9%	89.1%	21.8	88.2%	3.7
Top performing students	76.2%	95.0%	27.3	94.1%	5.0
Low performing students	39.6%	72.6%	8.6	55.1%	0.5

limit their access to better education options. Nonetheless, some students, particularly those who have low test scores, are not reaping the same school improvement benefits from choice as others. Additional factors, such as school admittance policies, may play as significant a role as family preferences in eventually determining where students end up.

WHY STUDENTS STAY IN NEIGHBORHOOD SCHOOLS

In this section we explore why students stay in their neighborhood schools. The most straightforward answer—students simply want to attend their assigned school—does not seem to explain most cases. Of the sixty-eight students we interviewed, fifty-nine (86 percent) wanted to attend a high school outside their neighborhood.[22] Their feelings are in step with most eighth graders in CPS: of those who returned a CCSR student survey in 2007, only 8 percent reported that they did not fill out an application to attend any school outside their assigned attendance boundary.[23]

The students in our qualitative sample described many reasons for wanting to go to other schools. Most wanted to leave their neighborhood school as a means of improving their educational opportunities. Others wanted to leave their neighborhood to attend school with family and friends because they valued being around people they knew. A number applied to schools because they liked their uniforms, extracurricular activities, or sports teams. And several students applied to schools for no discernable reason; they simply wanted to try something different.

Despite this overall desire to attend a school outside attendance boundaries, only eleven students in our sample eventually did so the following year. Discussions with students revealed two factors that limited their ability to leave their assigned schools: transaction costs and the application process. Specifically, concerns about managing the logistics of travel kept many students from attending other schools. In addition, students made several basic mistakes during the application process, and these mistakes reduced their likelihood of being accepted at another school. We discuss each of these factors in more detail next.

Transaction Costs

Sixteen students described their parents' and their own concerns about traveling outside their neighborhood as the primary reason they did not attend another school. Juan, for example, described how, despite his having older brothers who went to high schools in other parts of the city, his mom wanted him to go to school in their immediate neighborhood.

A: My mom mostly just told me, like, she doesn't want me to go far [to] school, so she's like just, just go to [the neighborhood school]. So she just told me.

Q: So your mom told you pretty much to go to [the neighborhood school]?

A: Yeah.

Q: Why? How come she didn't want you to go to a far school?

A: Because she's, like, I dunno, because supposedly, like, she thinks, I'm not, like, I don't wake up in time and stuff.

As Juan's remarks illustrate, many of these parents were concerned that their children would not be able to manage the logistics of attending school far from home. In particular, they worried that transportation inconvenience, time pressures, and even waning motivation would create challenges too difficult for their children to overcome.

Such concerns led several parents to discourage, and in some cases prohibit, their children from considering a full range of high school options even when they preferred to go to a school outside the neighborhood. Both Melissa and Derek, for instance, were initially interested in applying to and possibly attending other public schools in the city. Yet their parents' insistence that they stay close to home kept both of them from doing so. In Melissa's case, her mom insisted she go to the neighborhood high school because it was a short walk from their home. As a result, Melissa felt that even applying to other high schools was out of the question: "The reason I didn't apply is because, since my mom told me I was going to [the neighborhood school] she's, like, 'Oh don't, just don't apply to any other schools because I'm not gonna let you go. I just want you to go to this school.'"

Derek applied to and was accepted at two other high schools, both of which have relatively high graduation and attendance rates. Yet he did not attend either one because his dad thought they were too far away. He explained what happened this way: "My dad said stuff like, 'It's too far, man. Like you're gonna have to get up at five or four,' and he made me change my mind."

Parents, however, were not the only ones concerned about school travel. Several students expressed their own worries about traveling far and made independent decisions to stay close to home. One student, Christina, explained how she eventually decided to go to her neighborhood school after some consideration: "I [thought about] going to another school, but then I started thinking about it, and I'm like, 'I'm going to be, like, too tired to wake up. [I can get] to my neighborhood school in two minutes or less. I can get there, like, fast and everything.'"

Debbie also considered other school options and even applied to four different schools. She said the one school she was accepted to, however, was "too far away. I would have to wake up earlier and take the bus. I don't want to do that." For students who valued proximity, getting up early, traveling on the bus, or even walking far was too much of a hassle to leave their neighborhood school.

Application Process

The second factor contributing to students staying in neighborhood schools was the difficulty of successfully navigating the application process. Difficulties included submitting incomplete applications, applying to schools that did not match individual qualifications, and submitting too few applications. Seven students failed to submit applications on time, submitted incomplete applications, or failed to meet other requirements for particular schools. The reason for these missteps seems to be plain old-fashioned inattention and lack of follow-through. Antonio never talked with his parents about which high school to attend, but he had a friend who encouraged him to submit an application to a nearby selective-enrollment school. Although he was interested in attending the school, Antonio failed to show up for the admissions test required to complete his application. When asked what happened the Saturday morning of the test, Antonio explained:

> I set my alarm clock to go but then a thunderstorm came at like, 12:00, and turned the lights off. So my alarm clock was off the whole day. So I couldn't hear nothing, no alarm going off. So instead of going over there, I stayed at home until they called me and said, "What happened?" And I told them, "No, my alarm clock didn't go off." And they said if you wanted to take the test. And I said, "Yeah." But then the teacher wasn't there. So the test was mostly canceled. And then I couldn't go. [My parents] were mad because I should have put an alarm clock on my cell phone because if the lights turned off, because I really know that it was a bad thunderstorm that day.

From Antonio's story we see that he missed the test not once but twice after being called by the school to reschedule. His comment also suggests that his parents were aware that he was taking the test but were not involved in making sure he took it. This incident highlights how parents may place primary responsibility on their children for selecting and applying to schools.

Examples like Antonio's, however, were the exception. Most students failed to leave their neighborhood schools simply because they could not: of the forty-three students who successfully applied to schools, twenty-five (58 percent) were not accepted anywhere. These students in essence had no opportunity to leave their neighborhood schools even though they preferred to do so.

CPS does not collect any districtwide information about the school choice process, and there is no detailed information about the criteria used by neighborhood schools to accept or reject students, so we can say little about school practices that lead directly to such high rejection rates. Nonetheless, patterns across students in our sample suggest that the way students apply to schools contributes to their low acceptance rates. One problem is that many students apply to schools whose requirements exceed the students' qualifications. For example, ten students in our sample applied *only* to selective-enrollment schools, and another fifteen applied to a mix of selective and nonselective schools. Yet none of the students was accepted to a selective program. This admittance rate is not surprising given that students who are accepted into selective-enrollment schools in Chicago tend to have stanine scores of about 7 or higher on their most recent standardized tests.[24] Only one student in our sample, however, met this benchmark.

A second problem is that many students in our sample did not apply to enough schools. From our analysis of districtwide student survey and CPS administrative data, we found a relationship between the number of applications students completed and whether they were accepted at and eventually attended a high school different from their assigned one. Of the eighth graders in 2006–2007 who applied to five schools or more, 74 percent attended a high school outside their neighborhood the following year. That number goes down to 65 percent for students who reported completing four applications, and 53 percent for those who reported filling out three applications. It drops to 33 percent when students filled out only one or two applications.[25]

This pattern holds even when we take into account other factors, such as achievement, that contribute to whether students attends their assigned high school. We analyzed the likelihood of a student attending a non-assigned high school, holding constant student demographic characteristics, prior achievement, and the graduation rate of the assigned high school. Our estimates predict that a student who submits five or more applications is twice as likely to eventually attend a non-assigned high school as is a student who submits only a few applications.[26]

Across CPS, however, only 38 percent of eighth-grade students reported applying to five or more schools in 2007 (see table 7.2). This pattern of submitting few applications accounted for the low acceptance rates of many students in our qualitative sample. Thirty-three students we interviewed applied to three or fewer schools, and only eight of these students gained admittance to a school outside the neighborhood. By contrast, nine of the ten students who applied to four or more schools were accepted to at least one school.

TABLE 7.2 **Number of applications submitted by 2006–2007 eighth-grade students in CPS**

Number of applications	Percent of students
None	7.6%
One	14.7%
Two	10.7%
Three	13.4%
Four	16.1%
Five or more	37.7%

Overall, our analysis shows that many students are not aware of basic admittance strategies, such as choosing options that match their qualifications and applying to "safety schools" in case top choices fall through. Students applying to college typically learn these strategies from school counselors. In the next section we examine the guidance eighth-grade students receive as they navigate the high school application process.

ADULT SUPPORT AND THE APPLICATION PROCESS

Given that many students were stymied during the application process, the obvious next question is why. We found that students typically receive little help from parents or school counselors during the application process in eighth grade. However, students who do report high levels of adult involvement from parents and school counselors apply to more schools.

Parent Involvement

Students highlighted four types of adult family member involvement in the school selection process: disengaged, marginal, active, and directive. Thirty of the sixty-eight students (44 percent) reported having disengaged families who provided no concrete help with selecting a high school.[27] Even when these students raised the issue of where to attend school, they were unable to get advice from guardians beyond being told to apply to good schools and avoid bad ones. For instance, Ron was told by his mom to apply to high schools because "she wanted to see, like, how smart I am. Like, if I'm smart enough to get into schools." Other than being encouraged to see which schools would accept him, however, he did not receive any assistance from her: "She told me, 'It's up to you to find a decision.'" Tasha reported a similar experience:

Q: Did you ever talk to your mom and say, "These are the five schools I want to go to; which one do you think I should go to?"?
A: I asked her, but she didn't know which one she wanted me to go to.
Q: What did she say when you asked her?
A: She said, "I don't know, just pick the one that you want, that you think you should go to."

Ron's and Tasha's experiences highlight how the responsibility of selecting a school can fall primarily to students even when they reach out for support from family members. Sometimes guardians actually avoid giving their children suggestions, preferring that the children make the decision on their own.

Nineteen students (27 percent) had marginally involved adult relatives. This group of students received suggestions from family members about possible schools to attend but were given little information about why these were good choices. Furthermore, students were ultimately in charge of where to go in the fall. Ed's mom, for example, wanted him to go to Pritzker College Prep but never told him why. According to Ed, "She just told me all the time, 'You should go to that school.' And I don't want to go there." Marisol described how her mother and sister did not want her to go to the neighborhood school so they pushed her to apply to several other schools. While she completed the applications, she too had little understanding of why she applied to the schools that she did.

Q: What high schools did you apply to?
A: I applied to Lakeview and another school kind of far away.
Q: Why Lakeview? Why'd you apply to that school?
A: [My sister and mom] just didn't want me to go to [my neighborhood school].
Q: Okay. So it was, "Any school would probably be better than [your neighborhood school]." Did you know anything about Lakeview at all?
A: Not really, no.
Q: Okay. Do you know why they picked Lakeview as a school to go to or anything like that?
A: No.

These two students, like many others, knew very little about the schools their parents suggested or why they suggested them. As a result, they had little sense of how the selection process was relevant to their educational needs, interests, or future outcomes. This might be one reason fewer than half of the students in our sample followed their families' advice about where to apply to school.

Some students, however, had actively involved adult family members who worked closely with them to identify schools that matched their unique educational needs. Renee told how she received extensive help from an adult cousin:

Q: So when [your cousin] sat down and talked to you about the different schools, what sort of stuff did you talk about with her?
A: What school I want to go to, and she just asked me the different career plans I had for myself. So that's how we got down to the [schools I applied to].
Q: Okay. What sort of things did your cousin say to you about those high schools? How did those conversations go?
A: She told me which ones to pick.
Q: And do you know where she got the information from? Did you have information about different schools?
A: On the Internet?

Unfortunately, cases like this were few and far between: only four students (6 percent) explicitly described adult family members providing intensive help in identifying potential schools.

Finally, nine students (13 percent) had highly directive parents who dictated where they would attend school. As reported in the preceding section, in each of these cases the parents required that their children go to a neighborhood school to keep them close to home.

In sum, the vast majority of parents were at best marginally involved in the school choice process. Thus, much of the work of identifying and deciding on schools fell to students.

School Counseling

Students applying to college typically learn the basic application strategies from high school counselors. Yet our sample students, who were about thirteen years old when they applied to high school, received little guidance about how to successfully navigate the application process from eighth-grade counselors.

The primary assistance eighth-grade counselors give to students as they apply to high school is informational and procedural. At the beginning of the school year, counselors visit eighth-grade classrooms to distribute and explain the CPS high school directory. The counselors discuss with classes how to use the directory to select schools that meet their interests, needs, and qualifications. In these presentations counselors might also make general suggestions about factors to consider, such as how far they want to travel to school or possible career aspirations. In addition, a few counselors highlight "good" schools, such as selective-enrollment or charter schools. Beyond providing basic information and general advice, however, counselors do not work individually with students to help them select potential schools. The main reason is that counselors' time is dominated by processing students' high school applications. As one counselor explained, "We can have four hundred eighth graders. And then only one counselor. So you multiply that by five [applications per student] so that means I have to process about two thousand applications at least every school year . . . And I'm going through and signing all those two thousand applications."

Given such time constraints, another counselor said she was selective about which students to give individual help:

> I don't have time to do every kid, and unfortunately the kids who don't care are definitely gonna get very little of my interest and educational background. I give them the book. I give them motivation. Now the kids that have high scores, I pushed them. When you are gifted or when you are talented or when you are a hard worker you deserve a little bit more. Unfortunately we have a lot of kids here in the middle range . . . I'm going to give [students] this information, but I'm going to give it to [them] in a way that makes [them] understand enough that [they] can make an educated decision. If [they] choose not to make a decision, that's okay. But it's an educated no-decision. So there's only so much we can do.

There are several points to note from this comment. First, time constraints can prompt counselors to make calculated decisions about who is and who is not worthy of individual attention. In this case, the counselor believes motivated, high-achieving students deserve extra support. The practical implication is that few students will receive individualized attention because, according to her, few meet such standards. Second, the comments also illustrate that some counselors feel their role in the selection process stops after they provide students with information about schools. Figuring out whether to apply, where to apply, and how many schools to apply to is ultimately students' responsibility. Once students are informed, this counselor believed they were capable of making educated decisions on their own.

Another counselor articulated the same perspective. When asked what advice he provides to his students, he stated, "I don't give advice to students for what high school they should apply to." The interviewer responded by posing a hypothetical question: if a student with high test scores and good grades came to the counselor for help, would he talk to the student about selective-enrollment schools, or would he just allow the student make her own decision unassisted? The counselor answered, "No, I would not attempt to swing her [to selective-enrollment schools]. Whenever a child is considering high school, I feel that it should be from his or her own point of view. 'What do I want?' All [they] have to do is make a selection based upon [their] interests as to where they want to go, what [they] want to pursue, what will make [them] happy for high school."

When pressed whether eighth graders are capable of making these decisions, the counselor added, "Yes, I think so, because if for no other reason they've heard from other students, 'Oh, this is a very good high school.' Or if not from word of mouth then from reading it or from watching it on TV or from parents' focus. But mainly it should come from the interaction between the child and the parent on what they think they would like to do."

As this exchange illustrates, the counselors we interviewed were extremely reluctant to provide prescriptive help to students as they considered their high school options. This particular counselor would not even encourage a high-achieving student to go to schools with strong academic programs. Another counselor said that she would not discourage students from attending schools having poor academic offerings. Furthermore, the counselor quoted in the preceding paragraph thought not only that choosing schools should be left to the students but also that students were fully capable of making this decision on their own. Being exposed to information from friends, media, and parents, he said, enabled students to make good decisions about where to go to school.

Counselors' reluctance to provide help was reflected in students' reports of their experiences in applying to schools. Aside from having the counselor visit their class to distribute the CPS high school directory and help complete application forms, virtually all students said that they did not have a discussion with their counselor about selecting high schools. Similarly, they had little help from teachers with the selection process. At most, a few students said they received random, and sometimes contradictory, advice from counselors and teachers about avoiding some schools or considering others. Overall, however, schools provided little systematic guidance to students about how to choose appropriate high schools.

Does Adult Support Matter?

Our qualitative analysis showed that students receive little help from parents or schools in navigating the school choice process. Here we use survey data on all CPS students to explore whether adult support matters for students who wish to gain access to non-assigned high schools. Specifically, we examine whether students who receive educational support from adults are more likely to apply to multiple high schools. Again, the number of applications is an important indicator because it was shown to be related to students' success in going to an non-assigned high school.

We use several indicators of adult support in our analysis.[28] A parent involvement measure assesses students' perceptions of their parents' support for their school performance. Questions ask students how often their parents or other adults encourage them to work hard, do their homework, and take responsibility for their actions as well as talk to them about selecting courses or programs in school or going to college. High ratings on this measure indicate strong parental support. Counselor help is an item in the survey that asks students how much they agree that a counselor at the school helped them plan for life after high school. We also include two measures of elementary schools' high school application culture: the percentage of students who submitted five or more high school applications the preceding school year, and the percentage of students who attended high schools outside their neighborhood in the preceding year. Table A6 in the appendix contains the results of our model. It is available online at http://www.vanderbilt.edu/schoolchoice/.

Parental and counselor support has a positive effect on students' application behavior. Thirty-eight percent of CPS eighth-grade students in 2006–2007 reported sending five or more applications. Had students received higher levels of parental support, the proportion would have increased to 44 percent.[29] Assuming that all students had agreed that their counselor was very helpful, the percentage of students applying to five or more high schools would have increased to 41 percent. This result suggests that students' application behaviors, and by extension their chances of being accepted to schools outside their attendance boundary, can be improved with additional adult guidance.

Elementary schools also matter in helping students navigate the application process. As the percentage of prior students who applied to multiple high schools increases, current students are more likely to apply to five or more high schools. Furthermore, if all elementary schools increased the percentage of prior students who applied to five or more schools by 10 percent, then 45 percent of current eighth-grade students would have applied to five or more high schools (instead of the 38 percent who actually did so).[30] The percentage of previous eighth graders in an elementary school who attended a high school outside their attendance area, however, is not related to the number of applications current students complete. This finding suggests that what most shapes students' application behavior are the procedures for supporting the high school application process in eighth grade rather than the absolute number of prior-year classmates who eventually attend a non-neighborhood school.

Even though students who have strong parental support will be better off compared with students who have weak parental support, elementary schools can supply critical assistance to disadvantaged students during the application process. Figure 7.2 shows the probability of applying to five or more high schools for students who have weak parental support (diamonds) and strong parental support (triangles) and illustrates how the probabilities change depending on the level of elementary school support.[31] The distance between the two lines represents the effect of parental support; the slope of the lines represents the effect of elementary schools' application culture. Students with weak parental support who are attending schools with a strong prior history of students engaging in the high school choice process (for example, 40 percent) have a similar likelihood of applying to five or more high schools as do students with strong parental support attending elementary schools with lower levels of prior students engaging in the process (for example, 20 percent).

In sum, support from parents and counselors seems to play an important role in shaping the number of high school applications students submit. The more adult involvement students report, the more likely they are to fill out multiple applications. Students who are attending elementary schools having a strong prior history of students filling out multiple applications are also more likely to complete more applications. Furthermore, elementary schools that have strong application cultures can compensate for weak parental support.

FIGURE 7.2   Elementary schools can bridge the gap for students with weak parental support.

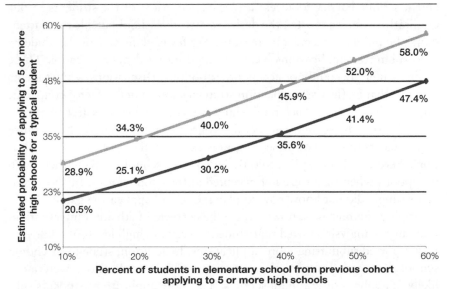

SUMMARY AND DISCUSSION

Our assessment of students' access to schools under school choice in Chicago is both encouraging and concerning. On the one hand, we found little evidence to support claims that families' and students' choices about where to go to school limit students' access to better educational opportunities. Earlier research suggested that the lack of high-quality information available to parents and the use of nonacademic factors in decision making led disadvantaged families to make poor choices about where to send their children, thereby indirectly limiting students' access to better schools. However, we found that academic considerations seem to influence families that participate in Chicago's choice system. When students opt out of their assigned neighborhood schools they tend to go to schools that have higher average graduation rates and test scores. Even though there are differences among groups, the overall improvement trend holds across race and socioeconomic status. Thus, the extent to which families' school choice decisions limit access to available educational opportunities may not be as significant as some observers believe. It is important to keep in mind, however, that we still know little about the quality of the decisions made by students who attend their neighborhood schools. Additional studies are needed to see whether these students also make choices that, given their options, put them in relatively better schools.

More generally our analysis suggests that the admissions process presents a serious barrier to access under choice. Most of the students in our qualitative sample reported the desire to attend a school outside their attendance boundary for academic reasons. Yet fewer than half of the students who submitted applications were accepted into a different school. These students literally could not access other options. Discussions with students revealed that ineffective application strategies were a major factor contributing to their low acceptance rate. Many students applied to selective-enrollment schools having strong academic programs; unfortunately, the entrance requirements of many of these programs exceeded the applicants' qualifications. Several others applied to only one or two schools, leaving them with no options when they were not accepted at their top choices. In short, students simply did not know how to play the school application game.

Application mistakes, however, can be corrected with adult intervention. Our survey analysis showed that students receiving high levels of adult support reported submitting more applications. In addition, students attending schools that had a culture of submitting multiple applications were more likely to apply to several high schools. The more applications students submitted, the more likely they were to attend a school outside their attendance area. Thus, by receiving more guidance during the choice process, high school applicants may make better decisions about applying to schools and hopefully increase the number of options from which they can choose.

Several implications stem from this work. In terms of policy, this study suggests that districts may need to develop targeted interventions to ensure that students who want to opt out of neighborhood schools have a serious shot at doing so. These efforts should include attempts to help students learn the most effective approaches to applying to schools, and individual counseling to improve the fit between schools' offerings and students' qualifications and interests. An early investment in this type of coaching could reap additional future benefits as students map out their strategies for maximizing post-secondary education opportunities. In addition, the existence of clear racial, class, and achievement patterns in the magnitude of difference between graduation rates of neighborhood high schools and schools of choice undermines the claim that school choice will increase equity. Targeted interventions aimed at disadvantaged students may be necessary if a community is to fully realize the goal of higher-quality schools for all students.

Our work also highlights, as other studies have done, the fact that students are often the primary decision makers in the high school selection process, deciding both where to apply and where to attend.[32] Given students' autonomy, future studies should pay more attention to the ways student preferences shape school choice outcomes. What sources of information do students draw on compared to parents? And what are the primary characteristics students look for in schools?

Although we were able to describe how students' application strategies limited their access, we could say little about the other side of the coin: how the larger education market shapes students' access. Tightening students' application strategies may improve chances of admission at the margins, but it will do little to offset the imbalance between the demand for high-quality schools and the short supply of them in urban districts. This imbalance is likely to continue to act as a fundamental constraint on access, giving schools significant power to admit or reject students.

Finally, researchers should look beyond families' stated educational preferences to examine the entire application process in school choice systems. There are many steps students must take between deciding to leave their assigned schools and being accepted into an alternative school. Yet there has been little research identifying the key points in the process that may derail students' attempts to attend a chosen school. Examining the application process in detail will deepen our understanding of the relative importance of individual behaviors and institutional practices in shaping access under choice.

8

Communication Breakdown

Informing Immigrant Families About
High School Choice in New York City

Carolyn Sattin-Bajaj

More than fifty years after the historic Supreme Court decision in *Brown v. Board of Education* to end the practice of race-based school assignments, considerable school segregation along racial or ethnic and class lines remains. In fact, according to a report from the Harvard Civil Rights Project, black and Latino students are three times as likely as white students to be in high-poverty schools, and twelve times as likely to be in schools in which almost everyone is poor.[1] These youth also attend predominantly minority schools in disproportionate numbers.[2] The severe isolation of low-income children of color, many of whom come from immigrant homes, constitutes a significant challenge to successful immigrant integration and to social equality more generally.[3] The latest results from the National Assessment of Educational Progress (NAEP) show that racial (or ethnic) and class-based disparities also persist in primary and secondary grades and affect students' academic performance.[4] Along with growing school segregation, many researchers, policy makers, educators, and citizens understand this so-called achievement gap to be one of the most pressing educational and social justice issues of our time.[5]

Scholars have long pointed to the concentration of low-income children of color in high-poverty, racially segregated, and low performing schools as a key explanatory factor of race- and income-based differences in academic achievement.[6] Since the early era of school desegregation, school choice policies—ranging from magnet and charter schools to vouchers, controlled choice, or open-enrollment plans—have been implemented, in part, to address these long-standing problems in education. Districts across the United States have adopted school choice with renewed vigor in recent years in the face of poor student performance on international exams, the widespread academic failure of disadvantaged students, and glaring inequities in students' access to high-quality educational opportunities.

According to the Education Commission of the States and the Center for Education Reform, forty states and the District of Columbia have charter school laws, and all but four states have some form of inter- or intradistrict open-enrollment policy.[7] The U.S. Department of Education estimates that 1.4 million of the country's 50 million public school students, or 2.8 percent of the total, are currently being educated in charter schools, only one of a variety of school choice options.[8] These figures are expected to rise with the Obama administration's avowed support for increasing the number of charter schools nationwide.[9] Finally, the National Center for Education Statistics reported that between 1993 and 2003, the proportion of children enrolled in assigned public schools declined from 80 to 74 percent, whereas the proportion of students enrolled in chosen public schools increased from 11 to 15 percent.[10]

Accessing high-quality educational options by students through participation in any number of school choice programs can require a significant amount of knowledge and time investment on the part of families.[11] Navigating these often complex and bureaucratic processes may be particularly difficult for low-income immigrant parents who, on top of the challenges associated with poverty, were raised and educated outside the United States, may face language barriers, and may lack some of the critical contextual knowledge they need to fully understand educational practices, policies, and expectations in their adopted country. Few studies have examined low-income immigrant families' experiences with school choice. Furthermore, little is known about how the expectations of parents' knowledge, behavior, and resources embedded in choice policies align with or depart from various immigrants' social practices, cultural models, and resources or about the implications of these convergences and divergences for immigrants' participation in school choice.

Given that children in immigrant families currently account for an estimated 25 percent of all primary- and secondary-school-age children in the United States, it is of growing importance that we understand how educational bureaucracies respond to their needs.[12] An investigation of school-based and districtwide approaches to informing families about school choice represents one entry point into understanding the challenges that immigrants may face in comprehending often unfamiliar educational policies and procedures. This chapter uses ethnographic data from research in three middle schools in New York City and analyzes school choice publications created and distributed by the New York City Department of Education (NYCDOE) to answer questions about how the district- and school-level communication strategies and materials facilitate or complicate Latin American immigrant families' understanding of the choice process. New York is home to one of the largest and most heterogeneous immigrant populations worldwide. The city's diversity, coupled with the fact that participation in school choice is mandatory for all students who wish to attend public high school in the district, make New York an interesting place to examine immigrant families' experiences with this one aspect of educational integration.[13]

Three main questions drive this chapter. First, what do the central district office personnel and school-based staff do to inform students and families about high school choice in New York? What materials do they provide, what events do they organize, and what resources do they dedicate to explaining the process? Next, in light of the materials, events, and school-based support that exist, how might Latin American immigrant parents' language proficiency, cultures, and educational backgrounds impact their understanding of the process and therefore their ability to assist their children in applying to appropriate and high-quality schools? Finally, in what ways, if at all, do district- and school-level communication and outreach efforts take into account the range of support that immigrant families may need if they are to understand and participate in the potentially foreign practice of school choice? The data for this chapter are derived primarily from ethnographic observations, focus groups with middle school guidance counselors, interviews with guidance counselors and school-based parent liaisons ("parent coordinators"), and informational materials developed and distributed by the NYCDOE and three middle schools.

The discussion begins with a brief review of some of the main conversations in the contemporary school choice literature. It also identifies some of the key gaps in this literature with regard to immigrants and school choice. This is followed by a summary of the extensive scholarship on conflicts between home and school as they relate to Latin American immigrant families' experiences with the U.S. school system. Next are described the methodology and research sites and an overview of the New York high school choice process, its goals, and the diverse portfolio of high schools from which students make their choices. An in-depth discussion of the study's main findings and their significance for current school choice and integration research follows. The chapter concludes with a discussion of policy implications and recommendations for future research.

SCHOOL CHOICE IN THE RESEARCH LITERATURE

School choice reforms have been at the center of public and political conversations about education and equity since their inception. Most empirical studies of school choice have focused on evaluating the outcomes of
these policies by examining three indicators. One indicator is the academic
achievement of students in choice programs compared to those in nonchoice
public schools.[14] A second factor is the impact of choice on school segregation.[15] Third, studies examine the implications of district choice programs
for existing public schools and students attending these schools.[16] Evidence
on the effects of school choice in each of these areas is highly contested, and
scholars are pursuing new and increasingly sophisticated ways to measure
the impact of school choice on student achievement and equity.[17]

The question of whether students who participate in choice differ from
those who do not is another chief concern in the literature. Decades of
research have shown that on average, students from higher socioeconomic
backgrounds enroll in chosen schools at higher rates than their disadvantaged peers. Studies in districts with open-enrollment plans, voucher programs, magnet school options, and interdistrict choice have all concluded
that there is in fact a "creaming effect," in which children of more highly
educated parents with more material resources are more likely than their
more disadvantaged peers to participate in school choice.[18]

The stratification trends are less clear in the case of charter schools, many
of which are located in impoverished urban neighborhoods and thus attract
a lower-income student population. However, activists and researchers alike
continue to debate the merits of charter schools and other choice programs
on equity grounds.[19]

Although social stratification and equity concerns have motivated studies of school choice for many years, an analysis of the trends in immigrant
families' participation in choice has been conspicuously absent from this literature. In fact, few studies disaggregate by immigrant origin, and therefore
little is known about how the enrollment patterns of children of immigrants
compare to those of their native-origin peers. Given the growing share of
children of immigrants in U.S. schools, however, it is increasingly important
to learn more about their experiences with this education policy. Research
on New York's mandatory high school choice process represents a unique
opportunity to capture a population of students and families often absent
from school choice analyses.

Despite the lack of empirical studies of immigrants and school choice,
there is much to learn from the existing evidence of the ways parents gather
information about choice programs and the various strategies that schools
and districts employ to inform them about choice options. As with partici-

pation in school choice, sources of information tend to vary by class and education level. Low-income parents and parents with limited education rely heavily on school-based sources of information and formal channels such as the radio, newspaper, and television.[20] In contrast, parents with high education levels tend to depend more on social, professional, or informal information networks.[21]

Researchers have discovered differences along racial and ethnic lines as well. Schneider and his colleagues found that black and Latino parents were more likely to use school-based and formal outlets, and they depended less on friends, family, or social contacts than white parents.[22] These findings were not surprising given the strong correlation between race or ethnicity and class background. The salience of social networks for families of high socioeconomic status links strongly to earlier work on the interaction between class background and the significance of social networks in a person's life.[23]

The role of school districts in providing information to families about school choice is also featured prominently in the scholarship. The parent information centers (PICs) that operated in six Massachusetts school districts having school choice plans are one of the most extensively researched examples of district-based information and outreach.[24] These centers were easily accessible by public transportation, and counselors gave visitors written materials in multiple languages about the available school options. Notably, counselors were not allowed to make specific recommendations to parents and students, and independent evaluations found that even after PICs were established, many parents selected low-quality schools.[25] Other districts, such as the large urban Southern California district in Andre-Becheley's qualitative study on intradistrict choice, rely on traditional outreach methods such as mailing flyers, distributing pamphlets and school directories, and advertising on television and in the print media, and these districts tend to be considerably less attentive to the varied needs of the public.[26]

Related studies have investigated the extent to which parents understand their district's school choice policies and how well informed they feel. Multiple studies have demonstrated that most parents, regardless of income, tend to have limited understanding of school choice policies and procedures and lack accurate information about test scores, demographics, and other data on the schools in the district.[27] Although this situation can be explained, in part, by the school districts' failure to make some of this basic information easily accessible to parents, it reflects a potentially larger underlying issue: the mismatch between district communication strategies and parents' information-gathering behaviors.[28]

CONFLICTS BETWEEN HOME AND SCHOOL FOR
LATIN AMERICAN IMMIGRANT FAMILIES

We know little about immigrants' experiences with school choice and, more specifically, the ways immigrant parents digest information about choice programs provided by districts, but the role of culture in exacerbating or attenuating school failure has been an object of scholarly inquiry for many years. Researchers have examined how differences between home and school cultures, practices, norms, values, and expectations have impacted child development, parent–child relationships, identity formation, and academic achievement.[29] These studies have covered considerable ground in illuminating how an individual student's background interacts with the social and cultural context of a school environment, a pedagogical practice, or policy to put the student at a relative advantage or disadvantage. The absence of this type of cultural analysis applied to questions about school choice participation represents one of the most significant lacunae in these literatures.

A substantial body of work also highlights the primacy of cultural values in explaining how and why many low-income immigrant parents interact with schools in the ways they do.[30] This scholarship highlights the need to investigate the assumptions about shared knowledge and values embedded in school policies and practices: a dangerous form of the "hidden curriculum."[31]

Much of the research on the involvement of low-income Latin American immigrant parents in their children's schooling in the United States shows that they tend to defer to teachers on academic matters, avoid challenging the school administration on educational decisions, and rarely make requests.[32] Their behaviors and attitudes, although corresponding to the cultural scripts and expectations of their countries of origin, are often contrary to common conceptions of what constitutes "good" and involved parenting in the United States. Their actions (or assumed "inaction," as the case may be) contrast starkly with the behavioral patterns of many middle-class parents, such as those in Lareau's studies, who do not hesitate to make demands of teachers or request additional support for their children.[33] As a result, Latin American immigrant parents are often demonized for not caring about their children's education. In this way, the children whose parents are not clued in to the implicit rules of the education game are doubly disadvantaged.[34]

This research literature substantiates the importance of considering institutional responsibility in perpetuating or combating educational inequality. Analysis of the information that districts and schools provide and what they do—and do not—make explicit may serve to identify the unarticulated aspects of the dominant culture that immigrants (and perhaps native groups as well) may have greater difficulty accessing. Such research may also help explicate the larger factors that contribute to the misalignment between home- and school-based practices.

RESEARCH METHODOLOGY

The research presented here involved observations of a series of events related to New York's high school choice process held at three large middle schools in Queens, New York; observations of citywide informational events; focus groups with middle school guidance counselors; and interviews with parent coordinators at these middle schools. Compilation and analysis of the school choice materials developed by the Office of Student Enrollment Planning Operations (OSEPO) at the New York City Department of Education also formed a key component of the study. These data were collected as part of a larger ongoing mixed-methods comparative study of the experiences of Latin American immigrant and African American families with high school choice in New York.

Ethnographic observations were conducted at school-based events for parents and students about high school choice, including workshops about how to fill out the high school application form and high school fairs held at individual middle schools. During these observations, participants went about their regular activities without interference, and I took notes on who attended the events, the format and content of the information provided by school personnel, whether translation and interpretation services were available, whether translation and interpretion included contextual information or consisted only of direct linguistic translation, the questions that parents asked, and the interactions between parents and school personnel and among parents. These observations enabled me to learn in detail about the school-based communication efforts, compare the various middle schools' approaches to outreach, and, perhaps most important, monitor interactions between students, parents, and school personnel at events specifically designed to inform parents about school choice.

Focus groups with guidance counselors at the middle schools constituted another main part of the data collection. These group discussions centered on the guidance counselors' roles in preparing middle school students and families for participation in high school choice, their explanations of the outreach strategies, and their perspectives on the strengths and drawbacks of the choice process generally. In addition, focus group prompts asked participants to reflect on their experiences in working with immigrant families on high school choice and the challenges that families encounter during the process. I also conducted informal and semistructured interviews with individual guidance counselors and parent coordinators at each middle school. These interviews followed a similar protocol to that used in guidance counselor focus groups. The aim of these interviews was to understand the roles played by the informants vis-à-vis the high school choice process, their participation in and assessment of the effectiveness of school-based and districtwide efforts, and their reflections on working with immigrant families on school choice.

Document analysis complemented the ethnographic observations and interviews by connecting the form and content of the school choice publications created by the NYCDOE with narratives from school personnel and observations of workshops and other outreach events. OSEPO produces a host of materials about high school choice, including the six-hundred-page *Directory of New York City Public High Schools,* which is distributed to each prospective eighth-grade student at the end of seventh grade. This office also develops shorter brochures and pamphlets that offer tips for parents about how to work with their children to select high schools. My analysis of these materials considered the type of media used (e.g., electronic, print), its accessibility (language, technological requirements), the content of the information, and the criteria emphasized in determining appropriate school selections. Finally, as with analysis of the live interpretations provided at events, to investigate the concept of cultural translation I examined whether the translated documents included contextual or background information or simply translated words and concepts in purely linguistic terms.

Site Selection

New York's historic and enduring role in the U.S. immigration narrative and its current leadership in urban school reform make it a fitting location to explore immigrant families' experiences in educational integration. With more than three million foreign-born residents, New York is one of the most dynamic centers of immigration in the United States and, in fact, the world.[35] The diversity and scope of immigration to the city are unparalleled; however, cities and towns all over the United States are now faced with the challenge of facilitating immigrant integration into unfamiliar institutions and policies. What makes New York an ideal place to study the integration experiences of immigrants and their children is that, unlike many other urban immigration hubs—which tend to have one or two dominant national-origin groups—New York is home to numerous large immigrant communities. According to the 2007 American Community Survey, the Hispanic immigrants in New York alone hailed from the Dominican Republic (358,376), Mexico (178,713), Ecuador (135,043), and Colombia (74,026) as well as many other countries across Latin America and Spanish-speaking parts of the Caribbean. Consequently, even a study that focuses exclusively on Latin American immigrant families and school choice stands to yield important new comparative data on integration.

As the largest single school district in the United States, the New York public schools contain a considerable immigrant-origin student population. Although the precise enrollment of children of immigrants is not publicly available, according to self-reported data in the Home Language Identification Survey, an estimated 42 percent of students speak a language other than English at home.[36] This figure serves as a rough proxy for the percentage of students from immigrant families. During the 2008–2009 school year, Hispanics were the largest racial or ethnic group of students enrolled in New York public schools (39.4 percent), followed by black (30.6 percent), Asian/Pacific Islander (14.6 percent), and white students (14.4 percent).[37] Moreover, students whose dominant language is Spanish constituted more than two-thirds of the English language learner (ELL) student population. The relevance of a study about Latin American immigrants and school choice is clear, then, given their substantial population share in New York as well as across the United States.

High School Choice in New York

School choice has been a fixture of the educational policy landscape in New York for decades. A long-standing district policy requires all eighth-grade students who plan to attend a traditional public high school to submit an application in which they rank as many as twelve high schools or programs.[38] According the NYCDOE Web site, "The high school admissions process is centered on two principles: equity and choice." In a system that is responsible for educating more than 1.1 million students, realizing these goals can be a difficult endeavor.

Each year, the roughly eighty-five thousand eighth-grade students who participate in high school choice must choose from among six hundred programs in the approximately four hundred public high schools across the five boroughs. These schools and programs vary widely in terms of size, quality, and academic outcomes. Although the district has shown gains in recent years on a number of educational indicators (including graduation rates and the percentage of students reaching proficiency on the NAEP), there continues to be an undersupply of high performing high schools. According to an analysis conducted by researchers at the Center for New York City Affairs at the New School, only 38.3 percent of high schools with graduating classes in 2007 had a graduation rate of 75 percent or higher.[39] This figure includes students graduating with a Regents diploma as well as those who received the less rigorous local diploma. Students who entered ninth grade in the fall of 2008 are now required to pass five Regents exams with a score of 65 or higher in order to graduate; local diplomas will no longer be awarded. If the Regents diploma is used as the threshold for graduation, Hemphill and Nauer's analysis shows that only 12.6 percent of high schools had a graduation rate of 75 percent or higher in 2007.[40]

Graduation rates constitute only one measure of school quality; however, given the significance of obtaining a high school diploma for lifetime earnings, graduation rates are a particularly important metric.[41] Schools in New York also vary dramatically in size, concentration of low-income students, safety record, teacher stability, and student satisfaction, among other characteristics. The unevenness in school quality is evidenced in the publicly available progress reports, annual school report cards, quality reviews, and learning environment surveys published by the NYCDOE.

New York high schools run the gamut in size, theme or specialization, and admissions criteria. Since 2002, more than two hundred small schools (with enrollments of fewer than six hundred students each) have been created, thereby significantly adding to the supply of small schools from earlier reform movements. Most students, however, continue to attend large, comprehensive high schools that serve more than fourteen hundred students each.[42] In addition to small schools and large, comprehensive high schools, students may attend career and technical high schools, small learning communities within high schools, and charter schools. Charter high schools, however, do not participate in the NYCDOE high school application process; instead, students must apply to each individual charter school through a separate lottery system.

High schools in New York use varying selection criteria, and there are seven mechanisms by which students gain entry into a particular school or program within a school. The most competitive (and often highest performing) schools admit students based on their scores on the Specialized High School Admissions Test (SHSAT), an exam that is offered annually to students in the fall of their eighth-grade year. Other schools—namely, those that concentrate on visual and performing arts—require students to audition. Screened schools tend to be academically rigorous, highly sought-after schools and programs, and they rank applicants based on their seventh-grade academic average, standardized test scores, attendance, and punctuality.

Most new small high schools fall into the category of "limited unscreened." They have no grade or test score requirements for acceptance but give priority to students who attend a school information session. Educational option ("Ed-opt") schools choose students according to a bell curve whereby 16 percent of students accepted are in the high reading range, 68 percent are in the average reading range, and 16 percent are in the low reading range. Zoned schools are large, comprehensive high schools that give priority to students who live in their geographic catchment area. Finally, unscreened schools have no admissions requirements, and a computer randomly selects students for admission based on available seats.

A variation of the current high school choice process has existed in New York since the 1970s.[43] The current iteration was launched in the 2003–2004 school year and is modeled after the matching process for American physicians, the National Resident Matching Program.[44] The official goals for the new matching formula were to increase the likelihood that a student would be assigned to his top-choice school and to distribute low-achieving students as evenly as possible across high schools.[45] To that end, the latest revision expanded to twelve the number of schools or programs that students could rank. During the 2008 matching process, the NYCDOE boasted a 90 percent success rate at matching students with one of their twelve choices.[46] In 2009, nearly 50 percent of all applicants received their first choice, and 80 percent were matched with one of their top three.[47] However, that same year, seventy-five hundred students were still rejected by all of their choices and had to participate in supplementary rounds.[48]

Each eighth-grade student receives an individualized application form in early October and is required to return a completed form by the first week of December. The application is printed with the student's final grade point averages from seventh grade, her latest (seventh grade) standardized test scores in reading and math, and average yearly attendance. These data determine a student's eligibility for certain screened schools and programs that have specific attendance, grades, and test score requirements. In addition, where applicable, the student's local zoned high school is listed at the top of the application. Not all students have a zoned high school, because twenty-one large high schools have, since 2002, been closed for poor performance.[49] Twelve additional high school closures were recently announced.[50]

Oversight of the high school choice process falls under the auspices of the Office of Student Enrollment and Planning Operations, which is housed in the district's central administrative offices in Manhattan. Much of the school choice policy and the related informational materials are developed in this office, but middle schools are granted considerable autonomy in determining how to work with students and families to complete the applications. OSEPO does not require that middle school personnel attend trainings about high school choice, but they organize optional workshops and offer support for guidance counselors upon request. District administrators reported to me in an interview that they expect middle school guidance counselors to review all of the high school applications before they are submitted. Yet there is negligible monitoring of school-based efforts concerning high school choice.

Sample

The three middle schools included in the study were selected based on two primary factors: their location in densely populated Latin American immigrant neighborhoods and the demographic features of the students enrolled at the school. I looked for schools with, relative to the districtwide averages, large Hispanic student populations (50 percent or higher), a high percentage of recent immigrant students (5 percent or higher), a high percentage of students classified as English language learners (20 percent or more), and a high proportion of students eligible for free lunch (a proxy for school poverty). In addition, I sought schools of similar size and grade distribution—in this case, large middle schools with more than fifteen hundred students in grades 6 through 8. The pertinent student demographic information for each of the three middle schools and districtwide averages are provided in table 8.1.

RESULTS

School Quality Excluded

The most striking aspect of the information that the NYCDOE and individual middle schools provided to students and families about high school choice was the exclusion of school quality from the list of important decision-making factors in school selection. This major criterion was conspicuously absent from the various publications and from the live presentations I observed. Instead, students' academic and extracurricular interests, school location, and school size were repeatedly highlighted as vital characteristics for families to consider when choosing schools. Furthermore, aside from a brief paragraph description hidden within the high school directory, families received no explicit instruction about the type of school quality information that was publicly available or how to access it. This is remarkable given the number of school-level reports that the NYCDOE produces containing detailed data on a range of school quality measures.

The *Directory of the New York City Public High Schools* was the most comprehensive resource that OSEPO published and distributed to families. This directory, the size of a telephone book, comprised more than six hundred pages of individualized descriptions of the approximately four hundred high schools in New York. Included were the school's address, contact information, programs offered, and eligibility requirements. At the beginning of the directory, general information about the school choice process was provided. This section reviewed the various types of schools and described

TABLE 8.1   **School and districtwide demographic information**

School name	Total enrollment	Race/ethnicity	% English language learners	% recent immigrant	% eligible for free lunch
New York City School District	1,018,546	American Indian: 0.41%, Asian/Pacific Islander: 14.6%, Hispanic: 39.3%, black: 30.6%, white: 14.4%	14.4%	N/A	73%
IS 725	2,103	American Indian: 0.10%, Asian/Pacific Islander: 10.9%, Hispanic: 80.4%, black: 6.7%, white: 1.8%	37.9%	10.8%	80.7%
IS 633	1,899	American Indian: 0.11%, Asian/Pacific Islander: 9.16%, Hispanic: 85.2%, black: 3.6%, white: 2.0 %	24.2%	8.6%	75.2%
IS 545	1,681	American Indian: 0.06%, Asian/Pacific Islander: 35.5%, Hispanic: 55.0%, black: 2.4%, white: 7.1%	19.9%	5.1%	71.5%

Note: Based on data from June 2009.

the various selection methods. A short list of the publicly available data reports and the Web site where they can be accessed appeared near the end of the preface. It was buried between a paragraph about the services available for students with special needs and a list of schools deemed in need of improvement (SINI) by the state. Each of the three main reports—the Progress Report, the Quality Review, and the Learning Environment Survey—was described in a single sentence. The elements that factor in to a school's progress report grade ("school environment," "student performance," and "student progress") were also identified and defined.

It is notable that this one-page description of the accountability reports was the only place in the entire directory in which some of the traditional school quality metrics—graduation rate, Regents passing rate, and credit accumulation—were mentioned by name. These important data points were not provided on the individual school pages, however, and the onus of finding this information was thus placed on students and parents. Furthermore, although the directory's discussion of these indicators was limited in scope and did not explicitly use the language of "quality," it was the only publication that made reference to using these data as a tool to evaluate and compare school performance.

The other high school choice publications that OSEPO has developed were revealing in the strategies that they suggested to parents and students for reviewing and selecting appropriate schools. For example, "Choosing a High School," a fifteen-page pamphlet distributed at events and available online, contained a "student interest inventory" consisting of questions about a student's interests and career goals, willingness to travel far distances to school, preferences for school size, and English language skills or need for English as a Second Language (ESL) services. In fact, every publication that was distributed at middle school events emphasized a student's interests, school location, and school size as important selection criteria. These factors were also repeated during each citywide and school-based presentation on how to choose schools.

The individual middle school events, although varied in audience size and in the availability and quality of interpretation services, offered nearly identical information and instructions to those in the OSEPO publications. All three middle schools held high school choice workshops for parents on evenings in mid- or late October. The turnout ranged from approximately 10 parents and students at IS 633, to between 150 and 200 parents and students at both IS 725 and IS 545. The format of the events was similar: an hour-long PowerPoint presentation led by a guidance counselor or the school's parent coordinator, followed by a brief question-and-answer session. The content of the presentation also was generally uniform because of the use of the same PowerPoint presentation template provided by OSEPO. In addition, a variety of printed materials was distributed to attendees at the start of each event. These included copies or shortened versions of NYC-DOE publications, a calendar of citywide high school choice events such as high school fairs and workshops, and a list of school open houses being held across the city.

The themes of students' interests, school location, and school type and size were prominent in each school's presentation, echoing the main messages transmitted in the OSEPO publications. In fact, all of the guidance counselors and parent coordinators leading the workshops discussed location—and, more specifically, the distance of a school from a student's home and the time required to travel to and from school—more frequently than any other topic. The presenters at all three schools even encouraged families to do a test run of the travel distances during regular school transit times.

This strong emphasis on school location as a key, or perhaps even a primary, criterion for applying to a school contrasted with the lack of discussion about school quality metrics at any of the school-based workshops.

Variation in Availability and Quality of Translation and Interpretation Services

To achieve the most basic level of equity, all parents must, at a minimum, receive information about high school choice in a language they understand. Often, however, schools and districts fail to meet even this minimum threshold. All OSEPO publications are available on the NYCDOE Web site in the nine most commonly spoken languages (English, Spanish, Haitian-Creole, Russian, Chinese, Korean, Urdu, Bengali, and Arabic), a fact that signifies the district's recognition of the linguistic diversity and translation needs of the families it serves.

In fact, in September 2006, after substantial lobbying by a coalition of community-based organizations, the NYCDOE created a Translation and Interpretation Unit to provide on-demand translation and interpretation services to schools and the district at large. This represented an important step forward in overcoming the persistent language barriers that immigrant parents face when dealing with their children's schools. However, few of the translated materials, particularly the high school directory, were made available in printed format to the families and schools in this and other studies.[51] As a result, despite the NYCDOE's ostensible commitment to providing translation and interpretation services, ultimately parents who were not literate in English had access to fewer sources of information.

The content of the school-based presentations about high school choice was virtually identical across sites, but the interpretation services provided at the middle school workshops were varied. Whereas at one school, a native Spanish-speaking guidance counselor translated each PowerPoint slide to Spanish in real time, another school provided interpretation only during a fifteen-minute question-and-answer session that occurred after an hour-long presentation in English. The latter event was the most extreme example of a school's failure to provide adequate translation and interpretation services. It illustrates the severity of the obstacles that non-English-speaking immigrant parents may face in learning about and understanding school choice.

IS 545 hosted its major high school choice informational event, "Everything You Ever Wanted to Know About the High School Application Process," in late October, slightly more than a month before the application was due. The event began with Megan Dowd, the school's parent coordinator, announcing to an audience of approximately two hundred adults and children that there would be no simultaneous interpretation during the main part of the presentation.[52] Instead, she would respond to Spanish-speaking parents' questions with the help of a volunteer interpreter after the English portion of the program was completed. After making this announcement, Ms. Dowd instructed the people requiring interpretation to move to the back of the auditorium so that they would be ready for the question-and-answer session at the end. Approximately one-third of the audience moved to the back of the auditorium.

The main presentation at IS 545 consisted of a roughly one-hour Power-Point slideshow in English led by a monolingual male guidance counselor. As he reviewed each slide, he provided additional commentary and offered tips to students and parents about how to effectively search for schools. At one point, when he was discussing the difference between the main round of choice and the supplementary round, he told the audience, "I highly recommend that you take advantage of the first round. List all twelve choices. That way you give your child a chance to get into a school he/she really wants to go to." Only parents who could follow along in English would have been able to understand this potentially valuable message.

Once the slideshow was finished, Ms. Dowd approached the group of parents and students at the rear of the auditorium awaiting interpretation. She explained that Mrs. Ramirez, a Spanish-speaking parent volunteer, would translate parents' questions and her answers. Mrs. Ramirez, a diminutive Latina woman whose children attended IS 545, stood in the aisle next to Ms. Dowd. One parent asked a question about the Ed-opt schools and the selection mechanism for these schools. Ms. Dowd responded in English to Mrs. Ramirez, explaining the bell curve allocation of slots to students based on their reading scores. Before she was able to translate into Spanish, Mrs. Ramirez had to ask Ms. Dowd to clarify her response at least three times. In this way, she evidenced her limited familiarity with the details of the high school choice process or, at a minimum, her confusion about the various school selection methods.

Ms. Ramirez's poor understanding of the high school choice process was only one of the weaknesses of the interpretation provided to parents at IS 545. When she spoke to parents in Spanish, Mrs. Ramirez's voice projected poorly over the conversations that individual parents were having at the front of the auditorium with guidance counselors; people in the audience struggled to hear both the questions that other parents were asking and Mrs. Ramirez's translated answers. Ten minutes after the interpretation session began, a voice came over the loudspeaker to announce that the school building would be closing and people had to get ready to leave. Most of the parents in the Spanish-speaking section, many of whom already appeared frustrated, got up and exited the auditorium.

The inadequate provision of interpretation services at IS 545 reflected the school's lack of awareness or negligence in taking into account the school community's needs when planning the high school choice event for parents. First, the assumption that the same people who require interpretation of the English-language presentation would be able or likely to generate specific questions and would benefit from a Q&A session proved to be faulty. Only four people raised their hands with questions, not all of which were answered before the meeting abruptly ended. The rest of the group sat quietly, straining to hear and staring at Ms. Dowd and Mrs. Ramirez with blank faces. Next, because of the limited time allocated and the chosen format of the interpretation session, virtually none of the information covered in the hour-long presentation was conveyed to the Spanish-speaking parents. Finally, the parents who sat for interpretation missed a valuable opportunity to speak with their child's guidance counselor individually (many eighth-grade counselors were in attendance). Instead, they wasted time and learned very little about high school choice while other parents took advantage of the guidance counselors' presence at the event.

At the other end of the spectrum, IS 725 offered immediate, comprehensive, and well-informed interpretation services to Spanish-speaking parents in the audience. Mr. Sanchez, a guidance counselor originally from the Dominican Republic, stood at the front of the auditorium next to Ms. Perolli, his colleague, who was leading the workshop in English. After each PowerPoint slide and commentary in English, Mr. Sanchez translated her explanations to Spanish. The fact that Mr. Sanchez is a bilingual guidance counselor who works directly with students on high school choice meant that he was intimately familiar with the process and could understand and then translate all of the details and nuances that Ms. Perolli covered in her presentation. This benefited the Spanish-speaking members of the audience, because they received all the information that had been provided in English. For example, one of the PowerPoint slides showed a sample application form. When she reached this slide, Ms. Perolli advised,

> You should list the programs according to preference. If you are not crazy about your zoned school but you are willing to have your child go there, put it last. Anything you put below your zoned school doesn't matter because once they get down the list to the zoned school they will automatically assign you to the zoned school [meaning that the student was not matched to any of the schools higher up on the list]. If you don't put the

zoned school, there is a chance that your child won't get any of the schools on his list and will have to go to the supplementary round.

Mr. Sanchez's verbatim translation relayed to Spanish-speaking parents Ms. Perolli's suggested strategy of putting the zoned school last in order to ensure the student a seat in at least one school. Parents do not receive this sort of additional information when they read translated materials alone. If equitable access to information is to be achieved, immigrant parents need careful, detailed interpretation of everything that guidance counselors say in English. An estimated seventy-five hundred students, or nearly 9 percent of the eighth graders who applied in 2009, did not get matched to any high school in the first round of applications.[53] This figure attests to the importance of knowing how to use one's zoned school as a default option. Students who do not get a first-round match must participate in the supplementary round, where there is a much smaller pool of generally less desirable schools from which to choose. By translating all of Ms. Perolli's commentary offered during the workshop, Mr. Sanchez ensured that Spanish-speaking parents received equivalent information and guidance to that of the other families in the audience.

The Limits of Linguistic Translation

The availability of interpretation services is one measure of a school's effectiveness in informing non-English-speaking parents about high school choice. Another measure is the degree to which the translations approximate the information provided to parents in English. However, even when accurate translations and interpretation are given, they may not be sufficient to explicate the intricacies of complex bureaucratic processes such as high school choice. Rather, immigrant parents who were born, socialized, and educated in countries having different school practices, policies, social mores, and cultural models may require translations that include contextual background and clearly articulated expectations. Thus, a third consideration is whether the translations take into account parents' potentially limited knowledge of certain norms, expectations, and quotidian school practices and therefore make them explicit.

In conducting this research, I witnessed the failure of direct linguistic translations to effectively communicate information to parents on a number of occasions. These ethnographic data also contain poignant examples of school personnel going beyond simply translating directly and instead including additional details and culturally relevant references in their explanations. In one case, the parent coordinator leading a workshop actually articulated parental rights that are often assumed to be universally known.

These illustrative moments differentiate cultural from linguistic translation, supplying evidence of the relevance of the concept of *cultural translation* and highlighting the potential value of including culturally sensitive, contextual details in translated communication to immigrant parents.

The limits of linguistic translation were perhaps most powerfully revealed when, at one middle school event, a Spanish-speaking woman repeatedly expressed confusion about the meaning of the phrase "Specialized High School Admissions Test." Nine of the most elite and competitive schools in the New York public school system require students to take a standardized exam for admission. Each year more than twenty thousand students sit for the Specialized High School Admissions Test to vie for approximately four thousand spots at these schools.

A key component of New York's portfolio of schools, the specialized high schools and the entrance exam itself were referenced in each of the NYC-DOE publications and at every citywide and middle-school-based workshop. The direct Spanish translation of the phrase "Specialized High School Admissions Test" to *examen especializado* or "specialized exam" was sprinkled throughout the school choice materials and was used countless times in presentations. During my observations, however, it became evident that many Spanish-speaking parents did not understand what the phrase actually referred to. For example, after hearing Mrs. Ramirez use the term *examen especializado* during the question-and-answer session at IS 545, one woman stood up and asked aloud,

Que es especializado? Es como en mi pais con las humanidades o letras? No es como en nuestros paises, verdad? *What is specialized? Is it like in my country, [choosing an academic track like] humanities or letters? It's not like in our countries, right?*

Neither Mrs. Ramirez nor any of the other Spanish-speaking parents in the audience responded to the woman's question—perhaps because they did not hear her or because no one else understood what the phrase meant. Regardless of the reason, the comment itself serves to demonstrate her evident confusion with a grammatically correct, and yet conceptually limited, translation of an important element of the larger choice process. High-achieving students who may be strong candidates for gaining admission to one of the prestigious exam schools stand to lose out if they or their parents do not know what it takes to apply to these widely coveted schools.

A focus group with guidance counselors and the parent coordinator at IS 725 elicited another example of the weakness of linguistic translation without embedded cultural knowledge. In this instance, the unsuccessful translation attempt involved notices sent home to parents about the Learning

Environment Survey—a survey distributed to teachers, students, and parents at every school and used to evaluate the school environment. Although it is not directly related to high school choice, this example brings to life the ways in which apparently straightforward attempts at communication with immigrant families may miss the mark.

During a discussion with the guidance counselors and Ms. Torres, the parent coordinator, about the school's outreach and communication strategies with families generally, Ms. Torres recounted, "The flyers [sent home to parents about filling out the Learning Environment Survey] are translated into Spanish, but parents still come in with the flyers, and they don't know what they mean."

Ms. Torres and the rest of the guidance staff did not understand what could have possibly been wrong with the flyers. This puts into sharp relief the mismatch between school personnel's comprehension of what they should be doing to explain policies, procedures, and concepts to parents and the depth and the breadth of support that some parents may need if they are to understand the messages sent from their children's school. If parents do not have a notion of what the Learning Environment Survey is or why they should fill it out, and if they have no reference point in the education system in their countries of origin, simply translating the words into Spanish may not be enough to convey meaning and produce understanding.

The Possibilities of Cultural Translation

In the midst of numerous missteps in the middle schools' and district's outreach to families, I observed a few instances in which school personnel took alternative and possibly more promising approaches to informing parents about high school choice. In these cases, they inserted contextual information and provided cultural translations in explaining the process. These enhanced translations explicated normative practices that are often taken for granted and did so in language and concepts with which immigrant parents could identify.

In many low-income Latin American immigrant families, the tendency to view school personnel as the ultimate authority on a child's academic education and to avoid confronting or challenging them may be even more exaggerated given the deeply rooted cultural history of such traditions.[54] Explicitly stating the school's expectations of parents as well as their rights to ask questions, request meetings, or appeal for specific support or services (for themselves or for their children) may be one way to help low-income and immigrant parents develop some of the cultural capital that has historically produced educational advantages for children in middle-class homes.

The articulation of parental and student rights and responsibilities constitutes a critical element of cultural translation. School personnel's impromptu comments made in the course of their planned presentations about high school choice often contained the most valuable insights and suggestions; some of these comments also exemplify this form of cultural translation. At one point during the workshop held at IS 633, Ms. Jean-Baptiste, the Spanish-speaking parent coordinator, mentioned the importance of attending open house events at prospective high schools. After reviewing some of the open house dates that had been scheduled, Ms. Jean-Baptiste then told parents that if they were unable to attend a scheduled open house, they should contact the high school directly to set up a tour. With this unscripted remark, she named for an exclusively immigrant audience (of approximately ten adults) some of their privileges and responsibilities as parents of eighth-grade students applying to high school in New York. Whether or not it was conscious, by telling parents about their right to call schools and request visits, Ms. Jean-Baptiste's remark equipped them with cultural capital that may help them navigate school choice and learn about school options. Asserting the propriety of requesting a school tour represents important support for families who may not be familiar with the cultural norms and expectations in the United States. This is especially true for low-income Latin American immigrant parents who come from traditions in which making requests of schools is not customary nor condoned.

Reliance on the Internet as a Primary Method of Disseminating Information

The increasing ubiquity of the Internet and growing computer literacy across many age, income, geographic, and racial or ethnic groups have led companies, governments, individuals, and school districts alike to rely progressively more on Web-based sources of information. The New York City Department of Education is no exception. The practice of referring students and families to Web sites and other electronic resources related to choosing a high school was widespread in New York.

Immigrant families experienced considerable difficulty accessing translated versions of the high school directory in printed form. Although the directory was made available in nine languages on the NYCDOE's Web site, parents in all three middle schools I studied complained about the school's failure to provide printed Spanish copies. These results echo Hemphill and Nauer's findings that, for the past two years, the directory was unavailable in any language other than English.[55] There are serious costs and time implications associated with downloading and printing a six-hundred-page document. Furthermore, other than the single-page description of each high school in the directory, virtually no information about individual schools was readily accessible in printed format. The same was true of school-level performance reports, such as the *Learning Environment Survey Report, Quality Review Report, Progress Report,* and the *Annual Report Card.* These reports can be retrieved only through the main NYCDOE Web site. As a result, access to information about school quality was even more elusive for the people on the disadvantaged side of the digital divide.

The NYCDOE also depended heavily on third-party sites to provide tools to assist families with school choice. In a number of OSEPO publications, students and parents were referred to Internet-based resources such as Hop Stop.com or the Metropolitan Transit Authority to get estimated travel times to schools. During workshops and presentations, guidance counselors and parent coordinators repeatedly suggested that parents visit these Web sites. Moreover, many of these Web-based resources are available in English only, thereby compounding the difficulties for people who cannot read English. For many immigrant families, the NYCDOE's reliance on Web sites and electronic documents may combine with their existing language barriers, lack of familiarity with the U.S. education system, and poverty to dramatically hamper their efforts to understand how to find a suitable high school for their child.

DISCUSSION
Barriers to Low-Income Immigrants' Access to School Choice Information

Immigrant parents with minimal English skills and limited financial resources face considerable challenges in learning about high school choice in New York and discovering how to successfully negotiate the process. Inadequate provision of translation and interpretation services constitutes perhaps the most basic and fundamental obstacle. The implications of a district's or a school's failure to meet parents' linguistic needs, however, may transcend the issue of an information vacuum. When parents make an effort to attend a school event and the school neglects to provide information that is comprehensible to them, these parents might take it as a signal that the school does not value them. Moreover, it might dissuade them from attending events in the future or from reaching out to their children's teachers and guidance counselors. Ultimately, poor or insufficient translation may alienate immigrant families and potentially multiply the struggles that many low-income immigrant-origin students already experience in school.

A more subtle, and yet similarly powerful, challenge to immigrant families' comprehension of school choice is related to the quality of the translations they receive. This question of quality refers to two main elements: first, it refers to interpreters' comprehension of the content material and their ability to translate the details that are provided in English. Direct translation of words may not be enough to explain a complicated bureaucratic process like high school choice. Therefore, a second aspect of quality refers to the level of cultural translation, or the degree to which a translation embeds additional contextual information about English terms, U.S.-specific concepts, and assumed knowledge about rights, expectations, and norms.

Employing bilingual guidance counselors may be one effective way to offer Spanish-speaking parents access to virtually identical information to that of their English-speaking counterparts. However, the realities of school budgeting and the supply of such personnel in the marketplace mean that not every middle school with a large Latino, immigrant-origin student population may be able to hire a bilingual guidance counselor. Therefore, districts must make translated materials widely available in printed form so that parents who need them can easily access information without incurring substantial costs.

Translated materials and live interpretation must be comprehensive and culturally sensitive to address persistent problems of information asymmetry. As these data show, linguistic translation alone is frequently insufficient to equip immigrant families with the information they need if they are to successfully negotiate school choice or many other educational policies. Even if certain information is not provided in the original version of a document or presentation, understanding the consumer public includes recognition that some knowledge is culturally bound and must be communicated. In fact, often what is not articulated in direct linguistic translations is more meaningful than what is, and it may be necessary to unpack the implicit social and cultural messages embedded in seemingly neutral policies such as school choice. Providing cultural translations represents one potential avenue to achieve this goal. Such translations may also serve to help immigrant parents generate valuable cultural capital and challenge the "hidden curriculum" that has previously contributed to cycles of social reproduction and inequality.[56] Finally, incorporating cultural translation into school outreach practices may resolve some of the seemingly endless communication breakdowns between school personnel and immigrant families that contribute to the range of home–school conflicts discussed earlier.

For immigrant families with low-level computer skills, restricted access to the Internet, and minimal English literacy, the limited availability of non-electronic and translated resources is another formidable obstacle to obtaining information about school choice. Although there are obvious benefits in cost savings and convenience in using its Web site to post announcements, reports, and documents, the NYCDOE excluded a considerable segment of the public when it replaced printed materials with electronic versions and reduced mailings in favor of e-mailed notices. The consequences for low-income Latin American immigrants may be especially severe, because access to computers tends to correlate directly with one's income level and because translated versions of many of the major NYCDOE reports and publications were available exclusively online.[57] The NYCDOE's reliance on third-party Web sites only intensifies the problem. Like the inadequate interpretation and translation, this uneven provision of information also symbolizes the district's inattention to the range of resources, skills, literacy levels, and languages that must be satisfied for families to be fairly and equally informed about the high school choice process. Finally, it may further serve to deter frustrated parents from engaging with their children's schools generally.

It should not be taken as a given that all families will investigate and consider traditional school quality measures—including graduation rates, test scores, and student satisfaction—in their selection process; some families may not be aware of the importance of or need to evaluate schools according to these metrics. In fact, many low-income Latin American immigrants come from countries and cultures in which competition, choice, and school quality comparisons are not a routine part of the educational process. These parents often assume, at least initially, that all schools in the United States are good or at least better than the schools in their countries of origin.[58]

OSEPO's publications and school-based workshops were nearly devoid of references to school quality as an important criterion for school selection; this amounts to one of the most serious limitations of the district's and schools' work to inform families about high school choice. Excluding from informational materials and events a discussion about what constitutes a high-quality school, how to access this information, and why seeking it is a critical part of the high school selection process puts those families who do not already know this at a distinct disadvantage. To address this potential source of inequality, all school choice publications and workshops should contain an explicit review of school quality metrics used by the city, state, and federal government to evaluate schools, a discussion of where school evaluations can be found, and instructions on how to use them.

Given the current emphasis in federal, state, and district accountability frameworks on traditional school quality indicators such as graduation rates and student academic proficiency, it is surprising that the official district school choice materials virtually ignore these data points. It is even more striking considering the substantial investment that the NYCDOE has made, both financially and politically, in creating publicly available school-level reports. The Office of Accountability of the New York City Department of Education has spent millions of dollars in the past four years to develop the progress reports, learning environment surveys, and quality reviews. In light of Hemphill and Nauer's data on the vast undersupply of high performing high schools in New York, however, the district's failure to mention school quality or these reports in its school choice publications and presentations may be better understood.[59] Encouraging families to investigate schools on the basis of these metrics might only call attention to the fact that the NYCDOE currently does not have enough good schools to meet student demand. Yet, until the NYCDOE reaches its goal of improving all schools, it has a responsibility not only to make these data available to the public but also to facilitate dialogue about the current condition of schools and ways to use data to make school choice decisions.

IMPLICATIONS

This preliminary research offers a small window into one district's high school choice process and shows how the weaknesses of its communication and outreach strategy may interrupt efforts to achieve equitable access to high-quality education. Through an examination of the obstacles that immigrants face in gathering information about school choice, this study also delves into the nuanced process of immigrant educational integration. The results illuminate how unsuccessful dissemination of information and inadequate translation and interpretation—about school choice or any other regulation, policy, or procedure—may explain long-standing conflicts and misunderstandings between schools and immigrant families and may thwart the larger social goals of facilitating immigrant families' integration.

The United States has seen spectacular growth in its immigrant population in recent decades, not only in traditional gateway cities but also, increasingly, in cities and states that have never before received large numbers of immigrants.[60] These post-1965 immigration waves have been accompanied by a rise in the number of children of immigrants being educated in U.S. schools. Thus, understanding immigrant families' experiences with integration across multiple social realms—not least of which is the education system—and learning about the various kinds of support these families may need if they are to be successful have taken on unprecedented urgency.

Informing immigrants of their rights and responsibilities as members of society and explaining bureaucratic procedures is only one element of the larger work of assisting integration. Yet, as this research shows, successfully reaching out to immigrant families and communicating critical information are more complicated than may be expected. Knowledge about how to nego-tiate institutional relationships, environments, and processes (e.g., finding an appropriate high school for one's child as part of a school choice plan) constitutes a valuable form of cultural capital that, by virtue of having been educated and socialized outside the United States, many immigrant par-ents may lack. Linguistic translation rarely includes essential background and contextual information—clues that immigrant parents need to be fully educated about the rules of the game. Effective support of immigrant inte-gration would include cultural translations of policies and procedures (edu-cational or other) and would make explicit social norms, expectations, and rights that are often assumed to be common knowledge. Hence, cultural translation should replace linguistic translation as the standard of service.

The problems with New York's approach to explaining high school choice to students and families do not only reside in the content of the mate-rials and in the translations provided. Many families, above all those of low-income immigrant backgrounds, may require individual guidance to make well-informed decisions about a child's educational pathway. In their study of how parents search for schools, Teske et al. found that low-income par-ents relied on people more than printed materials to obtain the type of "soft facts" that they were most interested in learning about a potential school.[61] Current opportunities for parents to speak directly with school personnel to ask questions about schools are inadequate. With caseloads of as many as four hundred students each, guidance counselors find it virtually impos-sible to spend time with each student. Schools having large numbers of low-income and immigrant-origin students should receive additional bud-get allocations to cover the cost of providing such necessary, personalized support in making school selections. In addition, schools' engagement with families concerning high school choice should begin well before students reach the eighth grade (or whenever decisions are required).

A number of gaps remain in the school choice literature and in the research on educational integration. Additional studies are needed that directly capture immigrant families' experiences with high school choice and include data based on their own narratives to illuminate the challenges they face, examine their sources of information, and reveal how and why immigrant students and families end up making the school selections they do. Current studies of school choice also tend to overlook the role of chil-dren in school choice decisions. Investigating the experiences of adolescent children of immigrants might be particularly telling given the complicated dynamics in families where children act as translators and cultural brokers for their parents.[62] Research that compares the school choice experiences of various immigrant groups—such as low-income Latin American and Chinese immigrants—may shed light on cultural and structural factors that complicate their negotiation of this or other bureaucratic processes. Comparative studies of immigrant and non-immigrant families may also deepen current understanding of the salience of immigration as an explanatory factor of variation in the ability or likelihood of participation in school choice. Finally, a focus on the supply side of this equation—the schools that eventually receive the students participating in the choice process—is also warranted. Further examination of how, if at all, schools reach out to students and families and whether they target certain students and ignore others would round out the picture of the multifaceted process of school choice.

PART IV

Competition and Segregation Effects of Choice

9

How Do Principals Respond to Charter School Competition?

Understanding the Mechanisms of the Competitive Effects of Choice

Marisa Cannata

Since the first charter school opened in 1992, the number of charter schools has risen to more than four thousand in forty states. The response to this dramatic growth has been a great deal of research comparing student achievement in charter schools to that in traditional public schools.[1] As this research area matures, researchers are delving deeper into charter schools to explore variation in achievement and operations within them, including finance, governance, student composition, teacher quality, management organizations, and instructional conditions.[2] Given the priorities of the Obama administration and recent changes in state policies, charter schools are expected to see further growth.

This increase in the number of charter schools—and the subsequent increase in choice and competition—may substantially impact the nation's education landscape as districts and communities respond by improving their own schools. To date, research on this area in general, and charter schools in particular, is mixed. Few studies have examined how principals in traditional public schools perceive and respond to competition from charter schools. Further, research on the competitive effects of charter schools has focused exclusively on noncharter public schools without considering the impact charter schools may have on private schools or the differential impact on magnet and traditional public schools.

This chapter addresses this gap by exploring the following questions. How do principals perceive the competition produced by charter schools, and how do their perceptions vary among private, magnet, and traditional public schools? What factors affect principals' perceptions of charter competition? And what is the relationship between charter competition and principals' leadership behavior?

CHARTER SCHOOL COMPETITION
Theoretical Framework

Charter schools are expected to have both direct and indirect effects on public educational outcomes.[3] Direct effects come from the flexibility and autonomy given to charter schools that theoretically enable them to be more efficient and effective. Most charter school research focuses on these direct effects and compares outcomes in charter and traditional public schools, although results are mixed and depend on the policy, organizational, and community context.[4]

The indirect effects of charter schools are hypothesized to come from the increased productivity of noncharter public schools due to increased charter competition.[5] Noncharter schools do not want to lose students (and the funding that follows them) to charter schools and thus should improve their own practices to retain students or attract those who have left for a charter school. This indirect effect of school competition should lead to greater variety and efficiency in all schools.[6] If charter schools are to achieve their full potential impact on education, their competitive effects would force other schools to improve.[7]

The mechanisms through which the competitive effects of charter schools are assumed to work depend on the perceptions and actions of noncharter school personnel. To be spurred to act, school personnel must perceive as detrimental the threat or actuality of losing students to charter schools—a loss that may also mean a loss in funding to the extent that school funding levels are based on the number of students.[8] A school's active response to these losses, then, should improve student outcomes. Noncharter schools may, for instance, adopt programs or practices used by the competing schools or may make their own programs and practices more efficient.[9]

This hypothesized mechanism of school competition points to potential limitations of such effects on noncharter schools. Noncharter schools may see charter schools as a release valve that eases overcrowding in a growing district or as a place for particularly unhappy parents and students.[10] Caps on the number of charter schools allowed in a district, and other legislative protections, blunt potential competitive effects and insulate noncharter schools.[11] Further, schools may respond to charter competition by spending more money on marketing rather than improving instruction and making substantive reforms.[12] The next section reviews existing research on the effects of school competition and the mechanisms through which they work.

Previous Research on Competitive Effects

As stated, previous research on the impact of charter school competition on noncharter public schools finds mixed results.[13] These may be explained in part by variation in the locations studied. For example, competition from charter schools has been linked with higher student achievement in Texas and Arizona but lower achievement in Ohio.[14] Charter schools in Florida appear to have a positive impact on student achievement gains in math, but there is no evidence of any impact in reading.[15] A study of charter competition in California found little evidence of any impact on achievement in noncharter public schools.[16] One recent study of charter school competition in eight locations, however, found little evidence of positive or negative effects on student achievement.[17]

Mixed results can also be explained by variations among studies focused on the same location. In North Carolina, one study used instrumental variables analysis and found positive and significant effects of charter competition on student performance, but a separate study used fixed effects and found a small negative relationship between the number of charter schools within specified distances and student reading gains, and no significant relationship between charter competition and student achievement gains in mathematics.[18] Multiple studies examining the competitive effects of charter schools on noncharter public schools in Michigan have disparate results. Two found positive impacts of charter competition on student achievement in elementary grades.[19] Bettinger found no evidence of any effects from charter competition.[20] Ni used longitudinal data on Michigan's schools to find that charter competition was associated with small negative effects in the short term, but larger negative effects on achievement in noncharter public schools in the long term.[21]

In addition to these studies involving charter schools, we can learn about potential effects of increased school choice on traditional public schools by studying the effects of competition between school districts or the competitive pressure of private schools. Although families choose their homes for a variety of reasons, school quality and property tax burden are among their primary motives. A literature review of research on public school district choice through 2001 concluded that, overall, competition had a positive impact on student achievement, especially in areas that exceeded a specified threshold of competition between public schools.[22] Few recent studies have considered the competitive effects of public school choice, although these also find a positive relationship.[23]

The research on the effects of private school competition on public schools is somewhat mixed, but generally it finds modest positive results.[24] Studies in New York and Milwaukee found positive effects of private school enrollment or private school vouchers on high school graduation.[25] Research using national data sets also found positive effects of private school competition on achievement and attainment in public schools, although other studies found mixed results or no effects from private school competition.[26] Jepsen found that the presence of positive effects of private school competition depends on the data set used, the aggregation level, the grade level, and the outcome measure.[27] Studies of private school competition in Georgia, Illinois, North Carolina, and Washington State found little evidence of positive effects.[28]

Much of the research on school choice and competition has focused on the outcomes of competition, that is, whether greater school choice leads to better educational outcomes in traditional public schools. Less research has focused on the processes through which competition provided by schools of choice is thought to affect those outcomes. A few studies relying on small samples indicate that principals or district officials in noncharter public schools do make changes in response to charter schools, although most districts responded by changing marketing practices rather than making substantive changes.[29]

Studies relying on larger samples, however, find less evidence that schools respond to charter schools in competitive ways. A survey of principals in California noncharter public schools found that principals felt little competitive pressure from charter schools, rarely changed their practices in response to charter schools, and felt that charter schools had no effect on their ability to recruit teachers and students.[30] Similarly, fewer than 5 percent of superintendents in Texas made curricular or programmatic changes in response to charter schools.[31] Overall, the limited evidence available on the processes through which school choice leads to improved outcomes suggests little perceived competition and few educational changes. This chapter adds to this research by exploring the factors that affect principals' perception of charter school competition and the extent to which their leadership behavior changes in response.

METHODS

Sample Characteristics and Data

To study the perceptions and effects of charter school competition on traditional public, magnet, and private schools, this chapter relies on a matched convenience sample of schools and their principals. Schools were selected from those with which the Northwest Evaluation Association (NWEA) has partnered to monitor student achievement through the administration of computerized adaptive tests in math, reading, and language arts every spring and fall of the school year. NWEA schools are linked to the public Common Core of Data (CCD) and Private School Survey (PSS) files to obtain school characteristics. The sample frame was defined as the set of schools that could be found in the 2005–2006 CCD and PSS files and were tested by NWEA in 2005–2006, with at least one grade having more than 50 percent testing coverage in both math and reading, and at least ten students tested. Special education, vocational and alternative schools, schools that were no longer testing with NWEA, and schools that did not have all the variables that we needed for school matching were excluded. The first selected sample that was contacted for participation consisted of all available 321 schools of choice and 337 best-matched traditional public schools selected from 5,864 potential matches.

The process of matching traditional public schools to schools of choice consisted of two stages. (Details are available in the online appendix at http://www.vanderbilt.edu/schoolchoice/.) In the first stage, CCD data on the schools were used to identify the best match. Matching criteria included location in the same state, geographical distance, grade range, ethnic composition, socioeconomic status, and size. Because of differences in grade configurations between schools of choice and traditional public schools, in some cases there was more than one match for a school of choice to match all the grade levels in the school. Some traditional public schools were also used as matches for more than one school of choice.

The second stage of the matching process entailed obtaining school participation in the teacher and principal surveys. When a traditional public school or its district declined participation or had recently closed or stopped testing with NWEA, a replacement was found for it. Unfortunately, the replacement was almost always of lower match quality than the original match. After these changes, the school sample comprised 224 charter, 60 magnet, 32 private, and 464 traditional public schools. Of these, only 116 (51.8 percent) charter, 34 (56.7 percent) magnet, 17 (53.1 percent) private, and 118 (25.4 percent) traditional public schools agreed to participate.

Principals and assistant principals were asked to fill out confidential online questionnaires. Completion rates for the principals were 80.4 percent for charter, 57.6 percent for magnet, 100.0 percent for private, and 74.9 percent for traditional public schools. Schools named multiple individuals as principals, and some schools included the principal and assistant principals. The 353 principals who completed questionnaires worked in 245 schools. Three of these schools operated two independent programs or campuses and are treated as separate schools. For schools in which both the principal and the assistant principal responded, only the principal response is included in this analysis. For three schools with no responses from the main principal and more than one assistant principal response, assistant principal responses were averaged to create one response per school. Because this chapter focuses on the competitive effects of charter schools, we used only magnet, private, and traditional public school data on principal perceptions of charter competition from states having charter school policies. The final sample size is 138 schools. Table A1 in the online appendix (http://www. vanderbilt.edu/schoolchoice/) includes descriptive statistics on the schools in the final sample and variables used in this chapter.

Data on the presence of charter schools surrounding the 138 sample schools came from the 2006–2007 CCD. Therefore, the data on actual charter competition, including location and number of students served, represent the universe of charter schools in the states where the sampled schools are located rather than only the charter schools in this sample. The latitude and longitude of the physical address of the magnet and traditional public schools came from the CCD, and information on the location of private schools came from the PSS.

Analytic Methods

Bivariate analyses were conducted to answer the first research question and identify overall mean differences in principals' perceptions of charter competition across school types. To answer the second research question, logistic regression analyses were performed using data on whether principals perceived any negative effect of charter competition either on recruiting teachers and students or on acquiring financial resources. The response options for the perceived competition variables may not represent a continuous measure because principals responded on a scale from 1 (very negative effect) to 5 (very positive effect). Further, few principals reported that charter competition had either a somewhat or a very positive effect on their schools; most respondents indicated either no effect or a somewhat or very negative effect. For this reason, linear regression is not appropriate, and a binomial logistic regression model with a logit link function was used.

The two outcome variables are the log odds that the principal perceived a somewhat or very negative effect (i.e., response of less than 3) of charter competition for students and teachers and for financial resources. The independent variables used are actual competition (the number of charter schools and percentage of charter school students within 2.5, 5, and 10 miles, and the minimum distance to a charter school), school characteristics (the principal's years of experience at the school, the percentage of students eligible for free or reduced-price lunch, the percentage of limited-English-proficient students, and dummy variables for school instructional level such as elementary, middle, high, or mixed grades), and school type.

The third research question explores the relationship between perceived and actual charter school competition and principal use of time. Ordinary least squares regressions were run to explore what predicts how principals spent their time.[32] The outcome variables are the relative amount of time the principal spent on routine management activities, instructional improvement activities, and public relations. The competition measures are the principal's perceived competition and actual competition, as in previous models. With three outcome variables and five measures of competition, this represents fifteen separate models. As with the preceding model, school characteristics and dummy variables for school type are included.

Variables

Perceptions of Charter Competition. Principals were asked about their perceived effect of charter school competition on five domains: acquiring financial resources, recruiting teachers, retaining teachers, attracting students, and retaining students. These domains were initially assumed to form a single measure of overall perceived charter competition, but factor analysis revealed that the domain of acquiring financial resources did not fit in that measure (it had low factor loadings and adversely impacted reliability). Thus, it is considered separately.

The binary outcome variable indicating whether the principal perceived a negative effect of charter school competition on acquiring financial resources comes from a survey item asking principals how charter schools have affected their school in acquiring financial resources. The five response options ranged from 1 (very negative) to 5 (very positive).

The binary outcome variable indicating whether the principal perceived a negative effect of charter competition on attracting teachers or students comes from survey items asking principals how charter schools have affected their school in recruiting and retaining teachers and in attracting and retaining students. The five response options ranged from 1 (very negative) to 5 (very positive).[33]

Actual Charter Competition. Measures of actual charter competition rely on distance from the sample school to charter schools in the same state, which is determined by using the latitude and longitude of their physical address provided by the CCD or PSS. It is restricted to only charter schools at the same instructional level (elementary, middle, high, or mixed grades). Using distance as a measure of charter school competition is consistent with previous research, as are the particular distance ranges used in this chapter and the use of market share, or the percentage of students in a given area attending a choice school.[34] The distance bands are as follows: ≤2.5 miles; >2.5 miles but ≤5 miles; and >5 miles but ≤10 miles. There are three types of charter competition measures: the minimum distance to a charter school; counts of charter schools within a specific distance; and percentages of students attending any school within a specific distance who are in charter schools.

Principals' Use of Time. Time on routine management is the extent to which principals spend time on activities related to building management, paperwork, and student discipline.[35] Principals were asked, "How often do you do any of the following during this 2007-08 school year?" with these response options: supervise clerical, cafeteria, and maintenance staff; monitor public spaces; deal with emergencies and other unplanned circumstances; work with students and their parents on discipline/attendance issues; and complete routine paperwork.

Time on instructional improvement is the extent to which principals spend time on activities related to school and instructional improvement.[36] Principals were asked, "How often do you do any of the following during this 2007-08 school year?" with these response options: demonstrate instructional practices and/or the use of curricular materials; observe a teacher during classroom instruction; examine and discuss student work; examine and discuss standardized test results of students from a teacher's class; create and implement the staff development program in the school; personally provide staff development; troubleshoot or support the implementation of school improvement efforts; monitor the curriculum used in classrooms to see that it reflects the school's improvement efforts; and monitor classroom instructional practices to see that they reflect the school's improvement efforts.

Time on public relations is the extent to which principals spend time on activities related to school publicity, community relations, and student recruitment.[37] Principals were asked, "How often do you do any of the following during this 2007-08 school year?" with these response options: promote the school's image in the community; communicate achievement results to the external community; attend or participate in events taking place in the community; host fundraisers or financial development efforts; and answer questions from potential students and/or their parents.

FINDINGS

On average, the closest charter school was slightly more than 9 miles away from the schools in this sample. The average school had fewer than one charter school within 2.5 miles of its location but slightly more than five charter schools between 5 and 10 miles away. About 2.8 percent of all students within 2.5 miles of the average school in this sample attended a charter school. About 23 percent of principals indicated that charter school competition affected their ability to attract and retain teachers and students in a negative way. Slightly fewer principals (19 percent) thought charter school competition negatively affected their ability to acquire financial resources.

Table 9.1 provides more details on principals' perceptions of charter school competition and suggests that principals overall perceived a small, slightly negative effect by charter schools on their operations. The average principal rating for a charter competition effect on acquiring financial resources was 2.78. This is closest to the response of "No effect" (response = 3) but is slightly in the direction of a small negative effect. Overall competition for teachers and students (2.88) was slightly higher and closer to "No effect." There was no evidence that magnet school principals had different perceptions of charter school competition on either financial resources or teachers and students than did principals of traditional public schools.

Private school principals, however, all indicated that charter school competition had no effect on their ability to acquire financial resources, a response that was statistically significantly higher than those of principals in traditional public schools. Private school principals only were also asked about perceived charter school competition for obtaining appropriate physical facilities, and all private school principals indicated there was no effect on this domain from charter school competition (data not shown). These small differences between non-charter public and private schools may point to the differential impact of competition across sectors. Principals of magnet and traditional public schools appear to feel more negative impact of charter schools on their finances and not on their ability to recruit students and teachers, whereas principals of private schools appear unaffected financially even as they face more competition in attracting students.

Table 9.2 presents the effects of three measures of actual charter school competition on perceived charter competition. The three columns under the label "Attracting and retaining students and teachers" show results from logistic regressions predicting whether principals indicated charter schools had a negative impact on their ability to attract and retain teachers and students. Principals of schools situated at greater distances from the closest charter school had smaller odds of saying that charter competition for teachers and students had a negative effect. The number of charter schools and the percentage of students attending charter schools within 2.5 miles were also associated with the odds that a principal perceived a negative effect of charter competition on teachers and students, indicating that when a school has more charter schools in close proximity, the principal perceives a more negative effect of charter schools on her ability to attract and retain teachers

TABLE 9.1   **Mean perceptions of charter school competition**

School type	Acquiring financial resources	Recruiting teachers	Retaining teachers	Attracting students	Retaining students	Overall competition for teachers and students
All schools						
Mean	2.78	2.95	2.96	2.78	2.83	2.88
SE	0.044	0.026	0.02	0.043	0.041	0.027
Min	1	1	1	1	1	1
Max	3.25	4	3.25	4	4	3.5
Traditional public						
Mean	2.69	2.97	2.97	2.83	2.92	2.92
SE	0.14	0.047	0.047	0.108	0.092	0.058
Min	1	1	1	1	1	1
Max	3	4	3	4	4	3.5
Magnet						
Mean	2.76	2.94	2.96	2.79	2.83	2.88
SE	0.051	0.034	0.024	0.049	0.047	0.033
Min	1	2	2	1	1	2
Max	3.25	3.25	3.25	3.25	3.25	3.25
Private						
Mean	3.00[a]	3	2.93	2.67	2.73	2.83
SE	0	0	0.067	0.159	0.153	0.083
Min	3	3	2	1	1	2
Max	3	3	3	3	3	3

a. The mean value is a statistically significant difference from the mean of traditional public schools at 5% significance level.

$N = 101$ for traditional public schools, 22 for magnet schools, and 15 for private schools. The response options were 1 = Very negative effect, 2 = Somewhat negative effect, 3 = No effect, 4 = Somewhat positive effect, and 5 = Very positive effect. It is possible for the maximum not to be a whole number because responses from multiple assistant principals were averaged for three schools. Overall competition for teachers and students is a composite of recruiting and retaining teachers and attracting and retaining students.

and students. Each additional charter school within 2.5 miles of the school was associated with almost twice the odds of perceiving a negative effect on attracting teachers and students. The impact of charter school enrollment share within 2.5 miles was smaller, but also positive and statistically significant. The charter school enrollment share of students from schools between 5 and 10 miles away was also associated with slightly greater odds of perceiving a negative effect of charter competition for teachers and students.

TABLE 9.2 **Effects of various measures of actual charter competition on principals' perceptions of charter competition**

	ATTRACTING AND RETAINING STUDENTS AND TEACHERS			ACQUIRING FINANCIAL RESOURCES		
	Minimum distance to charter	Charter school count	Charter enrollment share	Minimum distance to charter	Charter school count	Charter enrollment share
Minimum distance to charter school	0.891* (0.040)			0.988 (0.026)		
Distance radius						
≤ 2.5 miles		1.969* (0.473)	1.116* (0.048)		1.548 (0.360)	1.092* (0.044)
> 2.5 and ≤ 5 miles		0.972 (0.091)	1.029 (0.040)		0.832 (0.135)	1.041 (0.038)
> 5 and ≤ 10 miles		1.040 (0.028)	1.181* (0.072)		0.973 (0.036)	1.016 (0.050)
Private school	0.927 (0.843)	1.061 (0.943)	3.066 (2.961)			
Magnet school	0.341 (0.272)	0.351 (0.301)	0.584 (0.483)	0.656 (0.429)	0.731 (0.487)	0.714 (0.498)
Middle school grades	0.658 (0.424)	0.728 (0.498)	1.01 (0.688)	0.653 (0.403)	0.727 (0.464)	0.942 (0.615)
High school grades	1.373 (1.349)	1.814 (1.845)	1.367 (1.340)	0.352 (0.337)	0.44 (0.431)	0.45 (0.45)
Mixed grades	1.945 (1.947)	1.577 (1.432)	2.488 (2.448)	0.928 (0.904)	0.9 (0.857)	1.314 (1.33)
School enrollment	0.999 (0.001)	0.999 (0.001)	1.000 (0.001)	1.001 (0.001)	1.000 (0.001)	1.001 (0.001)
Principal experience at school	1.074* (0.036)	1.059 (0.032)	1.064 (0.036)	1.026 (0.037)	1.031 (0.037)	1.025 (0.041)
Percent minority students	0.994 (0.014)	0.990 (0.016)	0.988 (0.016)	1.028 (0.015)	1.028 (0.015)	1.027 (0.016)
Percent limited-English proficient	0.991 (0.023)	0.978 (0.029)	0.994 (0.024)	0.914* (0.034)	0.922* (0.035)	0.925* (0.035)
Percent free or reduced-price lunch eligible	1.024 (0.016)	1.022 (0.017)	1.038* (0.019)	0.994 (0.016)	0.991 (0.016)	0.994 (0.017)

*$p < .05$

$N = 138$. The dependent variable for the logistic models (which show odds-ratios and standard errors) is whether the principal perceived charter competition for attracting students and teachers and acquiring financial resources to have a somewhat or very negative effect.

There was little evidence that school type or other characteristics were related to principal perceptions of charter competition for teachers and students. The only statistically significant result was that principals in schools having a higher proportion of students eligible for free or reduced-price lunch had greater odds of perceiving a negative effect of charter competition (when I controlled for the percentage of students enrolled in charter schools within 10 miles of the school). There was a relationship between principal experience at the school and perceptions of charter school competition. Principals who had more years of experience at the school as either a principal, an assistant principal, or a teacher had a more negative perception of charter school competition for teachers and students. Perhaps principals who have been at their school longer have a better perspective on trends in teacher and student recruitment than those having less experience at the school.

The three columns labeled "Acquiring financial resources" in Table 9.2 present results for the relationship between actual measures of charter competition and principals' perception of charter competition effects on acquiring financial resources. As with the results for competition concerning teachers and students, actual measures of charter competition within 2.5 miles of the school were related to principals' perceptions of competition for financial resources, although there was no relationship between actual and perceived competition for charter schools that were farther away or using the location of the closest charter school. Also similar to the results for perceived competition for teachers and students, few school characteristics were related to principal perceptions of competition for financial resources. There was some evidence that schools with more limited-English-proficient students were less likely to perceive a negative impact of charter schools on acquiring financial resources. The reason may be that charter schools do not serve large numbers of LEP students and thus provide less competition for these schools. Unlike the results for competition for teachers and students, there was no relationship between principals' years of experience at the school and perceptions of charter competition on financial resources.

Table 9.3 examines the relationship between actual and perceived measures of charter competition and the ways principals use their time; my aim was to explore whether principals respond to charter competition by changing their leadership behavior. There is no evidence in these data that either actual or perceived charter competition was related to principal behavior and use of time.

DISCUSSION AND CONCLUSIONS

Overall, the principals in this study perceived little competition from charter schools affecting either their financial resources or their recruitment of

TABLE 9.3 **Effects of perceived and actual charter competition on principals' use of time**

	Routine management	Instructional leadership	Public relations
Minimum distance to charter school	0.006 (0.004)	0.001 (0.004)	0.003 (0.004)
Number of charter schools within distance radius			
≤ 2.5 miles	0.043 (0.039)	0.004 (0.042)	−0.017 (0.043)
> 2.5 and ≤ 5 miles	−0.003 (0.021)	0.018 (0.023)	−0.019 (0.024)
> 5 and ≤ 10 miles	−0.002 (0.006)	−0.008 (0.007)	−0.001 (0.007)
Charter enrollment share within distance radius			
≤ 2.5 miles	0.006 (0.008)	0.000 (0.008)	−0.005 (0.009)
> 2.5 and ≤ 5 miles	0.009 (0.009)	0.017 (0.01)	−0.001 (0.01)
> 5 and ≤ 10 miles	0.013 (0.012)	−0.001 (0.013)	−0.008 (0.013)
Perception of competition			
Attracting and retaining teachers and students	−0.195 (0.19)	−0.029 (0.206)	0.003 (0.208)
Acquiring financial resources	−0.092 (0.115)	−0.136 (0.124)	−0.258* (0.126)
Competition had a somewhat or very negative effect			
Attracting and retaining teachers and students	0.028 (0.131)	−0.129 (0.142)	−0.234 (0.144)
Acquiring financial resources	0.179 (0.143)	0.178 (0.154)	0.289 (0.157)

*p<.05

$N = 138$. The models also include school enrollment, principal years of experience in the school, percentage of students that are minority, limited-English proficient or eligible for free or reduced-price lunch, and dummy variables for school type and instructional level.

teachers and students. The lack of evidence that principals perceive much threat from charter schools is consistent with previous research on the mechanisms through which charter competition is expected to work.[38] This result is not surprising given that, in this sample, the closest charter school was, on average, more than nine miles away, a distance that is near the top of the range that research suggests most parents are willing or able to travel for a charter school.[39] Parents' ability to send their children to charter schools farther away is limited by access to transportation.[40] This may limit the generalizability of these findings to areas where charter schools are few in number or geographically dispersed. Communities that have denser charter populations may provide greater competitive pressures on noncharter schools, because charter schools are more likely to be in close proximity.

This study does provide some evidence about how close a charter school must be to apply competitive pressure on noncharter schools and thus provide an incentive to improve. The most consistent evidence for a relationship between whether principals perceive charter school competition to be impacting their school and actual measures of competition used in the existing literature is the number of charter schools and the student enrollment share of charter schools within 2.5 miles of the noncharter school. Charter schools that were farther away did not appear to impact principals' perceptions of charter competition. Research that uses broader measures of charter competition, such as the number or percentage of charter schools and students in the county, may be using inappropriate measures of competition. However, it may be that district officials' perceptions of charter school competition are more relevant given the district role in allocating resources to schools.[41] The data in this study cannot address this question.

The importance of a close geographic proximity and school density to perceived charter school competition has implications for the ways charter school policies may operate in rural communities or those having a smaller population density and thus schools that are more spread out. For example, some mostly rural states chose not to compete in the Race to the Top program because of concerns about the program's emphasis on charter schools.[42] Policy makers who are considering increasing the supply of charter schools should consider the potential differential impact in high- as well as low-density areas.

Although in general neither private, magnet, nor traditional public school principals perceived charter school competition to have much effect on their school, traditional public school principals were more likely than private school principals to report a negative effect of charter schools on their ability to acquire financial resources. This result is somewhat surprising given private schools' greater reliance on per-student funding acquired through tuition. It would be expected that the introduction of free alternatives to traditional public schools would create competition for private schools, as is the case in Washington, D.C., where Catholic schools have recently converted to charter schools because of loss of students.[43] One explanation for this finding may be that actual charter competition has a long-term negative effect on student achievement.[44] Arsen and Ni report in chapter 10 of this volume that long-term charter school competition is negatively related to districts' financial health and that districts with especially large populations of students requiring special services were least likely to be in a position to respond positively to charter competition and reallocate resources. To ensure that traditional public schools serving special-needs students have both the motivation and the resources to improve in the face of charter school competition, state policy makers should examine the financial impact of charter schools on these schools.

Finally, this study provides no evidence that principal perceptions of charter school competition, or actual charter competition, is related to the ways principals spend their time. This finding calls into question the mechanism through which greater school choice is assumed to affect traditional public schools. Improvements in noncharter schools due to competition from charter schools should be observable through the programs, curriculum, or behavior of the schools and their staffs, as well as in student achievement or other outcomes. However, it may be that the measures of principals' use of time are too broad to capture qualitative differences between principals' leadership behaviors. To examine the mechanisms of charter school competition effects, future research should explore additional measures of principal and teacher behavior in response to charter school competition.

10

Shaking Up Public Schools with Competition

*Are They Changing the Way
They Spend Money?*

David Arsen and Yongmei Ni

School choice policies have long been promoted in the belief that, by intro-
ducing increased competition to the education system, such policies will
improve the performance of traditional public schools (TPSs).[1] In this view,
choice policies will spur school administrators to reallocate resources from
less-productive to more-productive activities. Recent empirical evidence on
the competitive effects of school choice on student achievement and school
efficiency in traditional public schools, however, is mixed, with some studies
finding positive competitive effects and others finding no or negative effects.[2]

The diversity of results is not entirely surprising given variations across
states in the design and implementation of school choice policies as well as
differences in local education contexts. In general, however, research thus
far suggests that the competitive effects of school choice policies on school
effectiveness and efficiency are quite small. We have relatively little systematic information on the internal adjustments made by public school systems
when they are confronted by competition. Previous quantitative empirical
research tends to treat school organizations as black boxes, with researchers
looking for statistical linkages between changes in the degree of competition and changes in school efficiency. Yet changes in school resource allocation represent an essential dimension of any coherent competitive response.

This chapter looks inside the black box by examining the impact of
school choice competition on several aspects of district resource allocation.
We also consider whether adjustments in resource allocation are related to

districts' success in stemming further enrollment loss to choice competitors. The empirical work focuses on Michigan, where two statewide choice poli- cies—charter schools and an interdistrict choice policy—have been in effect since 1994 and 1996, respectively. The study uses fixed-effects techniques to examine thirteen years' worth of panel data. It separates the competitive effect of charter schools from that of Michigan's interdistrict school choice policy. Our analysis also controls for the short- and long-run effects of char- ter competition on TPS resource allocation. We direct particular attention to the most widespread prediction regarding how schools will respond to com- petition: the expectation that they will shift resources from noninstructional activities to instruction. Our results show, among other things, that districts do not shift resources to instructional activities in response to charter com- petition. Indeed, in areas with sustained high levels of charter school compe- tition, we find a significant negative impact on TPS instructional spending.

The remainder of this chapter is organized as follows. We present some conceptual framing of the ways choice policies might affect school resource allocation. Then we describe the Michigan educational context, focusing on the state's school choice and school finance policies. This is followed by a discussion of data sources and empirical methods and a presentation of our findings on the impacts of school choice policies on district resource alloca- tion. Next is an examination of changes in resource allocation in districts that do and do not stabilize their enrollment loss to charter schools. We con- clude by drawing some implications of the study.

CONCEPTUALIZING CHOICE POLICIES' IMPACTS ON SCHOOL RESOURCE REALLOCATION

The idea that school choice policies will create competition that compels public school personnel to use resources more effectively (or else lose stu- dents and funding to more efficient schools) is now familiar to most Amer- icans. Those who predict such improved school performance, however, seldom specify the precise nature of these adjustments to resource alloca- tion. Certainly the most common prediction is that increased competition will induce districts to focus their resources more intensively on instruc- tional activities that raise student achievement. A shift of resources from noninstructional to instructional uses is expected to increase school effi- ciency (measured by student outcomes per dollar spent), and this in turn is important to families making school choices.[3]

Indeed, one could predict that competition will induce schools to shift resources toward instruction even if it fails to improve school efficiency, because such a shift (revealed, for instance, in smaller class size or specialized instructional programs) should appeal to families choosing among multiple school options. Yet another argument also predicts an increase in instruction's share of total spending in response to school choice competition. When schools are forced to trim budgets because of the loss of revenue to competing schools, teachers may be better organized through their unions to avoid cuts in staffing or compensation than other school employees.

Nevertheless, the prediction that choice competition will spur broadly consistent or uniform responses among schools (such as an increase in instruction's share of total spending) is ambiguous even in theory. If one accepts that families have diverse preferences regarding alternative types of schooling services and that competing schools have an incentive to serve niche markets, then quite dissimilar shifts in resource allocation are possible among schools in a given local market. For instance, some parents may place a very high value on clean, safe buildings, and this preference could elicit a shift in district resources to custodians and security services. Other schools may seek to compete by improving their communication with and accessibility to parents (more secretaries and marketing staff) or improved transportation services or athletic programs.

So in general, one can conceptualize at least three ways in which increased school choice competition might affect district resource allocation. First, districts could systematically shift resources to certain functions or services while reducing spending on others. Here the most likely possibility—one consistent with conventional wisdom regarding the impacts of school choice policies—is that competition will lead traditional public schools to shift resources to regular classroom instruction and away from noninstructional spending. Second, no systematic patterns emerge, because districts respond to competition in dissimilar ways. And third, no patterns emerge in resource reallocation, because school districts by and large do not change their resource allocation in response to increased competition.

Any examination of resource reallocation in the public sector should account for the possibility that change may not unfold quickly. Economists anticipate that the positive long-run effects of competition on resource allocation and school quality will be more substantial than the short-run effects.[4] In the short run, an administrator who wants to raise school productivity has only limited options such as inducing the staff to work harder, getting rid of unproductive staff and programs, and allocating resources away from activities that are not achievement oriented. However, in the long run, some general equilibrium mechanisms are available to an administrator. For instance, administrators can propose higher salaries in order to attract high-quality teachers and thus draw people into teaching who would otherwise pursue other careers.[5]

Thus far we have very little systematic information on the budgetary responses of school districts to choice competition. To help fill this void, this chapter addresses two related research questions. First, how does resource allocation change in districts experiencing sustained choice competition? For example, how does the share of spending devoted to various instructional and noninstructional functions change? How does class size change? We also consider the impact of choice policies on district fiscal stress as revealed in their fund balances. Second, among districts exposed to charter competition, what types of resource allocation shifts are most effective in stemming further enrollment loss to charter schools? Are there discernable differences in the resource allocation adjustments among districts when they are threatened between those that do and do not succeed in limiting further enrollment loss to charters?

SCHOOL CHOICE CONTEXT IN MICHIGAN

In 1993, Michigan became the eighth state to adopt a charter school law. A charter school, officially designated a public school academy (PSA), is a state-supported public school that operates independently under a charter granted by an authorizing body. In Michigan, PSAs can be chartered by local school districts, intermediate school districts, the state board of education, or the governing boards of public community colleges or universities. Charter schools have no geographic boundaries. Students are free to choose to go to any charter school in the state on a space-available basis.

Originally, no limit was imposed on the number of charters that could be issued by any of the authorizing boards. However, in 1996, following a proliferation of charters issued by the board of Central Michigan University, the state legislature imposed a cap on the total number of schools that may be chartered by Michigan's fifteen public universities. This cap of 150 schools has limited new school development since 2000. However, there is no cap on the number of schools chartered by other organizations, and the number of charter schools has grown steadily in Michigan over the past decade. By 2006, Michigan had 226 charter schools enrolling about ninety-eight thousand students (or 6 percent of the state's public school population). In 2006, Michigan's charter enrollment was the third largest in the nation after California and Florida.

In addition to the charter school program, in 1996 the Michigan Legislature created an interdistrict choice program that allows students to choose public schools located outside their home districts. School districts can determine whether or not to accept nonresident students. However, they cannot prohibit students who live within their boundaries from attending public schools in another district that admits them. As of 2006, about three-fourths of Michigan's 554 local districts enrolled nonresident students under the interdistrict choice program. Student participation in interdistrict choice has increased substantially in recent years, climbing to 4.3 percent of all public students by 2006. The charter school and interdistrict choice programs are designed so differently that they are likely to have a different impact on TPSs. In our analysis, we include measures of the intensity of interdistrict choice as control variables to separate the effect of charter schools from that of interdistrict choice.

Participation rates in Michigan's school choice policies vary substantially by community type. Table 10.1 shows that charter school participation is clearly concentrated in Michigan's central city and low-income suburban districts (nearly all of which are adjacent to central cities). Central city districts also lose many students to low- and middle-income suburban schools through interdistrict choice. Together, Michigan's charter school and interdistrict choice policies have produced intense competitive pressure on the state's urban districts. Statewide, roughly one-third of the public school students residing in central city districts attend a charter school or a school in a district outside their district of residence. By contrast, choice policies have generated relatively minor competitive pressures on high-income suburban and rural districts.

Michigan's school finance system, commonly known as Proposal A, greatly facilitated the development of the charter school program. Approved in 1994, Proposal A shifted the responsibility for funding current operations from local districts to the state. In addition to state and federal categorical aid, school districts receive almost all their discretionary operating revenues from the state in the form of a per-pupil foundation grant. In 2006,

TABLE 10.1 **Enrollment loss to school choice programs in 2007, by school district type**

School district type	Total resident students	% lost to charters	% lost to other districts[a]	Total % lost
Central city	257,004	24.4	7.2	31.6
Low-income suburb	38,007	13.7	−7.3	6.4
Mid-income suburb	652,010	3.7	−2.2	1.5
High-income suburb	269,035	1.2	−0.9	0.3
Rural	340,630	2.0	0.3	2.2

Source: State of Michigan, Center for Education Performance and Information, and authors' calculations.

a. Represents net enrollment loss to interdistrict choice, so negative figures imply net gain.

the grant was approximately $6875.[6] That money goes directly to the school district where the students attend school. Under Proposal A, local voters can no longer increase local taxes to support school operations. Charter schools receive a per-pupil foundation grant equal to that of the district in which the school is located.[7] Thus, the amount of operating revenue received by districts and charter schools depends almost exclusively on the number of students they enroll. Essentially the only way schools can increase their revenue is to attract more students. In this sense, the school finance system in Michigan creates an ideal competitive market for schooling and makes Michigan an especially important case for studying the effects of charter schools on traditional public schools.

Funding for Michigan schools has been extremely tight in recent years, in large measure because of a sustained decline in the state's economy. Total employment in Michigan has fallen every year since 2000, amounting to an 18.4 percent reduction in state employment between June 2000 and September 2009. Michigan has had the highest unemployment rate of any state since 2006. Not surprisingly, overall financial support for Michigan public schools has suffered during this tough economic period. Figure 10.1 displays combined state and local operating revenue for all Michigan K–12 public schools—local and intermediate school districts and charter schools—from 1994 to 2008. After increasing by roughly 20 percent between 1994 and 2002, real per-pupil revenues fell by $1,507 between 2002 and 2008 (from $9,832 to $8,325), or 15.3 percent. A fuller gauge of this recent financial squeeze takes account of local districts' contributions to the Michigan Public School Employee Retirement System (MPSERS). This nondiscretionary obligation was shifted from the state to local districts when Proposal A was implemented. As figure 10.1 shows, after adjusting for the MPSERS funding responsibility, Michigan's per-pupil funding in 2008 fell below that of 1994. The significant funding gains during the first eight years of Proposal A have been entirely eliminated.

To its credit, Michigan's centralized school funding system has spread the consequences of economic decline much more evenly across local districts than otherwise would have been the case under the state's pre-1994 funding system. Each year since 2001, with minor exceptions, every district's per-pupil foundation grant from the state has increased (or decreased) by the same dollar amount. Consequently, changes in student enrollment have been the primary determinant of variations in revenue change across districts. As noted in table 10.1, Michigan's school choice policies have had a major impact on enrollment in urban districts. Between the turndown in state funding (affecting all districts) and the loss of students and funding to choice policies, Michigan's urban districts have suffered extraordinary

FIGURE 10.1   Total state and local revenues per pupil 1994–2008

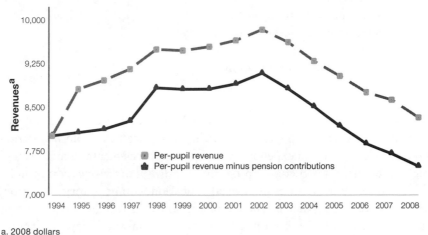

a. 2008 dollars

budget cuts. For example, between 2002 and 2010, total foundation revenue received by Michigan's fourteen central city school districts declined by
30 percent in nominal terms, and 47 percent in real terms. No one familiar with Michigan schools questions the fact that urban school administrators are acutely aware of the financial challenge posed by the state's school
choice policies. So how have they responded?

DATA AND METHODS

Data Sources

This analysis uses a statewide panel data set of Michigan school districts
from 1994 to 2006. The data were assembled from two main sources:
the Michigan Department of Education (MDE) and the State of Michigan's Center for Educational Performance and Information (CEPI). The
merged data set includes information by district for school choice enrollment, school finance, student demographics, and other school-level factors
over the thirteen years. Michigan's Single Record Student Database (SRSD),
managed by CEPI, was used in constructing the measure of charter competition (in 2002–2003 and 2003–2004).

   Measures of District Resource Allocation.   Several dimensions of district
resource allocation serve as the dependent variables in our first-stage analysis. First, we measure the percentage distribution of districts' total operating
expenditures (TE) across the following functional categories:

- Total instructional programs
  - Basic needs instruction
  - Added needs instruction
- Total support services
  - Instructional support
  - Business and administration
  - Operations and maintenance

Each of these functional categories includes expenditures on employee salaries and benefits, supplies, and purchased services. *Basic needs instruction* includes classroom expenditures on preschool, elementary, middle, and high school basic instructional programs. *Added needs instruction* includes the classroom expenditures on special education, compensatory education, and vocational education instructional programs. *Instructional support* consists of expenditures on both pupil and instructional staff support services, including, among other things, speech therapists, guidance counselors, and curriculum specialists. *Business and administration* contains spending on school-level administration and central district administration and business services. Finally, *operations and maintenance* consists of spending to keep the physical plant clean and safe. It does not include capital outlays.

As noted, conventional wisdom holds that charter competition will lead school districts to increase the share of their spending devoted to instructional programs. This notion unambiguously predicts an increase in the share of spending devoted to basic needs instruction. It remains an open question whether districts will compete to attract special-needs students whose instructional services are included in the category of added needs instruction. Similarly, the conventional wisdom predicts that districts will decrease the share of spending devoted to administration, operations, and maintenance in response to increases in the intensity of charter school competition.

To investigate changes in other dimensions of instructional spending, we also examine the impact of charter competition on TPSs' average pupil–teacher ratio (which proxies average class size) and average teacher salary. We expect charter competition to reduce pupil–teacher ratios, because administrators see this action as a strategy to improve student achievement and because parents prefer small classes for their children. There are distinct reasons to anticipate that competition will increase average teacher salaries, especially in the long run. First, to attract higher-quality teachers, administrators may propose higher salaries. Second, districts that are losing students to competitors may be forced to lay off teachers. If, in accord with union contracts, dismissals start with the least senior (and typically lowest-paid) teachers, average teacher salary will increase.

Finally, we examine the impact of charter competition on districts' general fund balance. This standard bottom-line measure of district budgeting is widely taken by district budget administrators and state officials as indicating district fiscal health or, alternatively, fiscal stress. In Michigan, state officials closely monitor budgeting in local districts having low fund balances; districts in which the fund balance turns negative must enter the state's mandatory deficit reduction program. We measure fund balance on a per-pupil basis to test whether sufficiently high levels of charter competition induce fiscal strain (lower fund balances) in school districts.[8]

Measures of Competition. Competition from charter schools is measured at the district level because the loss of students to charter schools influences total district revenues, forcing districts to decide how to adjust resource allocation among individual schools. Thus, in the first instance, it is the school district that experiences and responds to competitive pressure from charter schools.

Charter competition is measured in two ways. The first measure considers only the magnitude of the competition, whereas the second measure accounts for competition's magnitude and duration. We define the *magnitude* of charter competition faced by a district as the percentage of resident students in a district who attend a charter school.[9] Because student-level data are not available before 2002, it is impossible to identify the resident district of charter school students for earlier years. We assumed, therefore, that the percentage of students from each sending district in a given charter school for 1994–2002 is the same as in 2003. Based on the actual individual enrollment information in the 2003 SRSD data, we then imputed the percentage of students that each district lost to charter schools for 1994–2002.

To capture the second dimension of charter competition—its *duration*—we created three dummy variables that distinguish the effect of charter competition in the short run, medium run, and long run. Accordingly, if a district lost students to charter schools for no more than three years, we identified the charter competition as short run. Similarly, the loss of students for four to five years is defined as medium-run competition, and for longer than five years as long-run competition. Our second measure—a vector of variables measuring both the magnitude and the duration of charter competition—was obtained by interacting the percentage of students who transferred to charter schools with the three duration dummy variables.

For each of the measures of district resource allocation, we estimated two sets of models that differ only in the way charter competition is measured. In model 1, charter competition is measured only by its magnitude as the percentage of students living in a district who enroll in charter schools (regardless of the competition's duration, % CS enroll). Model 2 uses the set of variables representing both the duration and magnitude of districts' loss of students to charter schools (CS Short, CS Mid, and CS Long).

Estimation Strategies. Our basic model for estimating the effect of charter competition on school district resource allocation takes this form:

$$Y_{it} = CS_{it} B_1 + SDstructure_{it} B_2 + SDchar_{it} B_3 + IDC_{it} B_4 + I_t \delta + \theta_i + u_{it} \quad (1)$$

where Y_{it} is the expenditure variable of interest in district i in year t. The focus variables in this analysis are included in CS_{it}, which is measured in two ways, reflecting both the magnitude and the duration of charter competition experienced by district i at time t. $SDstructure_{it}$ is a vector of structural characteristics of district i at time t that have been found in previous research to affect districts' allocation of spending across alternative functions.[10] These variables control for some of the influence of district size and local residents' needs and preferences on district resource allocation.

$SDchar_{it}$ is a vector of district student characteristics that serve as control variables, including the percentage of students who receive special education services (which affects added needs instructional spending) and a vector of student racial characteristics that may affect family preferences or needs for different school services. IDC_{it} reflects interdistrict choice competition by the percentage of students transferring out of a district through the interdistrict choice program.[11] We estimate equation (1) through fixed-effect transformations with standard errors robust both to serial correlation and heteroskedasticity; that is the problem of unequal variance of u_{it}.

FINDINGS

Table 10.2 displays the results of the fixed-effect estimates pertaining to district resource allocation. Column 1 shows the results for the instructional spending regressions. Model 1, unexpectedly, shows that charter competition has a significant *negative* impact on the percentage of spending devoted to instruction. Model 2 shows that this negative effect is driven by districts experiencing sustained or long-run charter competition. Charter competition over the short and medium run, meanwhile, has no significant effect on the share of total spending devoted to instruction. On the whole, TPSs in Michigan show no indication of responding to charter competition by shifting resources to instructional uses. By contrast, districts respond to open enrollment competition from other districts by significantly increasing the share of total spending devoted to instruction.

To pursue these results further, we consider a number of more-refined measures of TPS instructional spending. As noted, instructional spending is composed of two major categories: basic instruction and added needs

TABLE 10.2   Charter school effects on TPS expenditures: Fixed effects

					DEPENDENT VARIABLE			
	% TE total instruction (1)	% TE basic instruction (2)	% TE added needs instruction (3)	Ln average teacher salary (4)	Pupil to teacher ratio (5)	% TE total instructional support (6)	% TE business and administration (7)	% TE operations and maintenance (8)
Model 1								
% CS enroll	−0.058** (0.022)	−0.013 (0.034)	−0.019 (0.019)	−0.178 (0.092)	−0.278 (1.953)	0.018 (0.020)	0.022 (0.013)	0.004 (0.015)
%IDC	0.041** (0.015)	0.027* (0.013)	0.004 (0.012)	−0.106* (0.051)	0.446 (1.034)	−0.011 (0.007)	−0.025* (0.013)	−0.005 (0.006)
R-squared	0.14	0.14	0.18	0.55	0.36	0.11	0.07	0.05
						0.11	0.07	0.05
Model 2								
CS Short	−0.043 (0.029)	0.072 (0.056)	−0.10* (0.050)	−0.116 (0.141)	−1.248 (3.153)	0.026 (0.025)	0.002 (0.03)	0.01 (0.024)
CS Mid	0.002 (0.040)	0.088* (0.042)	−0.061* (0.030)	0.02 (0.119)	−2.788 (2.379)	0.015 (0.026)	0.006 (0.027)	−0.018 (0.013)
CS Long	−0.066* (0.027)	−0.03 (0.034)	−0.008 (0.020)	−0.205* (0.097)	0.077 (1.939)	0.017 (0.020)	0.025* (0.011)	0.007 (0.013)
%IDC	0.042** (0.015)	0.029* (0.015)	0.003 (0.011)	−0.103 (0.051)	0.399 (1.037)	−0.011 (0.007)	−0.025** (0.012)	−0.006 (0.005)
R-squared	0.14	0.15	0.18	0.55	0.36	0.11	0.07	0.05

*p<.05, ** p<.01

Note: The full set of control variables for both models include Log(enroll), Log(TE/pupil), log(SEV/pupil), % FRL, % spec ed, % Asian, % black, and % Hispanic. The results for these variables are not reported here.

instruction (i.e., special education, compensatory, and vocational education programs). In general, as indicated in column 2 of table 10.2, charter schools do not have a consistent or significant impact on the share of TPS spending devoted to basic instructional programs. Only in the case of medium-run charter competition do districts increase basic instruction's share of spending. Districts' long-run response to competition, though not statistically significant, is to decrease the share of their spending allocated to basic instructional programs. Once again, the response of Michigan TSPs to interdistrict choice competition differs from their response to charter competition: as interdistrict transfers increase, districts shift a higher share of their spending to basic instruction.

An interesting equity question turns on whether charter competition induces TPSs to allocate more or fewer resources to programs for special-needs students. The results in column 3 of table 10.2 provide mixed evidence on this question. When charter competition is measured as a single variable without regard to its duration, it does not have a significant impact on the share of total spending that TPSs devote to added needs instruction. However, when we account for the duration of districts' exposure to charter competition, Michigan school districts devote a significantly *smaller* share of their spending to added needs programs during the first five years of charter competition. Over longer periods, charter competition has no significant effect. There is some evidence to suggest, therefore, that initially charter competition leads districts to divert resources away from special-needs programs serving high-cost students, perhaps in an effort to better compete for regular education students.

Table 10.2 also displays the fixed-effects estimates of charter competition's impact on other indicators of instructional program resources. There has been considerable speculation about how competition might affect TPS employee compensation. Again, contrary to expectations, the results in column 4 indicate a significant decline in average teacher salaries in districts experiencing sustained and high levels of charter competition. Meanwhile, under all specifications, we find that charter competition had no significant impact on average class size (pupil–teacher ratio).

We turn now to consider charters' competitive impact on TPS spending on support functions. The share of spending devoted to all support functions would exactly mirror the estimates for the total instructional spending share (column 1), because by definition expenditures for total instruction and total support services must sum to total expenditures. So charter competition is simultaneously associated with TPSs allocating an increasing share of spending to support services along with the declining share to instructional programs. In an effort to decipher why the relative spending on support services increases, especially over the long run, the results in columns 6–8 in table 10.2 disaggregate support service spending into its three major components: instructional support, business and administration, and operations and maintenance. For the most part, whether or not we account for the duration of charter competition, charter schools have no significant impacts on TPS expenditures for any of the support service functions, with one surprising exception. The share of spending devoted to administration increases in districts experiencing long-term charter competition. Once again, districts' response to rising levels of interdistrict choice competition differs from their response to charter competition. Interdistrict competition engenders a reduction in the share of TPS spending allocated to administrative functions.

Finally we consider the impact of charter competition on school districts' overall financial position as reflected in their fund balances. In Michigan, as elsewhere, districts with very low fund balances are monitored by state officials. Districts where the overall fund balance turns negative must enter a mandatory deficit reduction program monitored by the state department of education. In recent years, a growing number of Michigan districts—including several with high rates of charter school participation—have been forced to enter the state's deficit reduction program.[12]

The results in column 3 of table 10.3 indicate that higher levels of charter competition are strongly associated with declining district fund balances. This finding is consistent across both measures of charter competition. Rising levels of charter competition clearly generate financial pressure on Michigan's TPSs. As a matter of basic accounting, changes in fund balances reflect changes in revenues minus expenditures. On the revenue side, the incremental reduction in funds associated with a district's loss of a student to a choice school will vary depending on the design of a state's school finance system.13 The results in column 3 of table 10.3 imply that revenues decline more rapidly than costs in districts that lose students to charter schools. The regressions in columns 1 and 2 of table 10.3 examine this directly. These results indicate that the loss of students to charter schools has a significant negative impact on the revenues of Michigan school districts that is not accompanied by a corresponding decrease in their expenditures.

Taken as a whole, our findings do not indicate many strong or consistent impacts of charter competition on TPS resource allocation. The patterns that emerge, however, are not consistent with the conventional wisdom. Overall, Michigan school districts respond to charter competition by devoting a smaller share of their spending to instructional services, and a larger share to noninstructional support services. Charter competition, however, has no discernable impact on most of the more disaggregated measures of TSP resource allocation that we examine. We find some evidence that

TABLE 10.3 Charter school effects on district revenues, expenditures, and fund balances

	DEPENDENT VARIABLE		
	Total expenditure per pupil (1)	Local and state revenue per pupil (2)	Fund balance per pupil (3)
Model 1			
% CS enroll	−213.6 (1756.6)	−2678.0* (1119.8)	−3720.2* (1788.2)
%IDC	6441.7 (4291.9)	5008.1 (3432.8)	5091.1 (3785.5)
R-square	0.77	0.75	0.24
Model 2			
CS Short	3626.2 (2008.9)	1108.2 (1794.1)	−1135.8 (1740.6)
CS Mid	−563.9 (1220.6)	−1814.1 (1180.8)	−3826.8** (1359.6)
CS Long	−437.2 (1802.2)	−3037.1* (1503.4)	−3885.5* (1803.4)
%IDC	6456.7 (4303.4)	5041.7 (3439.5)	5103.2 (3796.8)
R-square	0.77	0.75	0.24

*p< .05, ** p<.01

charter competition leads districts to reduce their relative spending on added needs instructional programs and increase their relative spending on administration. In addition, higher levels of charter competition, when it persists beyond the short term, clearly generate fiscal stress in districts—as revealed by a significant reduction in their fund balances.

Two quite different explanations are consistent with the failure to observe more widespread and significant resource allocation changes in TPSs. First, it may be that TPSs are so wedded to conventional ways of doing things that they do not respond much to charter competition, even when that competition becomes quite intense. This result could be the consequence of either insufficient imagination to envision better ways to allocate resources or an inability to overcome the constraints established by public schools' bureaucratic organizational structure. Second, schools may in fact adjust their resource allocation in response to charter competition, but—as some market advocates predict—they might do so in quite dissimilar ways so that one observes few consistent patterns in the changes. We pursue this second possibility in the next section.

RESOURCE ALLOCATION IN DISTRICTS THAT DO AND DO NOT STABILIZE ENROLLMENT LOSS

Do the budgetary changes implemented by districts in response to charter competition influence their ability to stem further enrollment loss to charter schools? When TPSs in Michigan lose students to choice schools, they lose the entire per-pupil funding associated with those students. This loss in revenues generates pressure for expenditure cuts, and that makes it harder for districts to continue providing programs of the same quality, let alone improve educational services. In highly competitive local education markets, how TPSs adjust their spending should shape their prospects for stemming further enrollment loss. TPSs that cut the wrong programs could spur the loss of additional students and resources and trigger a downward spiral. Perhaps the muted impacts of charter competition on TPS resource allocation we have observed merely reflect the fact that districts modify their spending in quite dissimilar ways. Indeed, if certain budgetary changes are more successful than others in reversing the enrollment loss to charters, districts with the highest charter enrollment rates over the long run may be those that have made misguided budgetary changes.

As a first step it is necessary to establish that the trajectories of district enrollment loss vary among districts once they have been subjected to a significant level of charter competition. Do some districts stabilize or reverse their enrollment loss to charters while others continue to lose market share? In fact, we find both scenarios among Michigan school districts. Figure 10.2, for example, plots the share of resident students attending charter schools in six Michigan school districts since 1994. Between 1994 and

FIGURE 10.2 **Percentage of students transferring to charter schools in selected Michigan school districts**

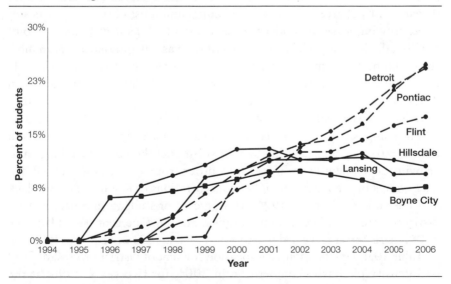

2001, the percentage of district residents attending charter schools increased sharply in all six districts, reaching roughly 10 percent in each. Thereafter the charter enrollment share stabilized or declined in some districts (Boyne City, Hillsdale, and Lansing) but continued to grow in Detroit, Flint, and Pontiac. Are there systematic differences in the resource allocation adjustments between districts that regain their equilibrium in the face of competition and those that continue to spiral downward?

To assess this question, we define groups of districts based on their intensity of charter competition in 2001, and then we observe changes in their resource allocation and charter penetration over the following five years. Our first group is composed of the 379 (of a total of 554) Michigan school districts that in 2001 had lost no students to charter schools. Next, we define the intensity of competition as "low" in the 142 districts where the percentage of resident students attending charters in 2001 was greater than zero and less than 6 ($0 < \%CS_{2001} < 6$). We follow Hoxby and Ni in defining competition as "threatening" in districts where charter schools attract greater than 6 percent of resident students, a threshold surpassed in 33 Michigan districts in 2001.[14] Finally, we disaggregate these threatened districts into the 18 districts in which the charter enrollment share did not increase between 2001 and 2006 ("stabilizes") and 15 districts in which the charter share "increases" over this subsequent five-year period.

The intensity of charter competition in Michigan TPSs varies by community type. Central city districts are much more likely to be threatened by charter schools than TPSs in other types of communities. Seventy-nine percent of Michigan's central city school districts (eleven of fourteen) were threatened by charter competition by 2001, and most of these districts suffered growing losses of students to charters in subsequent years. By comparison, the intensity of charter competition was low or nonexistent in most rural and high-income suburban districts. Moreover, among the relatively few (nineteen of five hundred) rural or middle- or high-income suburban districts that were threatened by charters as of 2001, all but four managed to reduce the share of resident students lost to charters by 2006.

The composition of students also varies significantly across these school district groups. Districts that would subsequently experience large and growing enrollment losses to charters differ from all the other school district groups by having much higher concentrations of low-income and black and Hispanic students. In 1994, 61.4 percent of students enrolled in these districts were from low-income families, and 46.5 percent were black. By 2006, these percentages had increased to 69.8 and 53.2, respectively.

Table 10.4 depicts resource allocation for school district groups, defined by intensity of charter competition in 2001, for two years: 1996 (at the

TABLE 10.4 **District resource allocation by intensity of charter competition, 1996, 2006**

	INTENSITY OF CHARTER COMPETITION						
	None (1)	Low (2)	Threatening/ stabilizes (3)	Threatening/ increases (4)	Total	(3)–(4)	(1)–(4)
1996 *% of total expenditures*							
Total instruction	66	64	65	59	65	6.0**	6.5**
Basic instruction	54	51	51	42	52	9.5**	11.6**
Added needs instruction	11	12	13	15	11	−2.4	−4.3**
Total support services	34	36	35	41	35	−6.0**	−6.5**
Instructional support	6	8	7	10	7	−2.5	−3.7**
Administration	13	12	13	14	13	−0.4	−0.8
Operations and maintenance	10	11	10	12	10	−2.2*	−1.7**
Fund balance	19	13	9	11	17	−2.2	8.3
2006 *% of total expenditures*							
Total instruction	64	63	64	56	63	8.5**	7.9**
Basic instruction	52	50	49	40	51	8.9**	11.4**
Added needs instruction	12	13	15	15	12	−0.2	−3.6**
Total support services	36	37	36	44	37	−8.5**	−7.9**
Instructional support	7	9	8	11	8	−3.5*	−4.1**
Administration	13	13	13	15	13	−2.1	−1.6*
Operations and maintenance	11	11	11	12	11	−2.0	−1.6
Fund balance	20	13	12	5	18	6.7*	15.6*

*p<.05, ** p<.01

Figures represent unweighted school district group averages.

start of Michigan's charter law implementation) and 2006. In both years, resource allocation is very similar across all district groups, with the exception of the districts in which charter competition was threatening by 2001 and continued to increase through 2006. In 1996, when the level of charter participation was so low that it is unlikely to have had discernable budgetary impacts, districts that would subsequently experience the greatest challenges were already allocating their spending quite differently from other districts.

In particular, they devoted a significantly smaller share of spending to instruction, including 11.6 percentage points less for basic instruction, than districts that by 2001 had lost no students to charters. On the other hand, these districts devoted significantly higher shares of their expenditures to added needs instruction, instructional support services, and operations and maintenance. As table 10.4 shows, the distinctiveness of this group's resource allocation—whether assessed relative to districts with no charter competition or to districts that were threatened and subsequently stabilized—did not diminish over the next decade as charter competition intensified. They continued to spend a smaller share on basic instruction and more on added needs instruction and support services, right up to the present, even as they lost ever-larger shares of students living within their borders to charter schools.

The districts that have experienced sustained and growing losses to charters also have significantly larger average class size, a disparity that only worsens relative to other TPSs over the decade. Average teacher pay, however, is not significantly different in these districts experiencing strongest charter competition at any point during 1996–2006. Finally, by 2006 their fund balances fall significantly below the levels in other Michigan school districts.

One interpretation of these results is that the leadership of these declining districts is largely responsible for their competitive failure. From the start, in this view, resources were misallocated, leaving these districts vulnerable to competition from charter schools that allocated resources more efficiently (or in any case more in line with parents' preferences). Moreover, when serious charter competition arose, these districts failed to learn from the market signals and continued to allocate spending pretty much as they always had, a practice that in turn led to further enrollment loss.

Such a view is unlikely to constitute an adequate account of the Michigan experience on at least two basic grounds. First, as revealed in table 10.4, from the start of Michigan's charter policy, declining districts—those that would eventually lose progressively larger shares of their students— had higher concentrations of high-need, high-cost students. Compared with other Michigan districts, these districts had higher percentages of students who were poor and disabled. These distinctive characteristics of the students they serve would normally increase the share of their spending directed to compensatory and special education instructional programs as well as certain noninstructional support services. So the distinctiveness of their spending is largely a reflection of the distinctive needs of their students. Indeed the desire of parents to place their children in educational settings with fewer high-need students is likely an especially salient consideration in their decision to move their children to choice schools.

Second, the success of districts that were threatened by charter competition by 2001 and then stabilized was not due to any distinctive changes in their resource allocation. We measured such changes between 2001 and 2006 for each of the functions depicted in table 10.4 for each of the school district groups. Resource allocation changes by the threatened and stabilized districts did not differ significantly from the changes made by either threatened districts that lost progressively more students to charters, on the one hand, or by districts that encountered no charter competition, on the other. Nor, once they encountered significant charter penetration, did the resource allocation of the threatened and stabilized districts become more similar to that in districts that had no charter competition. Resource allocation in these stabilizing districts was essentially indistinguishable from that in districts with no competition, both before and after they themselves confronted competition.

DISCUSSION

Michigan presents an interesting case of a state with relatively high participation rates in choice policies that have been in place for more than fifteen years. In addition, Michigan's school finance system generates strong incentives for schools to compete for students. In some states only part of the revenue follows students to charter schools when they leave TPSs, and districts have the authority to raise local revenue to replace funds lost to charter schools. In Michigan, however, students take the full amount of school funding with them to charter schools, districts cannot raise additional local tax revenue, and the state foundation allowance for K–12 education has remained at nearly the same nominal level over the past six years because of sustained weakness in the state's economy. The only way for schools to obtain more revenue is to compete aggressively for more students.

In general, our results do not support the hypothesis that competition from charter schools spurs regular public schools to shift resources to achievement-oriented activities. Charter competition has had relatively little impact on standard measures of district resource use in Michigan schools. In those instances where charter schools have influenced TPS resource allocation, the shifts do not conform to conventional predictions. Charter competition is associated with districts devoting a lower share of their spending to instruction and a higher share to noninstructional support services, such as administration. These are not short-run, transitory developments but rather are most pronounced in districts that have been subject to long-run competition. The presence of charter schools, meanwhile, has no significant effect on average teacher salaries or class size. In addition, changes in resource allocation cannot explain the differing trajectories of districts that do and do not turn back the competitive challenge. Districts exposed to long-run competition do, however, show a significant decline in their fund balances.

One potential limitation of our study is that our measures of resource allocation are too aggregated to distinguish some meaningful TPS adjustments. Further research with more-refined measures is warranted. We cannot be confident, moreover, that an identical analysis in other states would produce results similar to those from Michigan. The effects of charter competition are undoubtedly sensitive to important features of charter school policy as well as to the local contexts in which the policies are implemented.[15] Indeed, even within Michigan, the competitive effects of interdistrict choice appear far more salutary than those of charter schools.

About half of Michigan's charter schools are located in Detroit and other central cities, attracting students from these areas and nearby low-income suburbs. Many TPSs in urban districts have experienced great charter competition and have faced acute financial pressure because of the loss of students to charter schools. For example, about forty-four thousand students who live in Detroit attended charter schools in 2006. Together with eight thousand students attending suburban schools through interdistrict choice, Detroit Public Schools has lost about one-third of its students, amounting to about $400 million in revenue lost annually to the two choice programs.

Other central cities in Michigan, such as Flint, Pontiac, and Benton Harbor, have experienced similar proportionate losses. Educators in these districts are operating in extraordinarily turbulent settings. Among Michigan's fourteen districts with sustained and growing enrollment loss to charters, fewer than half the TPS students in 2002–2003 attended the same school in 2003–2004. These fourteen districts enroll about 15 percent of all TPS students in Michigan but enroll 70 percent of TPS students statewide who are black and eligible for free and reduced-price lunch. Large-scale closures of school buildings have been implemented, and teachers and administrators are being relocated from building to building.

There is little question, therefore, that charter schools are impacting resource allocation in Michigan's urban districts. We failed to uncover evidence, however, that these changes hold much promise for improving the quality of children's education.

Indeed the major implication of this study for policy makers is that we find no evidence to support the usual prediction that charter school competition on its own will induce school district personnel to shift resources to classroom instruction.

11

Charter Schools

Do They Cream Skim,
Increasing Student Segregation?

Ron Zimmer, Brian Gill, Kevin Booker,
Stéphane Lavertu, and John F. Witte

Few topics in education inspire as much debate as charter schools, which are publicly funded schools of choice that operate autonomously, outside the direct control of traditional school districts, under the authority of a quasi-contract, or charter, granted by a public body.[1] These schools first appeared on the educational landscape in 1992 and now include more than four thousand schools in thirty-nine states. The Obama administration is now trying to extend the reach of charter schools by increasing federal funding for them and encouraging states to remove caps on their numbers.

Many studies have sought to assess the educational impact of charter schools on their students.[2] But another key area of controversy—less often given careful empirical examination—is the effect of charter schools on the sorting of students across the system of public education as a whole. Critics of charter schools worry that they might skim the cream, enrolling high-ability students at the expense of lower achievers left in traditional public schools (TPSs), and that charter schools may further stratify an already racially stratified system.[3]

Indeed, when the concept of charter schools was introduced, some observers had concerns that charter schools would become enclaves of white students escaping the racial diversity of traditional public schools.[4] Critics also lament the fact that charter schools' skimming the best students from TPSs would reduce the peer interaction of high- and low-ability students within the traditional schools, pointing to a long and well-developed literature that highlights the benefits of the interaction of students having diverse backgrounds and ability levels.[5] These critics fear that charter schools might therefore have negative social and academic effects for students who remain in TPSs.[6] Supporters, in contrast, argue that charter schools will improve racial integration by letting families choose schools outside neighborhoods where housing is racially segregated, and by promoting fuller and richer integration in classrooms *within* schools where all students have chosen to attend.[7]

Whether schools become more or less integrated under a school choice program may be a function of family characteristics. For instance, parents who have greater economic means may have greater access to information and reliable transportation and therefore may be more likely than more disadvantaged parents to take advantage of choice; and because variance in income is related to race, school choice may lead to greater racial segregation than exists in TSPs.[8] In addition, if it is easier for parents to choose schools based on race and if parents have a preference for racially homogenous schools, then charter schools could create greater racial stratification than the TPS system.[9]

Particular charter school policies may also affect the impact of charter schools on the distribution of students by race and ability. For instance, low-income families may have greater access to charter schools if free transportation is provided. In addition, some states have tried to encourage the establishment of charter schools that serve at-risk students or require that schools be racially representative of the districts in which they are located. Other policies that regulate enrollment, charter authorizers, and charter types (e.g., conversions, start-ups, virtual schools), as well as the prevalence of school choice options due to magnet schools, open enrollment, vouchers, and No Child Left Behind (NCLB), also may affect the distribution of students by race and ability.[10]

In this study, we examine the effects of charter schools on the distribution of students by race and ability in seven locations: the school districts of Chicago, Denver, Milwaukee, Philadelphia, and San Diego, as well as Ohio and Texas statewide. The data come from states that encompass about 45 percent of all charter schools in the United States. In addition, the seven locations provide some variation in charter school and other policies that may affect the distribution of students by race and ability, including policies regulating who may establish charter schools, the types of schools that may become charter schools, the types and number of students whom charter schools may serve, and the provision of transportation.

In each location, we have student-level data over time, with unique student identifiers that allow us to follow students as they move between TPSs and charter schools. We assess how transferring students affect the racial and ability composition of the schools they leave and those they enter. The results suggest, overall, that charter schools are not systematically skimming high-achieving students or dramatically affecting the racial mix of students for transferring students. Also, variations in these results across sites do not appear to be related to variations in laws across the locations, making it difficult to prescribe specific recommendations. We first provide an overview of the previous literature, then describe the data and the analytical approach, and finally discuss the results and conclusions in detail.

PREVIOUS LITERATURE

Much of the previous literature on stratification used school-level data in an attempt to examine the effect of charter schools on the racial composition of schools. This literature has generally compared the racial makeup of charter schools relative to state and district averages.[11] It does not account for the fact that charter schools are not randomly dispersed within a state or even a district. In fact, one could argue that charter schools generally are located where they can attract students—primarily in low performing school districts or in areas within a district in which TPSs have performed poorly. These low performing districts and neighborhoods are likely to have high proportions of minority students, making it difficult for charter schools to be representative of statewide or districtwide populations.[12]

Moreover, comparisons have often been made sectorwide (all charters versus all TPSs in a community) rather than school by school. Sectorwide comparisons of the proportion of charter and TPS students in particular subgroups may be useful to describe the population being served, but such comparisons provide no information about the extent to which individual schools are integrated. In other words, the fact that the entire sector (charter or TPS) in a community serves a wide range of student populations does not tell us anything about integration. A community where the conventional public schools are one-third white, one-third black, and one-third Hispanic might have schools that are highly integrated (i.e., each school has a mix of students that looks like the districtwide average), or it might have schools that are fully segregated (i.e., one-third of the schools are 100 percent white, one-third are 100 percent black, and one-third are 100 percent Hispanic).

A better way to examine the effect of charter schools on the ability and racial distribution of students is to use longitudinal student-level data to examine the actual movement of students from TPSs to charter schools. This method admittedly does not provide a comprehensive picture of the student sorting resulting from charter schools, because it includes only the charter students who enter charter schools after having previously been enrolled in TPSs; it does not identify a counterfactual for students who enroll in charter schools beginning in kindergarten. Nonetheless, a partial picture of the changing peer environments of individual students who move to charter schools is preferable to a high-level comparison of charter school composition to district or state averages, a comparison that could mask enormous local variation in schools.

Only two studies—Bifulco and Ladd; and Booker, Zimmer, and Buddin—have used longitudinal student-level data to examine the sorting effects of students transferring to charter schools, and these works included charter schools in only three states.[13] Bifulco and Ladd examined data from North Carolina and found that charters have increased the racial isolation of black and white students. On average, black charter students left schools that were 53 percent black for charters that were 72 percent black. Similarly, white charter students left traditional schools that were 72 percent white for charters that were 82 percent white. Black as well as white charter students had more peers from college-educated parents at their charter school than at their previous TPS, but the percentage increase in college-educated parents was about six times as large for whites as for blacks. Overall, black students transferred to charters having lower average test scores than their previous schools, whereas white students transferred to charters having higher average test scores than their previous public schools.

Booker et al. used data from California and Texas to examine the effect of charter schools on the stratification of students in terms of ability and race. In both states, black charter students transferred to schools having higher concentrations of black students than the schools they attended previously. In Texas, white students also moved to schools having higher concentrations of whites than at their TPSs, but white students moved to schools with lower concentrations of whites than at their TPSs in California. Hispanic charter students in both states had fewer Hispanic peers than they had in their prior TPSs. In terms of measured ability, on average, transfer students had lower test scores than the average student at the TPSs they exited.

DATA

We collected longitudinal student-level data statewide from two states, and districtwide data from five large urban school districts. In total, seven states are represented in the data set.[14]

Snapshot of Charter School Policies in the Seven Locations

Before we delve into the data analysis, it is worth summarizing the charter school policies that might affect our results. Table 11.1 summarizes charter policies across the seven locations.[15] As the table reveals, local school boards can authorize charter schools in all locations, but some states also allow other entities to authorize charter schools, including county boards of education, the state, and nonprofit organizations. Ohio has the greatest range of entities that authorize charter schools.[16] In terms of types of charter schools, all locations allow public conversion and start-up charter schools; only Milwaukee and Texas allow private schools to convert to charter status. All locations except Texas allow "virtual" charter schools, in which instruction is delivered primarily by telecommunications technology to the students' homes. Despite being theoretically allowed in five of the seven locations, virtual charter schools are prevalent and identified as such only in Ohio.

As noted earlier, access to free transportation could be an important determinant of student distributions. In most locations, transportation is not required by charter laws, but it is generally specified in each charter contract. Only Philadelphia and Ohio require that transportation be provided. In addition, enrollment requirements may affect the distribution of students. In four of the seven locations, enrollment may be restricted to district residents or students within certain geographic areas. In some cases, states require charter schools to have racial balances similar to those of the districts in which they reside. Similarly, except for Philadelphia, each location gives, or has given, preferential treatment in the chartering process to schools that target at-risk or low performing students.[17]

The prevalence of other school choice options and location-specific policies also may affect the distribution of students by ability and race. For example, in addition to charter schools, students in Milwaukee have a wide array of choice options, including magnet schools, voucher private schools, nonvoucher private schools, open-enrollment programs, and within-district options that result from NCLB. The types of students taking advantage of charter schools may be different from those who reside in districts having more-limited choice options. In addition, each location has made policy changes during the years covered by our data. For instance, in Philadelphia the state took over the district in 2002 and turned over forty-five low performing schools to private managers. Some students may have exited these schools and enrolled in charter schools because they did not want to go through the transition to a new management structure.

Together, these policies and environmental factors could affect the distribution of students by race and ability. One must keep in mind the policies listed in table 11.1 when interpreting the results of our empirical analysis.

TABLE 11.1 Charter policies and environments across locations

Dimension	Chicago	Denver	Milwaukee[a]	Philadelphia	San Diego	Ohio	Texas[b]
Charter schools in the most recent year of our data	33	21	42	57	35	231	198
Types of chartering authorities	Local school board	Local school boards; state Charter School Institute in districts that have not retained exclusive authority to grant charters	Local school board, city of Milwaukee, University of Wisconsin-Milwaukee, and Milwaukee Area Technical College	Local school boards; state department of education for virtual schools	Local school board, county school board, or state	For conversions, local school boards. For start-ups: school boards; boards of vocational school districts; boards of ESCs; state universities; federally tax-exempt entities; or, when another authorizer fails to comply with its obligation as a sponsor, the state department of education	Local school board for conversions, and state board of education for open-enrollments (new starts)
Types of charter schools	Public conversion, start-ups, virtual	Public conversion, start-ups, virtual	Public conversion, private conversion, start-up, virtual, instrumentality, non-instrumentality, independent	Public conversion, start-ups, virtual	Public conversion, start-ups, non-classroom based (virtual)	Public conversion, start-ups, virtual	Public conversion, private conversion, start-ups

Dimension	Chicago	Denver	Milwaukee[a]	Philadelphia	San Diego	Ohio	Texas[b]
Transportation	Specified in charters	Specified in charters	Not addressed. Charters may coordinate transportation with existing traditional public schools with which they may share facilities.	Students who attend a charter located in their school district, a regional charter of which the school district is a part, or a charter located outside district boundaries at a distance not exceeding 10 miles by the nearest highway shall be provided free transportation.	Specified in charter (however, the Department of Education interpretation is that charter school students are entitled to transportation)	School districts must provide transportation to and from a charter school located within the district or within another district, but districts are not required to provide transportation if student lives more than 30 minutes away from school.	Neither regular public schools nor charter schools are required to provide transportation for students, although many do.

continued

TABLE 11.1 *continued*

Dimension	Chicago	Denver	Milwaukee[a]	Philadelphia	San Diego	Ohio	Texas[b]
Preferences for enrollment and enrollment requirements	Students enrolled prior and siblings	District residents	Students enrolled before the school became a charter. Racial balance of school may not differ from district. Charter schools may not use academic ability criteria; they may, however, define certain other criteria for enrollment, such as at-risk criteria.	District residents, children of parents who participated in the development of the school, and siblings. Charter school may limit enrollment to a particular grade level or area of concentration and may set reasonable criteria to evaluate prospective students.	District residents and siblings. Charter must specify means by which school's student body will reflect racial and ethnic balance of the general population living in the school district.	Students enrolled prior, district residents, and siblings. Racial balance of charter school may not differ from district, and charter school must comply with any desegregation order or regulations. School may choose to limit enrollment to students in a particular geographic area or at-risk students; school must enroll at least 25 students.	District residents if local charter
At-risk provisions	Preference in approval process is given to schools designed to serve substantial proportion of at-risk children.	Priority in the approval process must be given to schools designed to serve low-achieving students.	Local school boards must give preference in awarding charters to schools designed to serve at-risk children.	None	Priority is given to schools designated to serve low-achieving students.	School may restrict enrollment to at-risk students.	Initially gave preference to at-risk charter, but currently there are no preferences.

Dimension	Chicago	Denver	Milwaukee[a]	Philadelphia	San Diego	Ohio	Texas[b]
Other choice programs	The district has magnet schools, open-enrollment, and NCLB school choice option.	Colorado has a fairly liberal open-enrollment policy that allows students to enroll across district lines.	Wisconsin has a has the largest voucher program in U.S. (> 19,000 students); a number of magnet schools; and an interdistrict program to allow minority students to enroll in Milwaukee suburbs and white suburban students to enroll in MPS.	The d strict also has magnet school and NCLB school choice option.	The district also has magnet schools and intradistrict open enrollment as well as NCLB school choice option.	Varies by district, but many districts have magnet programs and NCLB school choice option. In addition, the state has a voucher program.	Varies by district, but most districts have magnet programs, some districts have open-enrollment and NCLB choice options.
Miscellaneous district policies and environments	Over past few years, Chicago has initiated the Renaissance 2010 initiative, which includes closing TPSs and opening new charter schools.	Unlike other states, Colorado charter schools have been used by suburban districts to deal with increasing enrollment.	In recent years MPS has initiated a small-schools program that has used many charter schools to reorganize large middle and high schools.	In 2001, the state took over control of the school district and initiated a number of reforms, including turning over the management of low performing schools to private management groups. However, these schools are not charter schools, but may affect the schooling choice families make.	San Diego has limited nonclassroom-based schools.	In many districts, charter schools consume a significant percentage of students and have created some fiscal challenges, resulting in some tension between districts and charter schools.	In 2006, the state initiated the Governor's Educator Excellence Award program, a grant program paying bonuses to school employees (including those in charter schools) who have performed above expectations in raising student performance levels.

a. We do not have data for independent charter schools in Milwaukee.
b. We observe only charter schools authorized by start-up charter schools in our data set.

Prior Achievement of Students Who Transfer to Charter Schools

First, we examine the prior achievement levels of students who enter charters, as compared to average districtwide achievement levels and to the achievement levels of other students in the TPSs from which they transferred. This analysis examines only students who switch to charter schools after they have been in TPSs. Because test scores are not available for students prior to kindergarten, it is impossible for us to test whether charter elementary schools are attracting the best students at the entry point. In addition, the analysis removes students who make "structural" moves— those who switch from elementary to middle schools and middle to high schools—because for such students, their previous school is no longer the relevant counterfactual (and we do not have data to indicate the TPS they would have attended if they had not attended the charter school). But we also conducted alternative analyses that included structural movers (on the assumption that the average achievement levels in their previous schools might be unbiased, if noisy, proxies for average achievement levels in the unknown counterfactual schools), and the results were quite consistent with those of table 11.2, with no substantive differences in any of the sites.[18]

Table 11.2 indicates that the results vary by location. For instance, in Milwaukee, test scores of students moving to charter schools are similar not only to districtwide averages but also to those of their peers in the TPSs they exited. However, in Chicago and Philadelphia, students who switch to charter schools have prior test scores that are similar to or slightly lower than district averages (as indicated by the negative z-scores), but slightly higher than the scores of their peers in the TPSs they exited. In Denver and San Diego, students transferring to charter schools have prior test scores that are not only below districtwide averages but also slightly lower than those of the students in the TPSs they exited.

These differences are more pronounced in Ohio and Texas. In each of these locations, students transferring to charter schools have test scores that are substantially lower than state averages. In addition, the average gaps between the prior scores of students exiting TPSs for charter schools and those of their TPS peers are larger than those in the other locations.

In sum, in all but one case (Chicago reading scores, which are virtually identical to the districtwide average), students switching to charter schools have prior test scores that are lower than districtwide or statewide averages, although the difference is usually small. Compared with their immediate peers in the TPSs they exited, students transferring to charter schools had slightly higher test scores in two of seven locations, whereas in the other five locations the scores of the transferring students were identical to or lower

TABLE 11.2   Average prior math and reading scores of charter movers and other students at the TPS that they leave.

	Overall	White students	African American students	Hispanic students
Chicago				
Prior math scores of movers	−0.03	0.30	−0.05	0.06
Prior math scores of TPS peers	−0.12	0.36	−0.17	0.03
Difference with TPS peers	**0.09**	**−0.06**	**0.12**	**0.03**
Prior reading scores of movers	0.02	0.35	0.01	0.02
Prior reading scores of TPS peers	−0.09	0.36	−0.12	−0.03
Difference with TPS peers	**0.11**	**−0.01**	**0.13**	**0.05**
Denver				
Prior math scores of movers	−0.32	0.16	−0.45	−0.34
Prior math scores of TPS peers	−0.16	0.13	−0.13	−0.25
Difference with TPS peers	**−0.16**	**0.03**	**−0.32**	**−0.09**
Prior reading scores of movers	−0.25	0.47	−0.18	−0.33
Prior reading scores of TPS peers	−0.17	0.22	−0.04	−0.29
Difference with TPS peers	**−0.08**	**0.25**	**−0.14**	**−0.04**
Milwaukee				
Prior math scores of movers	−0.02	0.61	−0.33	0.10
Prior math scores of TPS peers	−0.01	0.28	−0.15	0.05
Difference with TPS peers	**−0.01**	**0.33**	**−0.18**	**0.05**
Prior reading scores of movers	−0.04	0.52	−0.29	0.02
Prior reading scores of TPS peers	−0.04	0.21	−0.16	−0.02
Difference with TPS peers	**0.00**	**0.31**	**−0.13**	**0.04**
Philadelphia				
Prior math scores of movers	−0.11	0.47	−0.16	−0.20
Prior math scores of TPS peers	−0.17	0.26	−0.21	−0.20
Difference with TPS peers	**0.06**	**0.21**	**0.05**	**0.00**
Prior reading scores of movers	−0.05	0.53	−0.08	−0.23
Prior reading scores of TPS peers	−0.18	0.22	−0.19	−0.25
Difference with TPS peers	**0.13**	**0.31**	**0.11**	**0.02**
San Diego				
Prior math scores of movers	−0.29	0.11	−0.54	−0.43
Prior math scores of TPS peers	−0.12	0.10	−0.22	−0.21
Difference with TPS peers	**−0.17**	**0.01**	**−0.32**	**−0.22**
Prior reading scores of movers	−0.20	0.28	−0.42	−0.41
Prior reading scores of TPS peers	−0.11	0.14	−0.21	−0.23
Difference with TPS peers	**−0.09**	**0.14**	**−0.21**	**−0.18**

continued

TABLE 11.2   *continued*

	Overall	White students	African American students	Hispanic students
Ohio[a]				
Prior math scores of movers	−0.61	−0.33	−0.89	−0.60
Prior math scores of TPS peers	−0.41	−0.13	−0.68	−0.51
Difference with TPS peers	**−0.20**	**−0.20**	**−0.21**	**−0.09**
Prior reading scores of movers	−0.56	−0.30	−0.80	−0.51
Prior reading scores of TPS peers	−0.41	−0.14	−0.65	−0.49
Difference with TPS peers	**−0.15**	**−0.16**	**−0.15**	**−0.02**
Texas				
Prior math scores of movers	−0.46	−0.03	−0.83	−0.47
Prior math scores of TPS peers	−0.24	0.02	−0.41	−0.27
Difference with TPS peers	**−0.22**	**−0.05**	**−0.42**	**−0.20**
Prior reading scores of movers	−0.38	0.11	−0.64	−0.47
Prior reading scores of TPS peers	−0.21	0.07	−0.32	−0.31
Difference with TPS peers	**−0.17**	**0.04**	**−0.32**	**−0.16**

a. Because Ohio has virtual schools, which are fairly unique, we also ran the analysis excluding virtual schools. The overall results, those for African Americans, and those for Hispanic students are very similar. For white students, the patterns are similar, but with slightly smaller differences.

than those of their TPS peers. In terms of same-race comparisons, the analysis indicates lower prior scores for transfer students in five of seven sites for African Americans, and in four of seven sites for Hispanics. For white students the pattern was slightly different: in four of seven sites, white students entering charter schools had higher prior achievement scores than their white TPS peers in both subjects, and in one other site they had higher scores in one of the two subjects. These results for white students had little effect on the overall averages, because white students constituted a minority of charter students in every location, and fewer than one-quarter of charter students in the four locations had scores that were consistently higher than those of their white peers (as we show in the next section).

TRANSFERS TO CHARTERS AND RACIAL AND ETHNIC STRATIFICATION

In this section we compare the racial composition of the sending (traditional public) and receiving (charter) schools for students transferring to charters. Before presenting the results, we first provide context in table 11.3, a descriptive breakdown of the three major groups of students in charters and

TABLE 11.3   **Charter and traditional public school racial representation across all years**

| Location | CHARTER SCHOOL RACIAL BREAKDOWN ACROSS ALL YEARS | | | TPS RACIAL BREAKDOWN ACROSS ALL YEARS | | |
	Percent African American	Percent white	Percent Hispanic	Percent African American	Percent white	Percent Hispanic
Chicago	72.9	2.7	23.5	52.7	9.4	34.8
Denver	31.7	20.4	44.8	19.6	20.0	56.0
Milwaukee	40.7	23.0	27.1	63.8	14.1	14.4
Philadelphia	66.1	19.3	12.3	64.2	15.2	14.8
San Diego	22.9	20.4	40.4	14.5	27.1	39.4
Ohio	55.3	38.7	2.6	15.4	77.9	2.5
Texas	35.8	22.5	39.4	15.7	42.4	39.2

TPSs. African American students are overrepresented in charter schools in six of seven locations, a finding that is consistent with previous research.[19] Patterns for white students and Hispanic students are more mixed, varying across sites.

The totals in table 11.3 are useful for understanding the aggregate distribution of students by race within charters and TPSs. But they do not tell us the degree of integration in individual charter schools and TPSs and therefore may mask significant variation in the racial integration of schools. The 40 percent share of San Diego's charter enrollment represented by Hispanic students, for example, could result from Hispanics constituting 40 percent of the enrollment of every charter school in San Diego, or it could result from Hispanics constituting 100 percent of the enrollment of charter schools that account for 40 percent of overall charter school enrollment. Moreover, the totals in table 11.3 do not tell us about the effects on integration of students transferring to charter schools, because they do not tell us where the students would have been if they had not transferred.

Table 11.4 sheds light on these issues by comparing the peer environments (in racial composition) for charter switchers before and after switching to a charter school, separately for African American students, Hispanic students, and white students. (Totals across rows may not add up to 100 percent because other racial categories are omitted, but they constituted only small minorities in most sites.)

As is the case with table 11.2, this analysis examines only students who switch to charter schools after they have been in TPSs. We do not have data that would allow an examination of what the racial composition would have been in a TPS for students who never attended TPSs—most importantly,

TABLE 11.4   **Traditional public and charter peer environments for charter movers by racial and ethnic background of student**

	Percent African American	Percent white	Percent Hispanic
Chicago			
Charter school African American students attend	84.3	2.1	13.2
TPS School African American students attended	89.9	2.3	7.0
Difference	**−5.6**	**−0.2**	**6.2**
Charter school white students attend	55.7	11.8	29.8
TPS school white students attended	26.3	20.1	40.6
Difference	**29.4**	**−8.3**	**−10.8**
Charter school Hispanic students attend	44.0	5.3	49.3
TPS school Hispanic students attended	18.2	8.6	70.1
Difference	**25.8**	**−3.3**	**−20.8**
Denver			
Charter school African American students attend	51.0	14.6	31.0
TPS school African American students attended	42.2	15.3	41.9
Difference	**8.8**	**−0.7**	**−8.8**
Charter school white students attend	32.1	31.0	31.6
TPS School white students attended	25.2	28.7	38.9
Difference	**6.9**	**2.3**	**−7.3**
Charter school Hispanic students attend	21.9	11.6	64.0
TPS school Hispanic students attended	15.7	9.0	72.1
Difference	**6.2**	**2.6**	**−8.1**
Milwaukee			
Charter school African American students attend	65.5	13.2	13.8
TPS school African American students attended	73.0	10.5	9.7
Difference	**−7.5**	**2.7**	**4.1**
Charter school white students attend	27.4	38.9	23.0
TPS school white students attended	29.2	38.3	21.5
Difference	**−1.8**	**0.6**	**1.5**
Charter school Hispanic students attend	26.2	23.9	40.0
TPS school Hispanic students attended	25.5	19.2	47.0
Difference	**0.7**	**4.7**	**−7.0**
Philadelphia			
Charter school African American students attend	87.0	4.6	6.9
TPS school African American students attended	84.2	5.5	7.0
Difference	**2.8**	**−0.9**	**−0.1**
Charter school white students attend	36.1	48.7	10.9

	Percent African American	Percent white	Percent Hispanic
TPS school white students attended	39.5	39.7	12.3
Difference	**−3.4**	**9.0**	**−1.4**
Charter school Hispanic students attend	35.5	6.9	55.9
TPS school Hispanic students attended	38.1	12.0	45.4
Difference	**−2.6**	**−5.1**	**10.5**
San Diego			
Charter school African American students attend	33.7	20.0	32.1
TPS school African American students attended	25.3	16.1	39.2
Difference	**8.4**	**3.9**	**−7.1**
Charter school white students attend	15.8	42.1	30.2
TPS school white students attended	12.5	39.0	32.3
Difference	**3.3**	**3.1**	**−2.1**
Charter school Hispanic students attend	17.2	22.2	50.5
TPS school Hispanic students attended	15.8	19.0	49.4
Difference	**1.4**	**3.2**	**−1.1**
Ohio[a]			
Charter school African American students attend	78.9	16.5	2.1
TPS school African American students attended	74.1	20.0	3.0
Difference	**4.8**	**−3.5**	**−0.9**
Charter school white students attend	17.0	77.0	2.4
TPS school white students attended	14.9	79.0	3.1
Difference	**2.1**	**−2.0**	**−0.6**
Charter school Hispanic students attend	38.5	40.9	14.8
TPS school Hispanic students attended	31.8	42.1	21.6
Difference	**6.7**	**−1.3**	**−6.8**
Texas			
Charter school African American students attend	67.1	12.3	19.8
TPS school African American students attended	52.4	14.4	31.7
Difference	**14.7**	**−2.1**	**−11.9**
Charter school white students attend	17.3	54.8	24.2
TPS school white students attended	15.6	50.4	30.3
Difference	**1.7**	**4.4**	**−6.1**
Charter school Hispanic students attend	19.7	13.7	63.2
TPS school Hispanic students attended	15.1	12.4	71.4
Difference	**4.6**	**1.3**	**−8.2**

a. Because Ohio has virtual schools, which are fairly unique, we also ran the analysis excluding virtual schools. The results show similar patterns but are slightly more pronounced.

students who begin in charter schools in kindergarten. Also, the analysis removes students who are making structural moves, because the prior TPSs may not represent a strong counterfactual for the racial makeup of the school that the students would have attended had they not chosen to attend a charter. Finally, we should again note that we do not indicate the statistical significance of the differences because we do not want readers to infer that we find statistically significant differences to be substantively meaningful.

In most cases, the results in table 11.4 suggest that, on average, transferring students are switching to charter schools whose racial compositions do not differ dramatically from those of the TPSs the students left behind. Across the sites, however, African American transfer students are slightly more likely than white students or Hispanic students to move to charter schools having larger proportions of their own racial group.

This does not necessarily indicate a preference for a same-race environment; it could result simply from a preference among African Americans for charter schools (in which they tend to be overrepresented, as shown in table 11.3). In five of the seven sites, African American students transferred to charter schools having (on average) higher concentrations of African Americans than were present in the TPSs they exited. Across the seven jurisdictions, the average increase in the African American concentration experienced by an African American transfer student was 3.8 percent, versus an average increase of 1.3 percent in the white concentration experienced by transferring white students, and an average decline of 5.9 percent in the Hispanic concentration experienced by transferring Hispanic students.[20]

Some differences are also evident across jurisdictions. Philadelphia is the only site where transferring students of all three groups tend to switch to charter schools having higher concentrations of their own race. By contrast, in Chicago transferring students of all three groups tend to move to charter schools having *lower* concentrations of their own race. In all of the other sites, the results vary for different racial groups. Across twenty-one comparisons (seven sites with three racial groups each), we find only two cases in which the average difference between the sending TPS and the receiving charter school is greater than ten percentage points in the concentration of the transferring student's race.

EXAMINING THE RELATIONSHIP BETWEEN CHARTER POLICIES AND DISTRIBUTIONAL PATTERNS

Comparing the results in tables 11.2 and 11.4 to the policies described in table 11.1 reveals no clear relationship between charter policies and distributional outcomes across locations. For instance, both Milwaukee and Ohio have unique authorizing structures, but students switching out of Milwaukee's TPSs have similar prior test scores to students in the rest of the district and in the TPSs they exited, whereas Ohio students exiting TPSs for charter schools are below-average students from the perspective both of statewide averages and the TPSs they exited. Similarly, African American students in Milwaukee tend to transfer to charter schools having a higher proportion of African American students, whereas the opposite is true in Ohio.

We also speculated that other policies, such as transportation and enrollment requirements, could be important in determining the types of students who enroll in charter schools. Again, however, we find no obvious relationship. For instance, whereas charter schools in Ohio and Texas attract below-average students and whereas African American students in both locations are more likely to transfer to schools having a higher concentration of African American students, only Ohio requires that charter schools provide transportation. Similarly, although both Chicago and Texas have provisions favoring charter schools focused on at-risk students, Texas charter schools attract students with below-average test scores, and Chicago charter schools do not. In addition, students transferring to Chicago charter schools transfer to schools having a smaller share of their own race, but in Texas that is true only for Hispanics.

Finally, the presence of choice options also seems unrelated to the effect of charter schools on the distribution of students. For example, although Ohio and Texas have similar outcomes both by race and by ability, Ohio provides more choice options—including a voucher program.

The foregoing analysis is admittedly informal and represents only a first attempt to examine the relationship between charter policies and distributional outcomes. Estimating this relationship quantitatively would be preferable, but coding the policies for each location is difficult, especially because one must account for policy variations within the seven locations both geographically and over time. In addition, it would be difficult to tease out effects empirically with data from only seven locations. Nevertheless, this initial, informal attempt reveals no obvious relationship between policies and the distribution of students in race and ability.

CONCLUSIONS

In this study, we examine whether charter schools are skimming the best students from TPSs and whether students transferring to charter schools are transferring to schools having a greater concentration of students of their own race, thereby creating greater racial stratification. Much of the previous research has ignored the cream skimming questions altogether and has examined the racial distribution question using school-level data. Our study goes beyond much of the literature by using longitudinal student-level data across seven locations to track students who move from TPSs to charter schools, an approach that enables us to observe both their previous and their subsequent peer environments.

Overall, it does not appear that charter schools are systematically skimming high-achieving students or dramatically affecting the racial mix of students for transferring students. Students transferring to charter schools had prior achievement levels that were generally similar to or lower than those of their TPS peers. And transfers had surprisingly little effect on racial distribution across the sites: typically, students transferring to charter schools moved to schools having similar racial distributions as the TPSs from which the students came. There is some evidence, however, that African American students transferring to charters are more likely to end up in schools having higher percentages of students of their own race, a finding that is consistent with prior results in North Carolina.[21]

We also examined whether any distributional differences across locations can be explained by charter policies and environments across locations. However, we are unable to identify a systematic relationship between distributional outcomes and policies, suggesting that any differences across locations may be a function of nuanced characteristics of charter schools or their districts and states.

In sum, the results suggest that the worst fears of charter opponents regarding student sorting have not been realized: charters are not skimming the best students, nor are they creating white enclaves. But, by that same token, we find little evidence that they are systematically reducing stratification by race or ability.

12

Does Parental Choice Foster Segregated Schools?

Insights from the Netherlands

Helen F. Ladd, Edward B. Fiske, and Nienke Ruijs

The Netherlands differs from most other developed countries, including the United States, with respect to its strong historical commitment to parental choice of schools, its full public funding of all schools whether or not they are publicly or privately operated, and the fact that schools have substantial budgetary and operational autonomy. There is growing policy interest in the United States in giving parents more opportunities to choose schools for their children—in forms such as intra- or interdistrict choice and charter schools—and of reform proposals calling for more autonomy for schools.[1] The Dutch experience has the potential to provide insights for U.S. policy makers about how a system with more parental choice and school autonomy might play out over time.

A country of 16.5 million people, the Netherlands devotes a relatively small share of its gross domestic product to education, and its students do well by international standards. In particular, Dutch students outperform their peers in many other developed countries, including the United States, on international tests such as PISA and TIMSS.[2] Moreover, Dutch students whose mothers have limited education do better on PISA tests than comparable students in other countries within the Organisation for Economic Co-operation and Development (OECD). The determinants of these high achievement levels are complex and undoubtedly reflect not only the nature of the country's education system but also its attention to the overall well-being of its children. According to a recent UNICEF study, the Netherlands ranks at the top of twenty-one rich countries in child well-being, with the United States and the United Kingdom at the bottom.[3]

Of central interest for this chapter is the relationship between parental choice and school autonomy, on the one hand, and segregation of students by educational disadvantage, on the other. Studies from both the United States and around the world have shown that parental choice often leads to more-segregated schools than would otherwise be the case. Fiske and Ladd document such patterns for New Zealand; Cullen et al. do so for Chicago; and chapters in Plank and Sykes provide evidence of greater segregation in countries such as Chile, Sweden, and Australia.[4] In addition, charter schools in the United States often have a segregating effect.[5]

The Dutch context of parental choice is unusual in that for more than forty years the standard mechanisms described in the literature that often lead to segregation by socioeconomic disadvantage were overwhelmed by a different type of affinity or bond, namely religion. As a result of these bonds, and a related commitment to school autonomy, segregation by disadvantage was not an issue of significant policy concern. Not until the secularization of Dutch society in the 1950s and the influx of immigrants in the 1960s and 1970s did it become a salient issue.

One purpose of this chapter is to examine why, despite the country's long history of parental choice, segregation by educational disadvantage has only recently emerged as a policy issue in the Netherlands. A second is to document the levels and recent trends of school segregation in the country's four largest cities. The analysis indicates that segregation levels are very high—both absolutely and relative to comparable measures for the United States—and that they have been rising. In the final section, we examine how the Dutch commitment to parental choice and school autonomy makes it difficult for policy makers to alter the situation.

Our analysis focuses exclusively on primary schools, which in the Netherlands serve children from age four to age twelve. This focus is consistent with the Dutch view that primary schools are the most important part of the education system. In addition, because the Dutch primary school sector has more features in common with the U.S. system and those in other countries than does the Dutch secondary sector, its operations are more comprehensible and relevant to a non-Dutch audience. At the secondary level, Dutch students are tracked into a variety of high schools with differing program lengths. At that level, the segregation of students is closely connected to student performance in the primary grades and raises a number of issues beyond the scope of this chapter.

THE SEGREGATING EFFECTS OF PARENTAL CHOICE

Greater segregation of schools is consistent with the predictions of the following simple choice model in which there are only two types of families:

advantaged and disadvantaged. Consider first the advantaged families. The sociology and economics literatures provide at least three reinforcing motivations for such families to choose schools that serve children from similarly advantaged families. The first motivation, referred to in the literature as the *outgroup avoidance* theory, is that some advantaged families would prefer to minimize contact with the other group. In the school choice context, that means they would choose to remove their children from schools serving large numbers of disadvantaged children.[6]

An alternative motivation, sometimes referred to as *neutral ethnocentrism,* posits that members of each group prefer to be with members of their own group. For advantaged families, the school choice behavior associated with this motivation would be indistinguishable from that associated with the outgroup avoidance motivation.[7] The third motivation relates to school quality. To the extent that the quality of schools serving advantaged students is higher than that of schools serving disadvantaged students—perhaps because the former are able to command more resources and to attract higher-quality teachers—advantaged families who care about quality once again have an incentive to select schools serving advantaged students. A variant of this motivation is that advantaged families may prefer the types of programs offered in the schools serving advantaged students to those offered in other schools.[8]

It is somewhat harder to predict the behavior of members of the disadvantaged group. Ethnocentric preferences would push parents to choose schools serving other disadvantaged students like their children. Quality considerations could potentially reinforce this motivation, but only if parents believed that schools serving large concentrations of disadvantaged students would be more attentive than other schools to the particular needs of their children. More generally, quality considerations are likely to cut the other way. To the extent that disadvantaged families perceive that the quality is higher in the schools serving advantaged children, they have an incentive to try to send their children to such schools. However, various considerations, such as transportation costs and capacity constraints, may prevent them from doing so. Although the net effect on the behavior of the members of the disadvantaged group is ambiguous, the clear and unambiguous prediction for the advantaged families leads to the overall prediction that, unless policy makers actively intervene in the choice process, parental choice of school is very likely to make schools more segregated than they would otherwise be.[9]

THE HISTORICAL CONTEXT OF SCHOOL SEGREGATION

The twin principles of allowing parents to choose schools for their children and giving schools considerable operational autonomy are deeply embedded in the philosophy and organization of the Dutch education system. The 1917 Constitution provides for equal funding of all schools whether they are publicly or privately operated, and Article 23 gives any group of citizens, including those with specific religious orientations or educational philosophies, the right to establish its own publicly funded school provided it can attract a sufficient number of students.

As a result of these policies, only 30 percent of the Dutch primary students now attend what in the United States we would call traditional public schools. The other 70 percent attend schools having a religious orientation or a commitment to a specific type of educational program such as a Montessori or Dalton program. In return for their public funding, these privately operated schools are subject to the same general national curriculum guidelines and national teacher salary schedules as the public schools. Municipal governments have historically operated the public schools, but in 2006 operating authority for those schools was turned over to publicly appointed boards so as to make them more comparable to the privately operated schools and to preclude any temptation by municipalities to favor public schools. As a result, government policy makers currently have essentially no operational authority for any individual school.[10]

Whether publicly or privately operated, all schools are subject to national accountability standards implemented through the Dutch Inspectorate of Education. For primary schools, the inspectorate examines internal school processes and practices as well as student outcomes as measured by test scores in the students' final year. The internal school processes are rated on an absolute standard, and student achievement is judged in relation to expectations based on the mix of students in the school. The reports are public information; and although weak schools are subject to additional visits from the inspectorate, the inspectorate cannot close down schools. Only the minister of education can do that and only by taking away funding, something it has been reluctant to do unless the school has too few students.

Freedom of Education

Central to the Dutch primary school system is the concept of *freedom of education,* which means that parents as well as schools are free to engage in the kind of education of their choosing and to command public funding for their choices, subject only to the national controls just described.[11] As a result, there is no tradition of what in the United States we call a *common school* that serves the entire community and promotes a common sense of civic and other values. Instead, the schools reflect what was known as the *pillarization* of Dutch society.

Until the early 1950s Dutch society was organized around various sub-cultures, or *pillars,* defined by religious affiliation—Protestant, Roman Catholic, and secular. Dutch citizens for the most part lived within the confines of their particular pillar, each of which had its own churches, employers, newspapers, hospitals, and schools. Communication across the various religious fault lines occurred mainly among leaders at the top of the various pillars. This system of segregation by religious orientation broke down under the secularizing forces that swept through Europe after World War II, and churchgoing in the Netherlands among native Dutch is now low by U.S. standards, especially in the cities.

The one conspicuous exception is education, where nominal pillarization has persisted.[12] The various boards that operate primary schools continue to identify themselves as Protestant, Catholic, or public.[13] It is no longer the case, however, that a Catholic or a Protestant school caters only to students of that religion. Although Protestant and Catholic families are still most likely to enroll their children in schools of the corresponding religious orientation, a recent study based on survey data shows that 29 percent of Protestants and 23 percent of Catholics attend either a nonreligious school or a school of another religious persuasion.[14]

This historical commitment to freedom of education is so strong that the right to set up new schools has been extended to all groups. As a result there are now Islamic, Hindu, and Orthodox Protestant schools as well as schools with very specific educational philosophies. Although public schools must admit anyone who applies within a geographically defined catchment area, the privately operated schools can limit admissions to pupils whose parents concur with the particular value system of the school. Currently, it is mainly the new types of religious schools that tend to serve pupils of the respective religious orientation almost exclusively.[15]

Table 12.1 provides information on the schools and students in primary schools by school type, both for the four large cities (Amsterdam, Rotterdam, The Hague, and Utrecht) that are the focus on this study, and for the rest of the country. The table shows that in the big cities public schools are overrepresented and Catholic schools are underrepresented. The "Other" category includes Islamic and Orthodox Protestant schools, among others.

Weighted Student Funding As a Response to Disadvantage

Historically, there was considerable socioeconomic integration within the schools of the original three pillars, with wealthy and poor Catholics, for example, sitting side by side in the same schools, especially in the smaller communities. Nonetheless, even under that system there were still some

TABLE 12.1   **Primary students by school type, 2005–2006**

	Four big cities	Rest of country	Whole country
Schools and students			
Total schools	596	6,360	6,956
Total students	169,864	1,379,224	1,549,088
Students by school type (percent)			
Public	39.1	29.7	30.8
Roman Catholic	22.4	35.6	34.2
Protestant	25.0	24.3	24.4
Special program	6.6	4.7	4.9
Other	6.9	5.7	5.8

Distribution of students by type of school is based on the 6,842 schools for which we can identify the type of school. Of these schools, 581 are in the four big cities. Calculations by authors based on data from the Central Agency for the Financing of Schools (CFI).

concentrations of disadvantaged students. The influx of low-skilled immigrants that began in the 1960s (an influx described in more detail later) highlighted the issue of educational disadvantage, especially in the large cities, where it generated significant concentrations of educationally disadvantaged pupils of color. The fact that many of these students lagged behind other students was offensive to the Dutch sense of equity and its desire not to leave any particular group behind. Consistent with their commitments to parental choice and school autonomy, however, the Dutch simply accepted this new form of segregation—based on levels of disadvantage rather than religion—and focused their attention on alleviating the disadvantage itself. They did so by modifying their school funding system so as to minimize any adverse educational impacts of concentrations of disadvantaged students.

Specifically, in the mid-1980s the Dutch added student-based weights to their school funding program under which money follows pupils to the schools they attend. The weights were based on the backgrounds of the students, with additional weights of 0.25 for native Dutch students whose parents had limited education and 0.9 for first- and second-generation immigrants whose parents had little education. The effect was to direct more resources per pupil to the schools having large concentrations of disadvantaged students than to other schools. Our research has confirmed that schools serving substantial numbers of disadvantaged pupils do, in fact, have more resources, especially teaching slots, than those serving more privileged pupils.[16] In this way, the Dutch have continued to maintain the commitment to parental choice and school autonomy in the face of growing concentrations of disadvantaged students.

WHY SEGREGATION IS NOW EMERGING AS A POLICY ISSUE

Three factors help explain why segregation of disadvantaged pupils has now become a salient issue in the Netherlands. First is the influx of large numbers of low-skilled and poorly educated immigrants, especially in the big cities. This influx has led to a proliferation of what the Dutch refer to as "black schools" and has placed new pressures on an education system that historically worked well to support a pluralistic society. Second, the secularization of society permitted the development of a consumer mind-set among parents, who now make their choices of school based on perceptions of educational quality rather than simply on religion. This change, as one would expect, has led to white flight from black schools. And finally, in the wake of the terrorist attacks in the United States on September 11, 2001, Dutch politicians have been more willing to talk about the potential disadvantages of Islamic schools and, more generally, of the potentially adverse effects of segregated schools on the social integration of immigrants.[17]

Influx of Non-Western Immigrants

Among the immigrants to the Netherlands, the most policy relevant are those from non-Western countries.[18] The four main categories of such immigrants are those from the former Dutch colonies of Surinam and Antilles, and guest workers from Morocco and Turkey.[19] These immigrants began to arrive during the economic boom of the 1950s and 1960s, when many workers from the former colonies of Surinam and Antilles came to the Netherlands in search of greater economic opportunity. Since then, additional immigrants from those countries have moved to the Netherlands to study or to take advantage of the high-quality social services. Starting in the 1960s large numbers of unskilled Moroccan and Turkish workers were recruited under contract to work in the Netherlands. Although the initial expectation was that they would return to their home countries, most have stayed. Even after the end of official recruitment of these guest workers in the early 1970s and the introduction of tighter controls on immigration, the immigrant population continued to grow through the process of family reunification and marriage. More recently, these groups of non-Western immigrants have been augmented by asylum seekers from countries such as Somalia and Iran. Figure 12.1, based on data from the Central Bureau for Statistics (CBS), depicts the rising proportions of migrants from 1972 to 2007.

The vast majority of these immigrants has settled in the country's biggest cities. Although non-Western immigrants account for about 10 percent of the overall population, they account for more than 35 percent of the population of Rotterdam, more than 30 percent of Amsterdam and The Hague,

Figure 12.1   Percent of migrants in the Netherlands

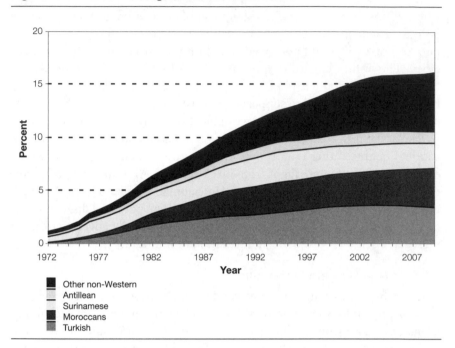

and slightly more than 20 percent of Utrecht. In all four of these cities they account for far higher percentages of the school population.

The policy relevance of these immigrants, particularly those in the four main categories, largely reflects their low skills, limited educational background, low income, and limited familiarity with the Dutch language. In terms of Dutch language skills, the Turks and the Moroccans are particularly weak, with the Antilleans and the Surinamese having somewhat better language skills because of their former colonial ties. Of most relevance for the education of their children is that more than 70 percent of the Turkish and Moroccan parents and about 55 percent of the Surinamese and Antillean parents have no more than a junior-level secondary education. In contrast, only 20 percent of the parents of native Dutch primary school pupils have comparably low levels of education.[20] These low levels of education translate directly into low-skilled jobs or, in many cases, to unemployment.

The low socioeconomic status of these non-Western immigrants differentiates them from previous immigrants who historically have been welcome in the Netherlands, and also distinguish them from the three historical pillars of the Dutch society. Although each pillar had its fair share of families with low socioeconomic status (SES), none of the pillars themselves could be categorized as low SES. Thus this new segment of society stands out because its members are a different color compared with native Dutch persons and typically have very low SES.

Although the presence of immigrants in the big-city school systems is undoubtedly at the root of current concerns about school segregation, non-Western immigrants are not currently increasing as a share of the primary-school-age population in the four big cities. Data on children in the five- to ten-year-old age group (as a proxy for the four- to twelve-year-old age group relevant for primary schools) show that the share exceeds 50 percent in both Amsterdam and Rotterdam and is only slightly less than 50 percent in The Hague, with little movement in the percentages over the 2003–2008 period. The share is lower in Utrecht, where it has a slight downward trajectory. In an additional set of thirty-two big cities, to which we refer briefly later, we observe very little change in the average proportion of (disadvantaged) immigrant children in primary schools over the longer 1997–2005 period.

Immigrants and the New Consumer Mind-Set in the Selection of Schools

We have previously alluded to the secularization of Dutch society, a development that has opened up new opportunities for families to base schooling decisions not only on religion but also on other criteria, including the mix of students in the school and perceptions of school quality. Because the immigrants differ from the established groups within Dutch society in that immigrants are overwhelmingly disadvantaged, this secularization has opened the door for the pressures discussed earlier. The educated native Dutch now have clear incentives—whether they reflect outgroup avoidance, ethnocentrism, or a search for quality—to enroll their children in schools having few immigrants. The immigrants, in turn, have mixed incentives, with ethnocentrism leading them to self-segregate but quality-related incentives in some cases leading them to enroll their children in integrated schools.

Survey research confirms these new motivations and behaviors in the Dutch context. In 2003, a group of researchers based at the University of Amsterdam surveyed more than nine hundred parents in neighborhoods having schools that were significantly whiter or blacker than the neighborhood itself, where "black" refers to non-Western immigrants. The researchers asked the parents about the choices they made for their children. They concluded that both native Dutch and immigrant parents typically deemed the white schools most suitable and the schools serving large proportions of immigrant students (i.e., the "black schools") the least suitable. According to the survey, the native Dutch parents avoided the black schools because of both the mismatch between home and school and the schools' poor academic standards. When immigrant parents avoided a black school, they typically did so because of the poor reputation of the school.[21]

The more that parental choices are influenced by the ethnic mix of a school's students, the more segregated the schools are likely to become over time and the more difficult it is for policy makers to ignore the fact that schools are segregated.

Political Considerations

Although the number of immigrant children is not currently increasing as a share of the student population in the big cities, these children are increasingly becoming the focus of political attention. A major catalyst for that attention is undoubtedly the destruction that occurred in New York City on 9/11, an event that raised political consciousness about Muslims in many countries, including the Netherlands. In the aftermath of that event a new radical populist, the late Pim Fortuyn, emerged and established a new political party that raised harsh questions about Dutch policy toward immigrants. In so doing, he put the issue of immigrants, especially Muslim immigrants, squarely on the public policy agenda. The views of Fortuyn—and, recently, the more extreme views of Geert Wilders—have allowed other, more moderate politicians to take stronger positions on policies toward immigrants than previously had been possible. One of the central policy concerns became the extent to which the residential and school segregation of immigrants kept them from being successfully integrated into Dutch society.[22]

Emblematic of these concerns are the fierce debates about the Islamic schools, of which there are more than forty throughout the country at the primary level, and two at the high school level. Almost all of the seventy-six hundred pupils in these primary schools are first- or second-generation immigrants whose parents have limited education. Like all schools, these Islamic schools follow the standard Dutch curriculum and use Dutch as the language of instruction. Moreover, most teachers and managers are non-Muslim. Religious and cultural values are expressed mainly through religious education classes and policies such as separate gym classes for boys and girls and the wearing of head scarves by girls.[23]

Supporters see Islamic schools as promoting self-esteem and cultural pride. Opponents view them as divisive and undermining of important Dutch values ranging from tolerance to the role of women.[24] Some politicians have called for limiting any expansion of Islamic schools.[25] Significantly, some of the most heated debates regarding Islamic schools take place between fundamentalists and moderates within the Muslim community itself.

PATTERNS AND TRENDS IN THE SEGREGATION
OF DISADVANTAGED IMMIGRANTS

Much of the recent empirical work on school segregation in the Nether-lands has focused on the question of whether schools are "too white" or "too black" relative to the population in the neighborhood.[26] One of these studies shows, for example, that as of 2005–2006 more than half the pri-mary schools in both Amsterdam and Rotterdam were more than 10 per-centage points whiter or blacker than the comparable percentage mix of children in the neighborhood. Specifically, in Amsterdam 23 percent of the schools were whiter and 33 percent were blacker, with one-third of the lat-ter being "too black" (as defined by the authors) in that they were more than 20 percent blacker than the neighborhood. In Rotterdam, 19 percent were whiter and 32 percent were blacker, with almost half of the latter being "too black." By this measure, The Hague appears to be the least segregated in that almost 60 percent of the schools in that city reflect the demographics of the surrounding neighborhoods.[27]

Although such an approach provides useful information on the extent to which schools reflect the ethnic mix of their surrounding neighborhoods, it provides little or no information about the overall degree to which schools are segregated within the city. Whenever the neighborhoods themselves are highly segregated, for example, even if the ethnic mix of students in every school reflected the mix of students within its neighborhood, no schools would emerge as "too white" or "too black." Yet school segregation would still be very high.

Our empirical analysis follows the U.S. tradition of segregation research and is designed to measure the extent of segregation across schools within cities regardless of the extent to which it is correlated with residential seg-regation. We use multiple measures to look at trends over time and to make comparisons to comparable measures in the United States, where segregation by race historically has been high and the subject of significant policy concern.

Methodology and Data

We examine here the extent to which educationally disadvantaged immigrant pupils at the primary level are segregated from other pupils. For this purpose a disadvantaged immigrant is defined as a first- or second-generation non-Western immigrant whose parents have limited education. Such pupils can be identified through administrative data because of the existence of the sys-tem of weighted student funding described earlier. In particular, these are the students eligible for the additional funding weight of 0.9 because of their educational disadvantage. Our data cover the years 1997–2005, a period during which the criteria for the weights remained unchanged. We cannot extend the analysis to a more recent year because of the elimination in 2006 of immigrant status as a criterion. Starting in that year, the weights are based solely on the educational attainment of a child's parents.[28]

Drawing on the U.S. literature on school segregation, we use five separate measures that reflect various aspects of the extent to which disadvantaged immigrants are segregated from other students. The five measures are grouped into two categories and calculated separately for each city. Measures of *isolation* highlight the extent to which disadvantaged immigrant pupils are concentrated in schools with other pupils similar to themselves, and hence are isolated from more-advantaged students. Note that these measures are likely to be higher in cities having higher proportions of disadvantaged immigrants than in other cities. Measures of *imbalance* highlight the extent to which pupils of the two types are unevenly distributed across schools and are invariant to a city's overall proportion of disadvantaged immigrants.

- Measures of isolation are as follows:
  - Fraction of disadvantaged immigrant pupils in schools having more than 50 percent of such pupils
  - Fraction of disadvantaged immigrant students in schools having more than 70 percent of such students
  - Isolation index (I), a measure of the extent to which disadvantaged immigrant pupils are in schools with other pupils like themselves[29]
- Measures of imbalance are as follows:
  - Dissimilarity index (DIS), a measure of the extent to which disadvantaged immigrants are unevenly distributed across schools[30]
  - Segregation index (S), a gap-based measure of segregation that, like the dissimilarity index, measures the extent to which schools are unbalanced[31]

Although the interpretation of the segregation index is somewhat less intuitive than that of the dissimilarity index, we include it among our measures so that we can compare levels of segregation in Dutch cities with those in the United States based on this measure.[32]

Levels and Trends in the Four Large Cities. Figure 12.2 illustrates the level and trends over time in the five measures of segregation aggregated across the four big cities, with the outcomes for each city weighted by the number of primary school pupils each year.

The top line indicates that almost 80 percent of the disadvantaged immigrant students in the four cities are in schools having more than a majority of students like themselves and that the percentage increased, but only slightly, over the nine-year period. The proportion of such students in schools having

FIGURE 12.2   **Five measures of segregation of disadvantaged immigrants (DI) versus all other primary school students, combined results for the four big cities, 1997–2005**

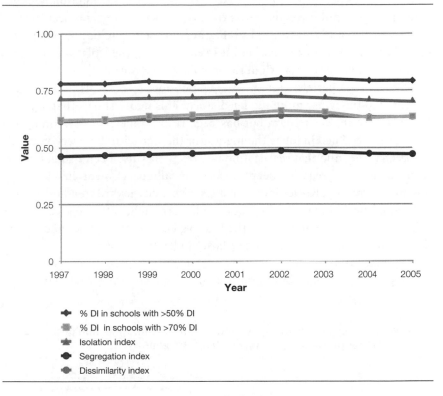

% DI in schools with >50% DI
% DI in schools with >70% DI
Isolation index
Segregation index
Dissimilarity index

more than 70 percent disadvantaged immigrants is correspondingly lower but still exceeds 60 percent in all years, reaching a peak in 2002. Consistent with those two measures, the isolation index indicates that the typical disadvantaged immigrant student living in one of the four cities was in a school having 70 percent or more disadvantaged immigrant students throughout the period. All of these measures are clearly high. The last one implies, for example, that typical disadvantaged immigrant children have relatively few native Dutch-speaking schoolmates, a situation that could make it difficult for them to develop their Dutch language skills.

Although the two measures of imbalance—the dissimilarity index and the segregation index—have different values, they tell the same story, namely that schools in the four cities were highly unbalanced throughout the period, but not much more so in 2005 than in 1997. The dissimilarity index indicates, for example, that more than 60 percent of the pupils would have to be moved to other schools to achieve balance, and the segregation index indicates that the gap between the exposure rate of a typical native Dutch student to disadvantaged immigrant pupils and the maximum possible average exposure rate in each city is 45 percent of the maximum exposure rate. The similar trends across the five measures largely reflect the fact that the share of disadvantaged immigrants in the four cities has remained relatively constant over time. Had it been growing, the isolation measures might well have risen more than the imbalance measures.

City-specific patterns for the segregation index, as illustrated in figure 12.3, tell a somewhat more nuanced story. This figure shows that segregation is lowest in Amsterdam but has been rising somewhat over time, that segregation in The Hague is the highest of the four cities in every year and has been rising, and that segregation in Utrecht has also been rising. Only in Rotterdam has segregation been consistently falling. As we discuss later, the downward trend in Rotterdam coincides with a downward trend in residential segregation in that city. The bottom line, though, is that segregation by this measure is rising in three of the four big cities in the Netherlands. Identical patterns emerge for the dissimilarity index (not shown).

A similar analysis for thirty-two other large Dutch cities shows that although disadvantaged immigrants are less isolated than in the four big cit-

FIGURE 12.3   **Trends in segregation index of disadvantaged immigrants (DI) versus all other primary students, by city, 1997–2005**

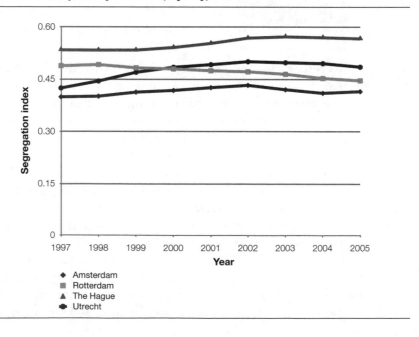

ies, segregation is increasing in those smaller cities as well.[33] The lower levels of isolation in these cities are not surprising given that disadvantaged immigrants account for only about 15 percent of their primary school students. Still quite high, however, are measures of imbalance such as the average dissimilarity index in the thirty-two cities, which exceeds 0.50. Moreover, by all five measures, disadvantaged immigrants in these cities became increasingly segregated between 1997 and 2005.

Comparisons to Segregation in the United States. The levels of segregation reported here are high, not only in absolute terms but also relative to segregation levels in the United States. In a recent study of the one hundred largest school districts in the southern and border states in the United States, researchers found that the average enrollment-weighted racial isolation of black students was 0.46, a number that is far lower than the comparable measure of immigrant isolation of 0.70 in the big Dutch cities. Similarly, for those same one hundred U.S. districts, the researchers reported a white–nonwhite dissimilarity index of 0.43, which is also far lower than the average of more than 0.60 for the Dutch cities.[34]

Additional U.S data are reported in table 12.2. The entries in the table are the percentages of black students in schools having more than 50 percent nonwhite students in 1972 (a few years after the major initial U.S. efforts to desegregate schools) and in 2000 for various regions of the United States. The increases in many of the percentages over the period reflect the resegregation that was occurring in many parts of the United States at the end of the twentieth century. Of note is that even the highest percentage in the table—the 78.3 percent for the northeastern cities in 2000—is lower than the comparable average of close to 80 percent in the four big Dutch cities.

To be sure, some U.S. metropolitan areas feature far higher levels of segregation than those of the one hundred districts in the southern and border

TABLE 12.2 **Percentages of black students in 50–100 percent nonwhite schools by U.S. region**

Region	1972	2000
Northeast	69.9	78.3
Border	67.2	67.0
South	55.5	69.0
Midwest	75.3	73.3
West	68.1	75.3
United States	63.6	71.6

Source: Charles Clotfelter, After Brown (Princeton University Press), 2004, Table 2.1, p. 56.

states or the averages across regions. As of 2000, the highest metropolitan-wide segregation indexes in the United States were in Detroit (0.630); Monroe, Louisiana (0.590); and Cleveland (0.585).[35] All these segregation indexes exceed the 2005–2006 segregation indexes for the four big Dutch cities, the highest of which is 0.57 in The Hague. Such measures for the United States are calculated for whole metropolitan areas, which include not only central cities with large black populations but also suburban districts that tend to be white. As a result, much of the overall segregation reflects differences between, rather than within, districts. For that reason, the overall metropolitan-wide measures are not fully comparable to the city-specific segregation measures for the Dutch cities. The Dutch measures would most likely be somewhat higher than reported in the table if they were based on the cities and their surrounding communities. Thus we conclude that the segregation of disadvantaged immigrant pupils in the four major Dutch cities exceeds that of black students in most major U.S. cities.

Trends in Residential Segregation. Finally, we turn to the trends in residential segregation in the four big Dutch cities so that we can compare them to trends in school segregation. The residential trends are based on publicly available data from the Central Bureau for Statistics (CBS) on the proportions of non-Western immigrants in each neighborhood.[36] Because there are fewer neighborhoods than schools, the levels of neighborhood and school segregation are not directly comparable. In general, all else held constant, the larger the units of observation, the lower the measured segregation. The relevant comparisons are those in levels across cities and the trends over time.

In table 12.3, we report two measures of segregation at the neighborhood level: the dissimilarity index and the gap-based segregation index. Recall that these are measures of unevenness and hence are invariant to the overall percentages of non-Western immigrants either across cities or within cities over time. As before, the values differ between the two measures, but the patterns and trends are relatively comparable, although not identical. We report changes both for the period 1999–2005, which is relatively comparable to the period for which we have calculated school-level segregation, and for an extended period through 2008.

Table 12.3 reveals that residential segregation is highest by far in The Hague throughout the period. Amsterdam features the lowest level among the four cities at the beginning of the period but not at the end because of the small increase in Amsterdam and the relatively large decrease in Rotterdam during both 1999–2005 and the full period. The trends in the other two cities are far less clear. The changes over time in The Hague differ across the two measures but in any case were very small. In Utrecht both measures sug-

TABLE 12.3 Trends in residential segregation, non-Western immigrants versus all others at the neighborhood level, four big cities, 1999 and 2003–2008

	Amsterdam	Rotterdam	The Hague	Utrecht
Dissimilarity index				
1999	0.363	0.417	0.465	0.396
2003	0.373	0.391	0.467	0.413
2004	0.374	0.387	0.471	0.419
2005	0.382	0.385	0.472	0.413
2006	0.386	0.379	0.473	0.406
2007	0.387	0.375	0.472	0.401
2008	0.384	0.370	0.470	0.394
Change 1999–2005	0.019	−0.032	0.007	0.017
Change 1999–2008	0.021	−0.047	0.005	−0.002
Segregation index				
1999	0.161	0.195	0.283	0.163
2003	0.173	0.192	0.281	0.181
2004	0.176	0.189	0.282	0.190
2005	0.180	0.189	0.282	0.188
2006	0.181	0.186	0.281	0.186
2007	0.182	0.181	0.281	0.187
2008	0.178	0.177	0.276	0.184
Change 1999–2005	0.019	−0.006	−0.001	0.025
Change 1999–2008	0.017	−0.018	−0.007	0.021

Note: Calculated by the authors based on data from the Central Bureau of Statistics. Calculations include all neighborhoods with at least 50 people. In 2005, the numbers of neighborhoods by city were 92 in Amsterdam, 78 in Rotterdam, 107 in The Hague, and 96 in Utrecht. The number of neighborhoods differs slightly from year to year.

gest that segregation increased between 1999 and 2005, but discrepancies between the two measures in the more recent years generate a mixed picture.

Comparing these trends to those in school segregation as shown earlier in figure 12.3 by city, we find that, with the exception of The Hague, the trends in school segregation mimic the trends in residential segregation. Specifically, both school and residential segregation fell in Rotterdam and rose somewhat in Amsterdam. In Utrecht, school segregation increased through 2002 and then declined somewhat, and that follows the general pattern of residential segregation. Only in The Hague, where both school and residential segregation are very high, do the patterns diverge; despite the absence of much change in residential segregation in that city between 1999 and 2005, school segregation increased quite significantly.

Although these trends in residential segregation contribute to our understanding of trends in school segregation, they tell us nothing about causal links. A reduction in residential segregation over time need not imply, for example, a reduction in school segregation. This analysis highlights the importance of looking at overall segregation and not only the extent to which the ethnic mix of schools differs from that in their surrounding neighborhoods. As we noted at the beginning of this section, The Hague has the highest percentage of schools that reflect their surrounding neighborhoods and hence, by that measure, appears the least segregated. But in terms of overall measures it features the highest levels of both school and residential segregation.

CURRENT EFFORTS TO RESTRICT SEGREGATION

Now that school segregation has been placed on the Dutch policy agenda, officials at both the local and the national levels are looking for ways to make the black schools less black and the white ones less white. In one of the earliest of these efforts, initiated in Gouda in 1981, nonwhite children, mostly Moroccan, were bused into white schools in affluent areas. The experiment ended in 1996, however, when major stakeholders, including parents and school boards, withdrew their support.[37]

This example highlights the problem faced by Dutch policy makers. The strong national commitment to freedom of education means that public officials have little or no direct authority to intervene to limit parental decisions about where their children will go to school or to force autonomous schools to change their admissions policies, which in the case of privately operated schools includes the right to require parents to subscribe to the particular religious or other values around which the school is organized. The only way changes can be made is in the typical Dutch manner of *polderizing*, or engaging in discussions in which all the relevant groups have an opportunity to have their say and, over time, coming to a consensus about what needs to be done on a voluntary basis.[38]

Concerned that segregation in schools undermines relations between various ethnic and other groups in Dutch society, officials in a number of cities have in recent years promoted voluntary agreements with school boards to encourage desegregation. Most of these agreements focus on student enrollment procedures, such as establishing a fixed enrollment time rather than allowing parents to enroll their children in a preferred school well before they are old enough to attend, a process that historically has benefited more-advantaged families. Other approaches include providing better information to disadvantaged parents about the options available to them and promoting exchanges and other contact between black and white schools.[39]

A Dutch institute for multicultural development recently published a list of agreements between the city and schools to reduce segregation in nineteen of thirty-five cities examined, but it noted that implementation of the agreements has been slow.[40] At the national level the Department of Education has recently initiated seven pilot projects to identify measures to combat segregation in each of the four largest cities as well as in Eindhoven, Deventer, and Nijmegen. Four other cities—Schiedam, Amersfoort, Tilburg, and Leiden—were subsequently added to the project, and an initial evaluation is scheduled for 2010.[41]

Some of the pilots build on policies the cities initiated on their own. By 2004 Rotterdam had introduced a series of measures to combat segregation, including the use of double waiting lists, a practice that allowed oversubscribed schools to give preference to children who would enrich the ethnic mix of the school's students. The city also encouraged local agencies to organize initiatives to encourage parents to exercise their right to choose among schools.[42] Such parental initiatives have been started at thirty schools.[43]

In 2007 Amsterdam launched ten pilots involving initiatives such as agreements between schools in support of voluntary parental initiatives, including a fixed enrollment date. Two new experiments in The Hague focus on supporting parental initiatives and fostering communication between students at black and white schools. In Utrecht experiments have focused on developing standard procedures for enrolling children in primary schools.[44] Outside the four big cities, the pilots involve similar measures, but most are quite limited in scope.[45]

The best-known, and most ambitious, pilot is under way in Nijmegen, where city officials are seeking to combat socioeconomic segregation by balancing the distribution of weighted students under a system that in the United States would be called "controlled choice."[46] All of the primary schools in Nijmegen, including the religious schools and those with alternative pedagogies, have agreed on a central subscription system in which there is a maximum number of students for each school.[47] Parents list the three to six primary schools they most prefer, and efforts are made to accommodate their wishes.

When a particular school is oversubscribed, priority is given to siblings of pupils already enrolled in the school and to children who live nearby. Subsequent priority is then given to either advantaged or disadvantaged students—with disadvantage defined by eligibility for weighted student funding—in order to reach a balance of 30 percent disadvantaged and 70 percent advantaged students at a school. If there are fewer places than students within one of the relevant categories, a lottery determines which students are placed in the school.[48] The policy also includes efforts to invest additional money in segregated schools that have large numbers of disadvantaged students.[49] Because this policy has been in effect only since April 2009, no results are available.

In summary, as of 2009 more than half of the larger cities in the Netherlands were making some form of effort to reduce segregation in their schools. These efforts differ widely in size and methods, and no single best practice has emerged. The various pilot projects of the Department of Education could potentially generate some models that are effective and acceptable in the Dutch education context, but progress in reducing segregation is likely to be limited at best.

Of the initiatives now under way, the one in Nijmegen is receiving the most attention because it represents the most aggressive effort to control choice and, if successful, could serve as a model for other cities. The situation in Nijmegen, however, is far from typical. The city has long had a progressive government, and most schools are operated by only two large school boards, thus simplifying the negotiation process. Even those boards had to be enticed to participate in the program with the offer of a new and favorable deal related to capital spending.

Several reasons are generally cited for the lack of overall progress in combating segregation in primary schools in the Netherlands, starting with residential segregation and with the basic policy problem mentioned at the beginning of this section. The constitutionally protected concept of freedom of education means that no one group, including public officials, has the authority to force other stakeholders—whether they be parents or schools—to behave in a certain way. For example, municipal officials cannot even require school boards to accept a fixed time of enrollment. Thus, any efforts to reduce segregation will have to reflect the voluntary commitment of a substantial number of stakeholders for whom private interests in maintaining the status quo may well exceed the public benefit to them of reducing segregation.

Other factors include the newness of the conversations regarding segregation, a lack of consensus about the causes or solutions to the problem, and, importantly, the fact that many Dutch citizens simply do not believe that segregation is a problem.[50] A 2007 study of thirty-five cities indicated that the main reason for the lack of programs to combat segregation in education was that segregation was not viewed as a serious concern.[51]

CONCLUSION

The first forty years of the Dutch experience with parental choice and school autonomy suggested that segregation by educational disadvantage need not emerge as a central characteristic of such a system. That conclusion no longer holds. With the influx of immigrants and the secularization of Dutch society, the pressures for segregation by disadvantage described in much of the worldwide literature on school choice have generated a highly segregated school system.

Our data show that segregation by immigrant status in primary schools is already high in many Dutch cities—and as high as, or higher than, among blacks in many cities in the United States—and that segregation continues to rise in several cities despite little or no increase in the proportion of immigrants in the school-age population. Although a number of efforts have been initiated to reduce segregation, especially in the country's largest cities, these efforts have thus far shown little success.

We do not address in this chapter the extent to which school segregation represents an educational or social problem. On the one hand, any given level of segregation in the Netherlands could be less problematic from an educational perspective than in the United States because the program of weighted student funding helps offset the adverse educational effects of disadvantage. On the other hand, it is quite plausible that having such segregated schools is highly counterproductive with respect to the goal of integrating immigrants into Dutch society, a goal that has long been built on principles of inclusiveness and equity.

The long-standing tradition of freedom of education is by no means the only determinant of the high levels of segregation in the Netherlands. Our comparison of school and residential trends suggests that residential segregation is also a contributing factor. Whatever their role in creating the problem, however, the twin aspects of freedom of education—the right of parents to choose their children's school and the operational autonomy afforded to schools—make it very difficult for the Dutch to do anything about their high levels of school segregation. Any proposal to reduce segregation, whether through voluntary agreements among schools or governmental policies, will inevitably involve a trade-off with a deeply held Dutch value.

Notes

Chapter 1

1. For a discussion of the school choice debates, including interviews of prominent research-ers and advocates, see Jeffrey R. Henig, *Spin Cycle: How Research Is Used in Public Debates: The Case of Charter Schools* (New York: Russell Sage Foundation, 2008).
2. James S. Coleman, Thomas B. Hoffer, and Sally Kilgore, *High School Achievement: Public, Catholic, and Private Schools Compared* (New York: Basic Books, 1982).
3. James S. Coleman and Thomas B. Hoffer, *Public and Private Schools: The Impact of Communities* (New York: Basic Books, 1987).
4. For examples, see *Sociology of Education* 55 (1982) and 58 (1985); see also Thomas Hoffer, "Perspectives on Private Schools," in *Handbook of Research on School Choice*, ed. M. Berends, M. G. Springer, D. Ballou, and H. J. Walberg (New York: Routledge, 2009), 427–428; Derek Neal, "Private Schools in Education Markets," in *Handbook of Research on School Choice*, 428–460; Helen M. Marks, "Perspectives on Catholic Schools, in *Handbook of Research on School Choice*, 479–499; Derek Neal, "The Effect of Catholic Second-ary Schooling on Education Achievement," *Journal of Labor Economics* 15 (1997): 98–123.
5. Hoffer, "Perspectives on Private Schools"; Neal, "Private Schools in Education Markets"; Jeffrey Grogger and Derek Neal, "Further Evidence on the Effects of Catholic Secondary Schooling," *Brookings Wharton Papers on Urban Affairs* 1 (2000): 151; William Evans and Robert Schwab, "Finishing High School and Starting College: Do Catholic Schools Make a Difference?" *Quarterly Journal of Economics* 110 (1995): 941–974; Neal, "The Effect of Catholic Secondary Schooling on Educational Achievement."
6. Mark Berends and Genevieve Zottola, "Sociological Perspectives on School Choice," in *Handbook of Research on School Choice*, 35–53; Maureen T. Hallinan and Warren N. Kubitschek, "School Sector, School Poverty and the Catholic School Advantage," *Catholic Education: A Journal of Inquiry and Practice* 14 (2010): 143–172.
7. See John F. Witte, "The Milwaukee Voucher Experiment," *Educational Evaluation and Policy Analysis* 20 (1998): 229–251; John F. Witte, *The Market Approach to Education: An Analysis of America's First Voucher Program* (Princeton, NJ: Princeton University Press, 2000).
8. For findings on Milwaukee, see Jay P. Greene, Paul E. Peterson, and Jiangtao Du, "The Effectiveness of School Choice in Milwaukee: A Secondary Analysis of Data from the Mil-waukee Voucher Experiment Program's Evaluation," *Harvard University Education Policy and Governance Occasional Paper* 97 (1997): 1; Paul E. Peterson and William G. Howell, *The Education Gap: Vouchers and Urban Schools* (Washington, DC: Brookings Institution Press, 2006). For arguments about using experimental designs in education, see Caroline Hoxby and Sonali Murarka, "Methods of Assessing Achievement of Students in Charter Schools," in *Charter School Outcomes*, ed. M. Berends, M. G. Springer, and H. J. Walberg

(New York: Taylor and Francis Group, 2009) 7–37; Robert Boruch, Dorothy de Moya, and Brooke Snyder, "The Importance of Randomized Field Trials in Education and Related Areas, in *Evidence Matters: Randomized Trials in Education Research*, ed. F. Mosteller and R. Boruch (Washington, DC: The Brookings Institution Press, 2002), 50–79; Peter H. Rossi, Mark W. Lipsey, and Howard E. Freeman, *Evaluation: A Systematic Approach*, seventh edition (Thousand Oaks, CA: Sage, 2004).

9. Cecilia E. Rouse, "Private School Vouchers and Student Achievement: An Evaluation of the Milwaukee Parental Choice Program," *Quarterly Journal of Economics* 113 (1998): 553–602. Her analyses relied on multiple methods, including analyses of lottery data, lottery data with instrumental variables, and fixed-effects modeling. The results were not completely robust across all methods.

10. Julian R. Betts and Y. Emily Tang, *Value-Added and Experimental Studies of the Effect of Charter Schools on Student Achievement* (Seattle: National Charter School Research Project, Center on Reinventing Public Education, University of Washington, 2008); Bettie Teasley, "Charter School Outcomes," in *Handbook of Research on School Choice*, 209–226; see also Henig, *Spin Cycle: How Research Is Used in Public Debates*.

11. Diana Jean Schemo, "Charter Schools Trail in Results, U.S. Data Reveals," *New York Times*, August 17, 2004.

12. CenterforEducationReform,August2004,http://www.edreform.com/_upload/NewYork TimesAd.pdf.

13. Henig, *Spin Cycle*, 80.

14. David Cohen, *Workshop on Understanding and Promoting Knowledge Accumulation in Education: Tools and Strategies for Education Research* (Washington, DC: National Academy of Sciences, 2003), 1.

Chapter 2

1. This chapter summarizes the content of the sixth of a series of annual reports mandated by Congress. We gratefully acknowledge the contributions of a significant number of individuals in its preparation and production. Marsha Silverberg of the Institute of Education Sciences was the contract officer's representative for this project and contributed greatly to the content and successful execution of the study. Staff from the Washington Scholarship Fund provided helpful information whenever they were asked to do so. We also benefited from the advice of a technical working group comprising Julian Betts, Thomas Cook, Jeffrey Henig, William Howell, Guido Imbens, Rebecca Maynard, and Larry Orr. Expert staff at Westat ably performed crucial support roles, including data management by Yong Lee, Quinn Yang, and Yu Cao; data collection management by Juanita Lucas-McLean and Bonnie Ho; and editorial and production assistance by Evarilla Cover and Saunders Freeland. The interpretation of the results presented here is the sole responsibility of the authors and should not be construed as representing the views of the U.S. Department of Education, the Institute of Education Sciences, or any of our respective institutions.

2. Title III of Division C of the Consolidated Appropriations Act, 2004, P.L. 108–199.

3. Patrick Wolf et al., *Evaluation of the DC Opportunity Scholarship Program: First Year Report on Participation*, U.S. Department of Education, National Center for Education Evaluation and Regional Assistance (Washington, DC: U.S. Government Printing Office, 2005), ix.

4. Perry Bacon Jr., "House Bill Draws Criticism from GOP," *Washington Post*, February 26, 2009, A06; Sam Dillon, "Democrats Limit Future Financing for Washington Voucher Program," *New York Times*, February 28, 2009, A11.

5. "Presumed Dead: Politics Is Driving the Destruction of the District's School Voucher Program," *Washington Post,* April 11, 2009, A12.

6. "Obama's School Choice: Democrats Want to Kill Vouchers for 1,700 Kids," *Wall Street Journal,* February 25, 2009, A12; "Democrats and Poor Kids," *Wall Street Journal,* April 5, 2009, A14; "Voucher Subterfuge: Hoping No One Notices, Congressional Democrats Step Between 1,800 D.C. Children and a Good Education," *Washington Post,* February 25, 2009, A18; "Don't Pull the Plug Yet," *Washington Post,* April 4, 2009, A16; "Parents Fight to Keep Children Out of D.C. Public Schools," *ABC News,* May 13, 2009, http://www.wjla.com/news/stories/0509/622478.html.

7. Bill Turque and Shailagh Murray, "Obama Offers D.C. Voucher Compromise," *Washington Post,* May 7, 2009, B01.

8. Bill Turque, "With Critics Quiet, Hearing Praises D.C. School Voucher Program," *Washington Post,* May 14, 2009, B01; "Vouching for Vouchers: A Senate Hearing Offers Good Reasons for Preserving the District's Education Experiment," *Washington Post,* May 14, 2009, A18; "Children First: A DC Scholarship Program Has Bipartisan Backing," *Washington Post,* August 3, 2009, A16.

9. Michael Birnbaum, "Limits Are Likely on D.C. School Vouchers," *Washington Post,* December 10, 2009, B01.

10. *Budget of the U.S. Government, Fiscal Year 2011* (Washington, DC: U.S. Government Printing Office: 2010), Appendix: Other Independent Agencies, 1244.

11. Patrick J. Wolf, "School Voucher Programs: What the Research Says About Parental School Choice," *Brigham Young University Law Review* 2008: 415–446; *Fighting for Opportunity: School Choice Yearbook, 2009–2010* (Washington, DC: Alliance for School Choice, 2010); Title III of Division C of the Consolidated Appropriations Act, 2004, P.L. 108–199, Section 309.

12. See, for example, Robert Boruch, Dorothy de Moya, and Brooke Snyder, "The Importance of Randomized Field Trials in Education and Related Areas," in *Evidence Matters: Randomized Trials in Education Research,* eds. Frederick Mosteller and Robert Boruch (Washington, DC: The Brookings Institution Press, 2002), 74; Peter H. Rossi, Mark W. Lipsey, and Howard E. Freeman, *Evaluation: A Systematic Approach,* seventh edition (Thousand Oaks, CA: Sage, 2004), 239–240; Edward Tufte, *Beautiful Evidence* (Cheshire, CT: Graphics Press, 2006), 145.

13. Jay P. Greene, "Vouchers in Charlotte," *Education Matters* 1, no. 2 (2001): 55–60; William G. Howell, Patrick J. Wolf, David E. Campbell, and Paul E. Peterson, "School Vouchers and Academic Performance: Results from Three Randomized Field Trials," *Journal of Policy Analysis and Management* 21, no. 2 (2002): 191–217; Daniel P. Mayer et al., *School Choice in New York City After Three Years: An Evaluation of the School Choice Scholarships Program,* MPR Reference No. 8404-045 (Cambridge, MA: Mathematica Policy Research, 2002).

14. By the 2008–2009 school year, 94 treatment group students and 202 control group students had "graded out" of the program. That is, 296 members of the impact sample were forecast to have exceeded twelfth grade based on their grade upon application to the program. Because students were always tested in their forecast grade (calculated by adding the years since application to their grade upon application), and because the SAT-9 does not have a test for grades 13 or higher, these students were not testable and thus were classified as grade-outs for the purposes of the 2009 test score analysis. These grade-outs were not invited to data collection events.

15. According to the statute, students in the district living in families with incomes below 185 percent of the poverty level who were already attending private schools were eligible for

the program. Because they were the lowest service priority, Washington Scholarship Fund (the program's administrator) offered scholarships only to existing private school students during the first year of partial program implementation. In that first year, 505 existing private school students were eligible applicants to the program, and 216 were awarded scholarships in a lottery separate from the lottery designed for public school students. The private school students subject to a lottery in that first year were not followed for purposes of the evaluation, because the nature of the treatment intervention was distinctive for them. Existing private school students sought scholarships in order to remain in private schools and not to switch from public to private schools.

16. Howard S. Bloom, "Accounting for No-Shows in Experimental Evaluation Designs," *Evaluation Review* 8, no. 2 (1984): 225–246.

17. For technical details regarding the evaluation methodology, see Patrick Wolf, Babette Gutmann, Michael Puma, Brian Kisida, Lou Rizzo, Nada Eissa, and Matthew Carr, *Evaluation of the DC Opportunity Scholarship Program: Final Report,* U.S. Department of Education, National Center for Education Evaluation and Regional Assistance, NCEE 2010-4018 (Washington, DC: U.S. Government Printing Office, 2010), Appendix A, http://ies.ed.gov/ncee/.

18. William G. Howell and Paul E. Peterson (with Patrick J. Wolf and David E. Campbell), *The Education Gap: Vouchers and Urban Schools,* revised edition (Washington, DC: The Brookings Institution Press, 2006), 29.

19. Our research team won a Department of Education competition a month later to conduct the program evaluation, with Westat serving as the prime contractor for the project.

20. Wolf et al., *Evaluation of the DC Opportunity Scholarship Program: First Year Report on Participation.*

21. Descriptive reports on each of the first two years of implementation and cohorts of students have been previously prepared and released (ibid.; Patrick Wolf, Babette Gutmann, Michael Puma, and Marsha Silverberg, *Evaluation of the DC Opportunity Scholarship Program: Second Year Report on Participation,* U.S. Department of Education, National Center for Education Evaluation and Regional Assistance, NCEE 2006-4003 (Washington, DC: U.S. Government Printing Office, 2006), http://ies.ed.gov/ncee/.

22. Excluded from this count are about a dozen private schools that serve a highly specialized clientele, including a ballet school and a handful of schools that exclusively enroll students with severe disabilities.

23. The Catholic Archdiocese of Washington, D.C., has a long history of operating parochial schools in neighborhoods throughout the district, including those areas largely populated by low-income and non-Catholic families. Privately funded K–12 scholarship programs that previously operated in the district disproportionately resulted in non-Catholic minority students attending Catholic schools, largely for academic reasons, as demonstrated in a separate research analysis (Julie R. Trivitt and Patrick J. Wolf, "School Choice and the Branding of Catholic Schools," *Education Finance and Policy,* forthcoming). Seven former Catholic private schools that enrolled a total of 112 treatment group students in 2007–2008 left the program and operated as public charter schools in 2008–2009.

24. The characterization of the results presented here differs slightly from the official evaluation published by the Department of Education. Whereas the official evaluation used a conservative threshold of determining statistical significance at $p < 0.05$, the discussion of the results presented here also presents marginally statistically significant results at the $p < 0.10$ level. In tables and figures, these findings are indicated by the # symbol. Additionally, the official evaluation includes an abundance of technical details, such as a detailed methodolog-

ical section, information about various sensitivity tests, and statistical tests for possible false discoveries that are the result of multiple comparisons. Readers interested in these technical details are encouraged to consult the official evaluation conducted by the U.S. Department of Education's Institute of Education Sciences, which can be found at http://ies.ed.gov/ncee/pubs/20104018/index.asp.

25. In previous analyses, the two cohorts of students in the impact sample had the potential to experience the same number of years in the program (e.g., three years after application). In spring 2009, the last year evaluation data were collected, cohort 1 students who applied in 2004 (14 percent of the sample) could have used their scholarships for five years, whereas cohort 2 students who applied a year later (86 percent of the sample) could have used their scholarship only for four years. For this reason, we refer to impacts as "after at least four years" because a small portion of the sample—both treatment and control—were in the study a year longer.

26. By 2008–2009 most of the students in the cohort 1 and baseline high school participant subgroups had graded out of the study, and thus we weren't able to continue to analyze the impact of the OSP on them as independent subgroups.

27. Each of these findings refers to one subgroup and not to the paired subgroup categories, and thus a significant finding refers to a treatment versus control difference and not a difference between, for example, males and females.

28. Interaction terms used to test the significance of the differences between the treatment impacts on each subgroup pair (e.g., SINI versus non-SINI) all proved to be insignificant. The practical meaning of this result is that, although some distinct subgroups demonstrated statistically significant impacts at the subgroup level, the impact of the treatment was not significantly different across subgroups. Moreover, these estimations of program impacts at the subgroup level inevitably are less precise, and therefore less likely to identify statistically significant impacts, than the overall analysis of impacts, because each subgroup is merely a portion of the much larger impact sample. For these reasons, the overall results of a statistically significant program impact on attainment should be given the greatest weight when the program is evaluated.

29. Treatment impacts were converted to months of learning based on the average monthly increase in reading scale scores for the control group across all years, weighted for the grade-level composition of the sample.

30. Interaction terms used to test the significance of the differences between the treatment impacts on each subgroup pair (e.g., SINI versus non-SINI) all proved to be insignificant. The practical meaning of that result is that, although some distinct subgroups demonstrated statistically significant impacts at the subgroup level, the impact of the treatment was not significantly different across subgroups. Moreover, these estimations of program impacts at the subgroup level inevitably are less precise, and therefore less likely to identify statistically significant impacts, than the overall analysis of impacts, because each subgroup is merely a portion of the much larger impact sample. For these reasons, the overall achievement results of a statistically significant program impact in reading and no significant impact in math are the clearest and most reliable achievement results from the year 3 analysis and should be given the greatest weight when the program is evaluated on the metric of student achievement.

31. The magnitudes of all these estimated achievement effects are lower than the threshold of 0.12 standard deviations, estimated by the evaluation's power analysis to be the study's minimum detectable effect size.

32. Wolf et al., *Evaluation of the DC Opportunity Scholarship Program: First Year Report*, C-7.

33. Thomas Stewart, Patrick J. Wolf, and Stephen Q. Cornman, *Parent and Student Voices on the First Year of the DC Opportunity Scholarship Program,* SCDP Report 05-01 (Washington, DC: School Choice Demonstration Project, Georgetown University, 2005), v.
34. See Michael D. Johnson and Claes Fornell, "A Framework for Comparing Customer Satisfaction Across Individuals and Product Categories," *Journal of Economic Psychology* 12, no. 2 (1991): 267–286.
35. Section 309, District of Columbia School Choice Incentive Act of 2003.
36. Jay P. Greene, "Vouchers in Charlotte," *Education Matters* 1, no. 2 (2001): 57–58.
37. Only students in grades 4–12 were administered surveys, so the satisfaction of students in early elementary grades is unknown.
38. William Evans and Robert Schwab, "Finishing High School and Starting College: Do Catholic Schools Make a Difference?" *Quarterly Journal of Economics* 110, no. 4 (Nov. 1995): 941–974; Jeff Grogger and Derek A. Neal, "Further Evidence on the Effects of Catholic Secondary Schooling," *Brookings-Wharton Papers on Urban Affairs: 2000* (Washington, DC: Brookings Institution Press, 2000), 151–193; Derek Neal, "The Effects of Catholic Secondary Schooling on Educational Achievement," *Journal of Labor Economics* 15, no. 1 (1997): 98–123; John R. Warren, *Graduation Rates for Choice and Public School Students in Milwaukee, 2003–2008, School Choice Wisconsin Report* (Milwaukee: School Choice Wisconsin, 2010).

Chapter 3

1. National Alliance for Public Charter Schools, *The Public Charter School Dashboard* (Washington, DC: National Alliance for Public Charter Schools, 2009).
2. Lewis Solomon, Kern Paark, and David Garcia, *Does Charter School Attendance Improve Test Scores? The Arizona Results* (Phoenix: Goldwater Institute, 2001); Ron Zimmer, Brian Gill, Kevin Booker, Stephane Lavertu, Tim Sass, and John Witte, *Charter School Operations and Performance: Evidence from California* (Santa Monica, CA: RAND, 2003); Tim R. Sass, "Charter Schools and Student Achievement in Florida," *Education Finance and Policy* 11 (2006): 91–122; Dale Ballou, Bettie Teasley, and Timothy Zeidner, "Charter Schools in Idaho," in *Charter School Outcomes,* eds. Mark Berends, Matthew G. Springer, and Herbert J. Walberg (Mahwah, NJ: Lawrence Erlbaum Associates, 2008), 221–241; Robert Bifulco and Helen F. Ladd, "The Impacts of Charter Schools on Student Achievement: Evidence from North Carolina," *Education Finance and Policy* 11 (2006): 50–90; Robert Bifulco and Helen F. Ladd, "School Choice, Racial Segregation and Test-Score Gaps: Evidence from North Carolina's Charter School Program," *Journal of Policy Analysis and Management* 26, no. 1 (2007): 31–56; Kevin Booker, Scott M. Gilpatric, Timothy Gronberg, and Dennis Jansen, "The Impact of Charter School Attendance on Student Performance," *Journal of Public Economics* 91, no. 5-6 (2007): 849–876; Timothy J. Gronberg and Dennis W. Jansen, *Navigating Newly Chartered Waters: An Analysis of Texas Charter School Performance* (Austin, TX: Texas Public Policy Foundation, 2001); Eric A. Hanushek et al., "Charter School Quality and Parental Decision Making with School Choice," *Journal of Public Economics* 91 (2007): 823–848; John F. Witte, David L. Weimer, Arnold Shober, and Paul F. Scholmer, "The Performance of Charter Schools in Wisconsin," *Journal of Policy Analysis and Management* 26, no. 3 (2007): 557–573.
3. Center for Research on Education Outcomes, Multiple Choice: Charter School Performance in 16 States (Stanford, CA: CREDO, 2009); Philip Gleason, Melissa Clark, Christina Clark Tuttle, and Emily Dwoyer, The Evaluation of Charter School Impacts: Final Report, NCEE 2010-4029 (Washington, DC: National Center for Education Evaluation and

Regional Assistance, Institute of Education Sciences, U.S. Department of Education, 2010); Christina Clark Tuttle, Bing-ru Teh, Ira Nichols-Barrer, Brian P. Gill, and Philip Gleason, Student Characteristics and Achievement in 22 KIPP Middle Schools (Washington, DC: Mathematica Policy Research, 2010); Ron Zimmer, Brian Gill, Kevin Booker, Stephane Lavertu, Tim Sass, and John Witte, Charter Schools in Eight States: Effects on Achievement, Attainment, Integration, and Competition (Santa Monica, CA: RAND, 2009).

4. Atila Abdulkadiroglu, Josh Angrist, Sarah Cohodes, Susan Dynarski, Jon Fullerton, Thomas Kane, and Parag Pathak, *Informing the Debate: Comparing Boston's Charter, Pilot and Traditional Schools* (Boston: The Boston Foundation, 2009); Kevin Booker, Brian Gill, Ron Zimmer, and Tim R. Sass, *Achievement and Attainment in Chicago Charter Schools* (Santa Monica, CA: RAND, 2009); Caroline M. Hoxby and Jonah E. Rockoff, *The Impact of Charter Schools on Student Achievement* (unpublished manuscript, Harvard University and Columbia Business School, 2004); Zimmer et al., *Charter Schools in Eight States*; Ron Zimmer and Richard Buddin, "Charter School Performance in Urban Districts," *Journal of Urban Economics* 60 (2006): 307–326; Caroline M. Hoxby and Sonali Murarka, *New York City's Charter Schools Overall Report* (Cambridge, MA: New York City Charter Schools Evaluation Project, 2007); Caroline M. Hoxby, Sonali Murarka, and Jenny Kang, *How New York City's Charter Schools Affect Achievement* (Cambridge, MA: New York City Charter Schools Evaluation Project, 2009); Ron Zimmer, Suzanne Blanc, Brian Gill, and Jolley Christman, *Evaluating the Performance of Philadelphia's Charter Schools*, WR-550-WPF (Santa Monica, CA: RAND, 2008); Emily Tang and Julian R. Betts, "Student Achievement in Charter Schools in San Diego" (unpublished manuscript, University of California, San Diego, 2006).

5. See Julian R. Betts and Emily Tang, *Value Added and Experimental Studies of the Effect of Charter Schools on Student Achievement* (Seattle: National Charter School Research Project, Center on Reinventing Public Education, University of Washington Bothell, 2009); Brian Gill, P. Mike Timpane, Karen Ross, Dominic Brewer, and Kevin Booker, *Rhetoric Versus Reality: What We Know and What We Need to Know About Vouchers and Charter Schools*, 2nd edition (Santa Monica, CA: RAND, 2007); Paul T. Hill, Lawrence Angel, and Jon Christensen, "Charter School Achievement Studies," *Education Finance and Policy* 1, no. 1 (2006): 139–150; Tom Loveless and Katharyn Field, "Perspectives on Charter Schools," in *Handbook of Research on School Choice*, eds. Mark Berends, Matthew G. Springer, Dale Ballou, and Herbert J. Walberg (New York: Routledge, 2009), 99–114; Gary Miron and Christopher Nelson, "Student Academic Achievement in Charter Schools: What We Know and Why We Know So Little, in *Taking Account of Charter Schools: What's Happened and What's Next?* eds. K. E. Bulkey and P. Wohlstetter (New York: Teachers College Press, 2004), 161–175; Bettie Teasley, "Charter School Outcomes," in *Handbook of Research on School Choice*, eds. Berends et al., 209–225.

6. *Accountability Report on Mayor's Charter Schools* (City of Indianapolis: Office of the Mayor, 2009).

7. David Skinner, "Indianapolis Mayor Bart Peterson: The Peyton Manning of Charter Schools," *Education Next* 7, no. 3 (2007): 33–39.

8. See Brian Peterson, *Transforming Urban Public Education Through Education Entrepreneurship* (New York: Living Cities, Inc., 2009); David Skinner, "Indianapolis Mayor Bart Peterson: The Peyton Manning of Charter Schools."

9. Bryan Hassel, *Fast Break in Indianapolis: A New Approach to Charter Schooling* (Washington, DC: Progressive Policy Institute, 2004).

10. *Accountability Report on Mayor's Charter Schools.*

11. Claire Smrekar, "Taking Charge of Choice: How Charter School Policy Context Matters" (paper presented at the National Center on School Choice conference "School Choice and School Improvement: Research in State, District, and Community Contexts," Vanderbilt University, Nashville, TN, 2009).

12. Hassel, *Fast Break in Indianapolis*; Peterson, *Transforming Urban Public Education Through Education Entrepreneurship.*

13. *Supporting Charter School Excellence Through Quality Authorizing* (Washington, DC: Office of Innovation and Improvement, U.S. Department of Education, 2007).

14. *Accountability Report on Mayor's Charter Schools*; Terri Akey, Jonathan A. Plucker, John A. Hansen, Robert Michael, Suzanne Branon, Rebecca Fagen, and Gary Zhou, *Study of the Effectiveness and Efficiency of Charter Schools in Indiana* (Bloomington: Center for Evaluation and Education Policy, Indiana University, 2008).

15. David Harris and Andrew J. Rotherham, "Get Mayors in the Schooling Game," *Act Locally SF,* March 27, 2007; David Skinner, "Indianapolis Mayor Bart Peterson: The Peyton Manning of Charter Schools."

16. National Association of Charter School Authorizers, *Principles and Standards for Quality Charter School Authorizing* (Chicago: NACSA, 2009).

17. Betts and Tang, *Value Added and Experimental Studies of the Effect of Charter Schools on Student Achievement.*

18. Abdulkadiroglu et al., *Informing the Debate: Comparing Boston's Charter, Pilot and Traditional Schools*; Josh Angrist, Susan Dynarski, Thomas Kane, Parag Pathak, and Christopher Walters, *Who Benefits from KIPP?* NBER working paper 15740, National Bureau of Economic Research, Cambridge, MA, 2010; Will Dobbie and Roland G. Fryer Jr., "Are High-Quality Schools Enough to Close the Achievement Gap? Evidence from a Bold Social Experiment in Harlem" (unpublished manuscript, Harvard University, 2009); Gleason et al., *The Evaluation of Charter School Impacts: Final Report*; Hoxby and Rockoff, *The Impact of Charter Schools on Student Achievement*; Hoxby and Murarka, *New York City's Charter Schools Overall Report*; Hoxby et al., *How New York City's Charter Schools Affect Achievement*; Larry McClure, Betsy Strick, Rachel Jacob-Almeida, and Christopher Reicher, *The Pereuss School at UCSD: School Characteristics and Students' Achievement* (San Diego: The Center for Research on Educational Equity, Assessment and Teaching Excellence, University of California, San Diego, 2005); Jonathan A. Supovitz and Sam Rikoon, *Early Achievement Impacts of the Harlem Success Academy Charter School in New York City* (unpublished manuscript, University of Pennsylvania, 2010).

19. See Center for Research on Education Outcomes, *Multiple Choice: Charter School Performance in 16 States*; Tuttle et al., *Student Characteristics and Achievement in 22 KIPP Middle Schools.*

20. Ballou et al., "Charter Schools in Idaho"; Caroline M. Hoxby and Sonali Murarka, "Methods of Assessing Achievement of Students in Charter Schools," in *Charter School Outcomes*, eds. Berends et al., 7–37.

21. Mark Berends, Ellen Goldring, Marc Stein, and Xiu Cravens, "Instructional Conditions in Charter Schools and Students' Mathematic Achievement Gains," *American Journal of Education* 116, no. 3, 303–335; Mark Berends and Genevieve Zottola, "Social Perspectives on Choice," in *Handbook of Research on School Choice*, eds. Berends et al., 35–53; Tom Loveless and Katharyn Field, "Perspectives on Charter Schools," in *Handbook of Research on School Choice*, eds. Berends et al., 99–114; Teasley, "Charter School Outcomes."

22. Mark Berends, Marc Stein, and John Smithson, "Differences Between Charter and Traditional Public School Teachers' Instructional Practices and Curricular Alignment to the

Mathematics Standards and State Assessment in Indiana" (paper presented at the National Center on School Choice conference "School Choice and School Improvement: Research in State, District, and Community Contexts," Vanderbilt University, Nashville, TN, 2009); Marc Stein, Ellen Goldring, and Genevieve Zottola, "Student Achievement Gains and Parents' Perceptions of Invitations for Involvement in Urban Charter Schools" (paper presented at the Annual Meeting of the American Educational Research Association, New York, 2008).

23. Majida Mehana and Arthur J. Reynolds, "School Mobility and Achievement: A Meta-Analysis," *Children and Youth Services Review* 26 (2004): 93–119.

24. The majority of the Indianapolis charter schools continue to use the NWEA assessment. However, Indianapolis Public Schools ended its contract with NWEA after the 2005–2006 school year.

25. NWEA requests, but does not require, that schools and districts report data on student eligibility for free or reduced-price lunch, special education designation, and English language learner status. Consequently, the frequency and method of reporting these non-required student-level measures vary too much across the charter and traditional public schools to be deemed reliable for inclusion in our analyses.

26. Our formal model is specified as follows:

$$y_{it} - y_{it-1} = \alpha Charter_{it} + \pi Mobility_{it} + \mu_i + \theta_{gt} + v_{it}$$

where $y_{it} - y_{it-1}$ is a measure of the achievement gain of student i in time t. In the model, t equals spring in the current academic year, and $t-1$ equals spring in the preceding academic year. $Charter_{it}$ is an indicator of whether student i attends a charter school in time t; $Mobility_{it}$ is an indicator of whether student i made a nonstructural move in time t; μ_i captures individual student fixed effects; θ_{gt} captures grade-by-year fixed effects; and v_{it} is a random shock.

27. Center for Research on Education Outcomes, *Multiple Choice: Charter School Performance in 16 States*; Zimmer et al., *Evaluating the Performance of Philadelphia's Charter Schools*; Ron Zimmer et al., *Charter Schools in Eight States*.

28. Booker et al., *Achievement and Attainment in Chicago Charter Schools*; Scott Imberman, *Achievement and Behavior in Charter Schools: Drawing a More Complete Picture* (Houston: University of Houston, September 28, 2007, http://www.ncspe.org/publications_files/OP142.pdf); Tang and Betts, "Student Achievement in Charter Schools in San Diego"; Witte et al., "The Performance of Charter Schools in Wisconsin"; Zimmer et al., *Charter School Operations and Performance: Evidence from California*; Zimmer et al., *Charter Schools in Eight States*.

29. Booker et al., *Achievement and Attainment in Chicago Charter Schools*; Timothy J. Gronberg and Dennis W. Jansen, *Texas Charter Schools: An Assessment in 2005* (Austin, TX: Texas Public Policy Foundation), 2005; Tim R. Sass, "Charter Schools and Student Achievement in Florida," *Education Finance and Policy* 11 (2006): 91–122; Tang and Betts, "Student Achievement in Charter Schools in San Diego."

30. Bifulco and Ladd, "The Impacts of Charter Schools on Student Achievement: Evidence from North Carolina"; Booker et al., "The Impact of Charter School Attendance on Student Performance"; Center for Research on Education Outcomes, *Multiple Choice: Charter School Performance in 16 States*; Katrina R. Woodworth, Jane L. David, Roneeta Guha, Haiwen Wang, and Alejandra Lopez-Torkos, *San Francisco Bay Area KIPP Schools: A Study of Early Implementation and Achievement, Final Report* (Menlo Park, CA: SRI International), 2008.

31. We conducted a series of sensitivity tests to explore the possibility that the overall charter school results presented in table 3.4 are influenced by selection bias. For the spring-to-spring

samples, the sensitivity tests indicate that the overall charter school effects in table 3.4 are robust. In other words, the spring-to-spring findings present evidence that the effect on math achievement of attending a charter school in Indianapolis in the first years of the mayor's initiative was positive. The sensitivity tests confirm the need to be cautious about the overall fall-to-spring charter school results presented in table 3.4. It is highly likely that the fall-to-spring findings are biased upward because of selection bias and the negative dip in fall test scores after students move to a new charter school. However, the sensitivity tests indicate that the fall-to-spring effect is either positive or similar to attending a traditional public school; the sensitivity tests did not indicate that students experienced a negative impact on fall-to-spring achievement gains when switching to a charter school.

32. Smrekar, "Taking Charge of Choice: How Charter School Policy Context Matters."

33. *Supporting Charter School Excellence Through Quality Authorizing.*

34. Adam Gamoran, Martin Nystrand, Mark Berends, and Paul LePore, "An Organizational Analysis of the Effects of Ability Grouping," *American Educational Research Journal* 24 (1995), 687–715; Fred M. Newmann, M. Bruce King, and Peter Youngs, "Professional Development That Addresses School Capacity: Lessons from Urban Elementary Schools," *American Journal of Education* 108, no. 4 (2000): 259–299; Brian Rowan, Richard J. Correnti, Robert J. Miller, and Eric M. Camburn, "School Improvement by Design: Lessons from a Study of Comprehensive School Reform Programs," in *Handbook of Education Policy Research,* eds. Gary Sykes, Barbara Schneider, and David N. Plank (New York: Routledge, 2009).

35. Berends et al., "Differences Between Charter and Traditional Public School Teachers' Instructional Practices and Curricular Alignment."

36. Ibid.

37. Marc Stein, Ellen Goldring, and Xiu Cravens, "Do Parents Do as They Say? Academic Preferences in Choosing Charter Schools," in *School Choice and School Improvement,* eds. Mark Berends, Ellen Goldring, and Marisa Cannata (Cambridge, MA: Harvard Education Press, 2011).

Chapter 4

1. We wish to thank Antonio Wendland, Ron Berry, and Ashley Inman for their assistance in obtaining and managing the data used in this investigation and for their help in preparing this chapter.

2. James S. Coleman, *The Adolescent Society: The Social Life of the Teenager and Its Impact on Education* (New York: Free Press, 1962).

3. James S. Coleman, "Academic Achievement and the Structure of Competition," *Harvard Educational Review* 29 (Fall 1959): 330–351.

4. James S. Coleman, "The Adolescent Society," *Education Next* 6 (Winter 2006): 40–43.

5. Coleman, *The Adolescent Society: The Social Life of the Teenager.*

6. Arthur G. Powell, Elaine Farrar, and David K. Cohen, *The Shopping Mall High School: Winners and Losers in the Educational Marketplace* (Boston: Houghton Mifflin, 1985).

7. Ibid., 19.

8. Theodore S. Sizer, *Horace's Compromise: The Dilemma of the American High School* (Boston: Houghton Mifflin, 1984), 54.

9. James S. Coleman and Thomas Hoffer, *Public and Private High Schools: The Impact of Communities* (New York: Basic Books, 1987).

10. Ibid., 303.

11. James S. Coleman, Thomas Hoffer, and Sally Kilgore, "Public and Private Schools" (contractors report prepared for the National Center for Education Statistics, November 1981).

12. Ibid.

13. Robert D. Putnam, "The Prosperous Community: Social Capital and Public Life," *American Prospect* 13 (1993): 4–13; Robert D. Putnam, "Bowling Alone: America's Declining Social Capital," *Journal of Democracy* 6, no. 1 (1995): 65–78; Robert D. Putnam, *Bowling Alone: The Collapse and Revival of American Community* (New York: Simon & Schuster, 2000).

14. Anthony Bryk, Valerie Lee, and Peter B. Holland, *Catholic Schools and the Common Good* (Cambridge, MA: Harvard University Press, 1993).

15. H. Naci Mocan and Erdal Tekin, "Catholic Schools and Bad Behavior: A Propensity Score Matching Analysis," *Contributions to Economic Analysis and Policy* 5, no. 1 (2006): 1–34.

16. David N. Figlio and Jens Ludwig, "Sex, Drugs and Catholic Schools: Private Schooling and Adolescent Behaviors," working paper no. 30, National Center for the Study of Privatization in Education, New York, 2001.

17. Clive R. Belfield, "Modeling School Choice: A Comparison of Public, Private-Independent, Private-Religious and Home-Schooled Students," *Education Policy Analysis Archives* 12, no. 30 (2004): 1–18.

18. Stephen Morgan, "Counterfactuals Causal Effect Heterogeneity and the Catholic School Effect on Learning," *Sociology of Education* 74 (2001): 341–374; Joseph Altonji, Todd Elder, and Christopher R. Taber, "Selection on Observed and Unobserved Variables: Assessing the Effectiveness of Catholic Schools," *Journal of Political Economy* 113, no. 1 (2005): 151–184; William N. Evans and Robert M. Schwab, "Finishing High School and Starting College: Do Catholic Schools Make a Difference?" *Quarterly Journal of Economics* 110, no. 4 (1995): 941–974; Derek Neal, "How Vouchers Could Change the Market for Education," *Journal of Economic Perspectives* 16, no. 4 (2002): 25–44.

19. Richard J. Murnane, Stuart Newstead, and Randall J. Olsen, "Comparing Public and Private Schools: The Puzzling Role of Selectivity Bias," *Journal of Business & Economic Statistics* 3, no. 1 (January 1985): 23–35; David Figlio and Joe Stone, "Are Private Schools Really Better?" *Research in Labor Economics*, 1999: 115–140.

20. Neal, "How Vouchers Could Change the Market for Education."

21. Helen Ladd, "School Vouchers: A Critical View," *Journal of Economic Perspectives* 16, no. 4 (2002): 3–24.

22. Sean Reardon, Jacob Cheadle, and Joseph P. Robinson, "The Effect of Catholic Schooling on Math and Reading Development in Kindergarten Through Fifth Grade," *Journal of Research on Educational Effectiveness* 2 (2009): 45–87.

23. Paul E. Peterson and Elaine Llaudet, "Heterogeneity in School Sector Effects on Elementary Student Performance," PEPG discussion paper 07-08, Program on Education Policy and Governance, Harvard University, Boston, 2007.

24. William Carbonaro, "Student Learning: Sector Differences in Achievement Gains Across School Years and During the Summer," in *School Sector and Student Outcomes*, ed. Maureen Hallinan (Notre Dame, IN: University of Notre Dame Press, 2006); William Carbonaro, "Public-Private Differences in Achievement Among Kindergarten Students: Differences in Learning Opportunities and Student Outcomes," *American Journal of Education* 113, no. 29 (2006): 31–65.

25. For labor market outcomes, see, for example, Samuel Bowles, with Herbert Gintis and Melissa Osborne, "Incentive-Enhancing Preferences: Schooling, Behavior, and Earnings," *American Economic Review* 91, no.2 (2001): 155–158; James J. Heckman and Yona Rubenstein, "The Importance of Non-cognitive Skills: Lessons from GED Testing Program,"

American Economic Review 91, no. 2 (2001): 145–149; Pedro Carneiro and James J. Heckman, "Human Capital Policy," in *Inequality in America: What Role for Human Capital Policies?* eds. James J. Heckman and Alan B. Krueger (Cambridge, MA: MIT Press, 2003), 1–11; George Farkas, "Cognitive Skills and Non-Cognitive Traits and Behaviors in Stratification Processes," *Annual Review of Sociology* 29 (2003): 541–620. For other outcomes, see James J. Heckman, Jora Stixrud, and Sergio Urzua, "The Effects of Cognitive and Non Cognitive Abilities on Labor Market Outcomes and Social Behaviors," *Journal of Labor Economics* 24, no. 3 (2006): 411–482.

26. These results and other detailed results discussed later that are not shown in the accompanying tables are available from the authors upon request.

27. Evidence for the usefulness of this taxonomy has been accumulating since Fiske's early research (Donald W. Fiske, "Consistency of the Factorial Structures of Personality Ratings from Different Sources," *Journal of Abnormal Social Psychology* 44 (1949): 329–344). Most notable is the work of such scholars as W. T. Norman, "Toward an Adequate Taxonomy of Personality Attributes: Replicated Factor Structure in Peer Nomination Personality Ratings," *Journal of Abnormal and Social Psychology* 66 (1963): 574–583; Lewis R. Goldberg, "Language and Individual Differences: The Search for Universals in Personality Lexicons," in *Review of Personality and Social Psychology*, vol. 2, ed. L. Wheeler (Beverly Hills, CA: Sage, 1981); and Robert R. McCrae and Paul T. Costa, "Validation of the Five-Factor Model of Personality Across Instruments and Observers," *Journal of Personality and Social Psychology* 52 (1987): 81–90. Recently, a number of behavioral economists have put the taxonomy to creative use; examples are Ernst Fehr and Simon Gächter, "Fairness and Retaliation: The Economics of Reciprocity," *Journal of Economic Perspectives* 14, no. 3 (2000): 159–181; Charles A. Holt and Susan K. Laury, "Risk Aversion and Incentive Effects," *American Economic Review* 92, no. 5 (2002): 1644–1655; Armin Falk, "You Get What You Pay For: Incentives and Selection in the Education System," PEPG discussion paper 08-06, Harvard, Boston, 2008; Tomad Dohmen, Armin Falk, David Huffman, and Uwe Sunde, "Homo Reciprocans: Survey Evidence on Behavioural Outcomes," *Economic Journal* 119 (2009): 592–612. As it relates to our scheme, the first two categories within this taxonomy—agreeableness and conscientiousness—resemble social capital as Coleman defined it in that they appear to identify a readiness to conform to social norms, whereas the other three categories—extroversion, neuroticism, and openness to experiences—seem to fall within our second category: individual psychological traits not easily shaped directly by others outside the family. Unfortunately, we cannot provide a direct test of the usefulness of the Big Five taxonomy, because the categories are not easily matched to the scales ECLS-K has made available.

28. See ECLS-K user's manuals, first, third, fifth, and eighth grades. The ECLS-K eighth-grade manual (sections 3-25 to 3-36) provides measures of reliability for most of the composite variables in the data set. The reliability is estimated as the variance on repeated estimates of ability compared with total sample variance. For the other variables the measurement is related to the consistency of each of the items and to the score scale as a whole.

29. Correlations for the conformity to social norms measures range from 0.12 to 0.60, and correlations for the psychological traits vary between 0.06 and 0.59. Correlations of items in the social norm index with those in the psychological trait index vary between −0.06 and 0.35.

30. Table 4.2 provides the descriptive statistics for mother's education, but that variable is not used separately in any of the models because it is a component of the socioeconomic status index.

31. See appendix B (http://www.vanderbilt.edu/schoolchoice/) for a discussion of the ordered probit model used in the analysis.

32. See appendix B (http://www.vanderbilt.edu/schoolchoice/) for the procedures used in the matched comparison analysis.

33. Rajeev H. Dehejia and Sadek Wahba, "Propensity Score-Matching Methods for Nonexperimental Causal Studies," *Review of Economics and Statistics* 84 (2002): 151–175.

34. That is, the "common support," following Sascha O. Becker and Andrea Ichino, "Estimation of Average Treatment Effects Based on Propensity Scores," *Stata Journal* 2, no. 4 (2002): 358–377.

35. The other methods used are caliper matching, radius (with a range of calipers), and Mahalanobis metric matching.

36. Becker and Ichino, "Estimation of Average Treatment Effects Based on Propensity Scores."

37. Alberto Abadie et al., "Implementing Matching Estimators for Average Treatment Effects in Stata," *Stata Journal* 4, no. 3 (2004): 290–311.

38. Gary King, Michael Tomz, and Jason Wittenberg, "Making the Most of Statistical Analyses: Improving Interpretation and Presentation," *American Journal of Political Science* 44, no. 2 (2000): 341–355.

39. Stef Van Buuren and Karin Oudshoorn, "Flexible multivariate imputation by MICE," v. 1.0 user's manual (Leiden: TNO Preventie en Gezondheid, 1999).

40. Stephen W. Raudenbush and Anthony S. Bryk, "Hierarchical Model for Studying School Effects," *Sociology of Education* 59, no. 1 (1986): 1–17.

41. Table C1 (http://www.vanderbilt.edu/schoolchoice/) presents complete results for estimates of homework completion and classroom disruption in English classes.

42. Because ECLS-K split the sample in half between the math and science teachers, there are not enough observations to estimate impacts using the matched comparison model.

43. Gary King, James Honaker, Anne Joseph, and Kenneth Scheve, "Analyzing Incomplete Political Science Data: An Alternative Algorithm for Multiple Imputation," *American Political Science Review* 95 (2001): 49–69.

44. In an ordered probit model a significantly positive coefficient indicates that increasing the relevant independent variable increases the probability that the noncognitive dependent variable will take on the highest value, and it reduces the probability that the dependent variable will take on the lowest value. The impact on the probabilities that the dependent variable will take on the intermediate values is a priori unclear. See William Greene, *Econometric Analysis*, 5th ed. (Englewood Cliffs, NJ: Prentice Hall, 2003), 875–879, for further details. We also calculated the marginal effects at the means of the independent variables without simulations. Estimated impacts were similar regardless of method used.

45. For example, we can observe that there is a 2.6 percent probability that tardiness will take the value of 3 ("some of the time"), a 22.4 percent probability that it will take the value 4 ("rarely"), and a 74.5 percent probability that it will take the value of 5 ("never").

Chapter 5

1. U.S. Department of Education, *Public School Choice Non-Regulatory Guidance*, January 14, 2009, http://www/ed.gov/policy/elsec/guid/schoolchoiceguid/pdf.

2. Office of Communications and Outreach, *Guide to U.S. Department of Education Programs* (Washington, DC: U.S. Department of Education, 2008).

3. Education Commission of the States, *Intra-district Transfer: 50 State Report,* 2008, http://mb2.ecs.org/reports/Report.aspx?id=268.

4. Roslyn A. Mickelson and Stephanie Southworth, "When Opting Out Is Not a Choice: Implications for NCLB's Transfer Option from Charlotte, North Carolina," *Equity & Excellence in Education* 38, no. 3 (2005): 249–263; Ruth Neild, "Parent Management of School Choice in a Large Urban District," *Urban Education* 40, no. 3 (2005): 270–297.

5. Julie B. Cullen, Brian A. Jacob, and Steven D. Levitt, "The Impact of School Choice on Student Outcomes: An Analysis of the Chicago Public Schools," *Journal of Public Economics* 89 (2005): 729–760; James J. Kemple, *Career Academies: Impacts on Students' Initial Transitions to Post-Secondary Education and Employment* (New York: Manpower Demonstration Research Corporation, 2001).

6. Jacqueline Ancess and David Allen, "Implementing Small Theme High Schools in New York City: Great Intentions and Great Tensions," *Harvard Educational Review* 76, no. 3 (2006): 401–416; Casey D. Cobb and Gene V. Glass, "Ethnic Segregation in Arizona Charter Schools," *Education Policy Analysis Archives* 7, no. 1 (1999); Hamilton Lankford and James Wyckoff, "Who Would Be Left Behind by Enhanced Private School Choice?" *Journal of Urban Economics* 50 (2001): 288–312.

7. Adam Gamoran, "Student Achievement in Public Magnet, Public Comprehensive, and Private City High Schools," *Educational Evaluation and Policy Analysis* 18, no. 1 (1996): 1–18.

8. Yu Yang, Yuan Li, Leroy Tompkins, and Shahpar Modarresi, "Using the Multiple-Matched-Sample and Statistical Controls to Examine the Effects of Magnet School Programs on the Reading and Mathematics Performance of Students" (paper presented at the annual meeting of the American Educational Research Association, Montreal, Canada, 2005).

9. James J. Kemple and Jason Snipes, *Career Academies: Impacts on Students' Engagement and Performance in High School* (San Francisco: Manpower Demonstration Research Corporation, 2000).

10. Caroline M. Hoxby, Sonali Murarka, and Jenny Kang, *How New York City's Charter Schools Affect Achievement* (Cambridge, MA: New York City Charter Schools Evaluation Project, 2009).

11. Lewis Soloman, Kern Paark, and David Garcia, *Does Charter School Attendance Improve Test Scores? The Arizona Results* (Phoenix: The Goldwater Institute, 2001).

12. E. P. Bettinger, "The Effect of Charter Schools on Charter Students and Public Schools," *Economics of Education Review* 24, no. 2 (2005): 133–147; Robert Bifulco and Helen Ladd, "The Impacts of Charter Schools on Student Achievement: Evidence from North Carolina," *Education Finance and Policy* 1, no. 1 (2006): 50–90; Randall W. Eberts and Kevin M. Hollenbeck, "Impact of Charter School Attendance on Student Achievement in Michigan" (paper presented at the annual meeting of the American Educational Research Association, New Orleans, 2002); Tim R. Sass, "Charter Schools and Student Achievement in Florida," *Education Finance and Policy* 1, no. 1 (2006): 91–122.

13. Richard Buddin and Ron Zimmer, "Student Achievement in Charter Schools: A Complex Picture," *Journal of Policy Analysis and Management* 24, no. 2 (2004): 351–371; Eric A. Hanushek, John F. Kain, and Steven G. Rivkin, "The Impact of Charter Schools on Academic Achievement," unpublished manuscript, 2002.

14. Paul T. Hill, Lawrence Angel, and Jon Christensen, "Charter School Achievement Studies," *Education Finance and Policy* 1, no. 1 (2006): 139–150.

15. Significant positive effects are reported by Jay P. Greene, Paul E. Peterson, and Jiangtao Du, "The Effectiveness of School Choice: The Milwaukee Experiment," *Harvard University Education Policy and Governance Occasional Paper* 97, no. 1 (1997). Mixed effects are reported by William G. Howell and Paul E. Peterson, *The Education Gap: Vouchers and Urban Schools* (Washington, DC: Brookings Institute Press, 2002); and Cecelia E. Rouse,

"Private School Vouchers and Student Achievement: An Evaluation of the Milwaukee Parental Choice Program," *Quarterly Journal of Economics* 113, no. 2 (1998): 553–602. No effects were found by John F. Witte, Troy D. Sterr, and Christopher A. Thorn, "Fifth-year Report: Milwaukee Parental Choice Program," unpublished paper, University of Wisconsin, 1995; Jonathan A. Plucker, Matthew C. Makel, John A. Hansen, and Patricia A. Muller, "Achievement Effects of the Cleveland Voucher Program on High Ability Elementary School Students," *Journal of School Choice* 1, no. 4 (2007): 77–88.

16. Alan B. Krueger and Pei Zhu, *Another Look at the New York City Voucher Experiment* (Cambridge, MA: National Bureau of Economic Research), 2002.

17. Witte et al., "Fifth-year Report: Milwaukee Parental Choice Program."

18. Greene et al., "The Effectiveness of School Choice: The Milwaukee Experiment."

19. Rouse, "Private School Vouchers and Student Achievement: An Evaluation of the Milwaukee Parental Choice Program."

20. Howell and Peterson, *The Education Gap: Vouchers and Urban Schools.*

21. Krueger and Zhu, *Another Look at the New York City Voucher Experiment.*

22. Umut Ozek, "The Effects of Open Enrollment on School Choice and Student Outcomes," working paper 26, Urban Institute, Washington, D.C., 2009.

23. Justine S. Hastings and Jeffrey M. Weinstein, "Information, School Choice, and Academic Achievement: Evidence from Two Experiments," *Quarterly Journal of Economics* 123, no. 4 (2008): 1373–1414.

24. Caroline M. Hoxby, *School Choice and School Productivity: Or Could School Choice Be a Tide That Lifts All Boats?* (Cambridge, MA: National Bureau of Economic Research, 2002).

25. Hastings and Weinstein, "Information, School Choice, and Academic Achievement: Evidence from Two Experiments."

26. Mickelson and Southworth, "When Opting Out Is Not a Choice."

27. Patricia A. Bauch and Ellen Goldring, "Parent Involvement and School Responsiveness: Facilitating the Home School Connection in Schools of Choice," *Educational Evaluation and Policy Analysis* 17, no. 1 (1995): 1–21; Justine S. Hastings, Thomas J. Kane, and Douglas O. Staiger, *Parental Preferences and School Competition: Evidence from a Public School Choice Program* (Cambridge, MA: National Bureau of Economic Research, 2005).

28. Ancess and Allen, "Implementing Small Theme High Schools in New York City"; Jennifer Jellison Holme, "Buying Homes, Buying Schools: School Choice and the Social Construction of School Quality," *Harvard Educational Review* 72, no. 2 (2002): 177–205; Lankford and Wyckoff, "Who Would Be Left Behind by Enhanced Private School Choice?"; Douglas L. Lauen, "Contextual Explanations of School Choice," *Sociology of Education* 80, no. 3 (2000): 179–209; Kristie J. R. Phillips, Charles S. Hausman, and Elizabeth Larsen, "Open Enrollment Choice Plans: Students Who Choose and the Schools They Leave" (presentation given at the Annual Meeting of the American Sociological Association, Boston, 2008).

29. Holme, "Buying Homes, Buying Schools: School Choice and the Social Construction of School Quality."

30. Ancess and Allen, "Implementing Small Theme High Schools in New York City."

31. Hill et al., "Charter School Achievement Studies."

32. David L. Levinson, Peter W. Cookson, and Alan R. Sadovnik, eds., *Education and Sociology* (New York: RoutledgeFalmer, 2002).

33. Dennis Epple and Richard E. Romano, "Competition Between Private and Public Schools, Vouchers, and Peer-Group Effects," *American Economic Review* 88, no. 1 (1998): 33–62.

34. Jeffrey R. Henig, *Rethinking School Choice: Limits of the Market Metaphor* (Princeton, NJ: Princeton University Press, 1994).

35. Cullen et al., "The Impact of School Choice on Student Outcomes: An Analysis of the Chicago Public Schools"; Brian A. Jacob, Lars Lefgren, and David Sims, "The Persistence of Teacher-Induced Learning Gains," NBER working paper, National Bureau of Economic Research, Cambridge, MA, 2008; Hastings and Weinstein, "Information, School Choice, and Academic Achievement: Evidence from Two Experiments"; Caroline M. Hoxby and Sonali Murarka, *Charter Schools in New York City: Who Enrolls and How They Affect Their Students' Achievement* (Cambridge, MA: National Bureau of Economic Research, 2009); Krueger and Zhu, *Another Look at the New York City Voucher Experiment*; Ozek, "The Effects of Open Enrollment on School Choice and Student Outcomes"; Plucker et al., "Achievement Effects of the Cleveland Voucher Program on High Ability Elementary School Students"; Rouse, "Private School Vouchers and Student Achievement: An Evaluation of the Milwaukee Parental Choice Program"; Patrick Wolf, Babette Gutmann, Michael Puma, Brian Kisida, Lou Rizzo, and Nada Eissa, *Evaluation of the DC Opportunity Scholarship Program: Impacts After Three Years* (Washington, DC: National Center for Education Evaluation and Regional Assistance, 2009).

36. Ozek, "The Effects of Open Enrollment on School Choice and Student Outcomes."

37. Office of Communication and Outreach, *Guide to U.S. Department of Education Programs* (Washington, DC: Office of Communication and Outreach, U.S. Department of Education, 2008).

38. Albert M. Camarillo, "Cities of Color: The New Racial Frontier in California's Minority-Majority Cities," *Pacific Historical Review* 76, no. 1 (2007): 1–28.

39. See Bauch and Goldring, "Parent Involvement and School Responsiveness"; Hastings et al., *Parental Preferences and School Competition*; Mickelson and Southworth, "When Opting Out Is Not a Choice."

40. See Charles T. Clotfelter, Helen F. Ladd, and Jacob L. Vigdor, "Teacher Credentials and Student Achievement: Longitudinal Analysis with Student Fixed Effects," *Economics of Education Review* 26 (2007): 673–682; Betheny Gross, Kevin Booker, and Dan Goldhaber, "Boosting Student Achievement: The Effect of Comprehensive School Reform on Student Achievement," *Education Evaluation and Policy Analysis* 31, no. 2 (2009): 111–126; Hoxby and Murarka, *Charter Schools in New York City: Who Enrolls and How They Affect Their Students' Achievement*; Jacob et al., "The Persistence of Teacher-Induced Learning Gains"; Bruce Sacerdote, "When the Saints Come Marching In: Effects of Hurricanes Katrina and Rita on Student Evacuees," NBER working paper, National Bureau of Economic Research, Cambridge, MA, 2008.

41. Kindergarteners were also excluded because they did not participate in state testing.

42. Hastings and Weinstein, "Information, School Choice, and Academic Achievement: Evidence from Two Experiments."

43. For a more detailed discussion about the coding of the control variables, please refer to the online link, http://www.vanderbilt.edu/schoolchoice/, for our appendix.

44. Donald B. Rubin, *Matched Sampling for Causal Effects* (New York: Cambridge, 2006).

45. For a more detailed discussion about PSM and its application in this study, please refer to the online link, http://www.vanderbilt.edu/schoolchoice/, for our appendix.

46. Additional information about the modeling and weighting procedures used in this study is included in the technical appendix, which is available online at http://www.vanderbilt.edu/schoolchoice/.

47. Holme, "Buying Homes, Buying Schools: School Choice and the Social Construction of School Quality"; Ancess and Allen, "Implementing Small Theme High Schools in New York City."
48. Phillips et al., "Open Enrollment Choice Plans: Students Who Choose and the Schools They Leave."
49. As is evident in the second models in tables 5.1 and 5.2, students who are zoned to higher-performing schools as well as students who choose to leave one higher-performing school to attend another higher-performing school are significantly more likely to score higher in language arts and mathematics than students who are zoned to lower-performing schools. However, the effect associated with using intradistrict transfer to leave a higher-performing zoned school and choose another higher-performing school disappears when the appropriate reference group is used. In other words, when compared to students who were zoned to a higher-performing school and did not exercise choice, students who were zoned to a higher-performing school and chose another higher-performing school are not likely to experience increases in academic achievement as a result of intradistrict transfer participation.
50. Phillips et al., "Open Enrollment Choice Plans: Students Who Choose and the Schools They Leave."

Chapter 6

1. Jeffrey R. Henig, *Rethinking School Choice: Limits of the Market Metaphor* (Princeton, NJ: Princeton University Press, 1994); Mark Schneider, Paul Teske, and Melissa Marschall, *Choosing Schools: Consumer Choice and the Quality of American Schools* (Princeton, NJ: Princeton University Press, 2000); Thomas Dee and Helen Fu, "Do Charter Schools Skim Students or Drain Resources?" *Economics of Education Review* 23, no. 3 (2004): 259–271.
2. John F. Witte and Christopher A. Thorn, "Who Chooses? Voucher and Interdistrict Choice Programs in Milwaukee," *American Journal of Education* 104 (1996): 186–217.
3. Examples include Henig, *Rethinking School Choice: Limits of the Market Metaphor*; Jeffrey R. Henig, "What Social Science Is—and Is Not—Resolving About the School Choice Debate: Reactions to 'School Choice and Culture Wars' and 'Liberal Equity in Education,'" *Social Science Quarterly* 79 (1998): 541–547; B. Kleitz, W. Gregory, T. Kent, and Richard Matland, "Choice, Charter Schools, and Household Preferences," *Social Science Quarterly* 81 (2000): 846–854; Gregory R. Weiher and Kent L. Tedin, "Does Choice Lead to Racially Distinctive Schools? Charter Schools and Household Preferences," *Journal of Policy Analysis and Management* 21 (2002): 79–92.
4. Natalie Lacireno-Paquet, Thomas T. Holyoke, Michele Moser, and Jeffrey R. Henig, "Creaming Versus Cropping: Charter School Enrollment Practices in Response to Market Incentives," *Educational Evaluation and Policy Analysis*, 24, no. 2 (2002): 145–158.
5. Dee and Fu, "Do Charter Schools Skim Students or Drain Resources?"
6. Mark Berends and Genevieve Zottola, "Social Perspectives on School Choice," in *Handbook of Research on School Choice*, eds. Mark Berends, Matthew G. Springer, Dale Ballou, and Herbert J. Walberg (New York: Routledge, 2009), 37.
7. Schneider et al., *Choosing Schools: Consumer Choice and the Quality of American Schools.*
8. Ted Kolderie, *Beyond Choice to New Public Schools: Withdrawing the Exclusive Franchise in Public Education* (Washington, DC: Progressive Policy Institute, 1990).
9. Joseph Murphy and Catherine Dunn Shiffman, *Understanding and Assessing the Charter School Movement* (New York: Teachers College Press, 2002).

10. Mark Schneider, Melissa Marschall, Paul Teske, and Christine Roch, "School Choice and Culture Wars in the Classroom: What Different Parents Seek from Education," *Social Science Quarterly* 79 (1998): 496–498.

11. Kleitz et al., "Choice, Charter Schools, and Household Preferences"; Claire Smrekar, "The Social Context of Magnet Schools," in *Handbook of Research on School Choice*, eds. Berends et al., 393–407; Schneider et al., "School Choice and Culture Wars in the Classroom"; Mark Schneider and Jack Buckley, "What Do Parents Want from Schools? Evidence from the Internet," *Educational Evaluation and Policy Analysis* 24 (2002): 133–144.

12. See Seymour Sudman and Norman M. Bradburn, *Asking Questions: The Definitive Guide to Questionnaire Design—For Market Research, Political Polls, and Social and Health Questionnaires* (Hoboken, NJ: John Wiley & Sons, 1982); Andrew Schwartz, Colleen Schwartz, and Tracey Rizzuto, "Examining the 'Urban Legend' of Common Method Bias: Nine Common Errors and Their Impact" (paper presented at the forty-first Annual Hawaii International Conference on System Sciences, Big Island, Hawaii, 2008).

13. Schneider et al., *Choosing Schools: Consumer Choice and the Quality of American Schools.*

14. Kleitz et al., "Choice, Charter Schools, and Household Preferences."

15. Weiher and Tedin, "Does Choice Lead to Racially Distinctive Schools?"; Paul Teske, Jody Fitzpatrick, and Gabriel Kaplan, *Opening Doors: How Low-Income Parents Search for the Right School* (Seattle: Daniel J. Evans Schools of Public Affairs, 2007).

16. Valerie E. Lee, Robert G. Croninger, and Julie B. Smith, "Equity and Choice in Detroit," in *Who Chooses? Who Loses? Culture, Institutions, and the Unequal Effects of School Choice*, eds. B. Fuller and R. F. Elmore with G. Orfield (New York: Teachers College Press, 1996), 70–91.

17. E. Goldring and K. Rowley, "Parent Preferences and Parent Choices: The Public–Private Decision About School Choice," *Journal of Educational Policy* 23, no. 3(2008): 209–230.

18. Schneider et al., "School Choice and Culture Wars in the Classroom."

19. Lee et al., "Equity and Choice in Detroit."

20. Schwartz et al., "Examining the 'Urban Legend' of Common Method Bias."

21. William D. Crano and Marilynn B. Brewer, *Principles and Methods of Social Research* (Mahway, NJ: Lawrence Erlbaum Associates, 2002).

22. Kleitz et al., "Choice, Charter Schools, and Household Preferences."

23. Weiher and Tedin, "Does Choice Lead to Racially Distinctive Schools?"

24. Donald T. Campbell and Donald W. Fiske, "Convergent and Discriminant Validation by the Multitrait-multimethod Matrix," *Psychological Bulletin* 56, no. 2 (1959): 81–105.

25. Ron Zimmer, Brian Gill, Kevin Booker, Stephane Lavertu, Tim R. Sass, and John Witte, *Charter Schools in Eight States: Effects on Achievement, Attainment, Integration, and Competition* (Santa Monica, CA: RAND, 2009).

26. Kevin Booker, Ron Zimmer, and Richard Buddin, *The Effect of Charter Schools on School Peer Composition* (Washington, DC: RAND, 2005).

27. Robert Bifulco and Helen Ladd, "School Choice, Racial Segregation, and Test-Score Gaps: Evidence from North Carolina's Charter School Program," *Journal of Policy Analysis and Management* 26 (2006): 31–56.

28. Zimmer et al., *Charter Schools in Eight States.* The schools were located in Chicago, Denver, Milwaukee, Philadelphia, and San Diego, along with one each in Ohio and Texas.

29. Henig, *Rethinking School Choice: Limits of the Market Metaphor*; Salvatore Saporito and Annette Lareau, "School Selection as a Process: The Multiple Dimensions of Race in Framing Educational Choice," *Social Problems* 46, no. 3 (1999): 418–439.

30. Center for Education Reform, *Annual Survey of America's Charter Schools: 2010* (Washington, DC: Center for Education Reform, 2010).

31. The two academic-related responses were academic quality and academic focus. The other reasons included size of school's enrollment, extracurricular activities, services for special-needs students, opportunities for parental involvement, safety at school, discipline at school, school location, and other.

32. Mayoral charters in Indianapolis also tested a majority of their eleventh-grade students in 2006–2007 (64 percent). Exclusion of these students did not change the results, and therefore they are included in this study. The number of students contacted is low for several reasons. We can track students only if they were previously enrolled in a school that contracted with NWEA for testing. Further, we cannot track students who have only ever been enrolled in their current charter school, homeschooled, or enrolled in a private school.

33. Although the level of response is consistent for most grades, we do see a slight decline from lower to higher grades in the way parents rated academic focus and quality as a top priority. Grades were classified as being elementary (K–5), middle school (6–8), or high school (9–11). There are no significant differences between elementary and middle school parents in their ATP rating, but there are significant differences between high school parents and parents of children in the lower two levels.

34. ($\chi^2 = 7.84$, P<0.05)

35. Standardization was based on all schools and grades contained in our database for Indiana, representing approximately seven hundred fifty schools across the state.

36. Claire Smrekar and Ellen Goldring, *School Choice in Urban America: Magnet Schools and the Pursuit of Equity* (New York: Teachers College Press, 1999).

37. William Howell, "Switching Schools? A Closer Look at Parents' Initial Interest In and Knowledge About the Choice Provisions of No Child Left Behind," *Peabody Journal of Education* 81, no. 1 (2006): 140–179.

38. Jack Buckley and Mark Schneider, "Shopping for Schools: How Do Marginal Consumers Gather Information about Schools?" *Policies Studies Journal* 31, no. 2 (2003): 121–147.

39. Smrekar, "The Social Context of Magnet Schools."

Chapter 7

1. Jennifer J. Holme, "Buying Homes, Buying Schools: School Choice and the Social Construction of School Quality," *Harvard Educational Review* 72, no. 2 (2002): 177–205.

2. Carol Ascher, Norm Fruchter, and Robert Berne, *Hard Lessons: Public Schools and Privatization* (New York: Twentieth Century Fund, 1996); Mark Schneider, Paul Teske, and Melissa Marschall, *Choosing Schools: Consumer Choice and the Quality of American Schools* (Princeton, NJ: Princeton University Press, 2000).

3. Mark Schneider, Paul Teske, Melissa Marschall, and Christine Roch, "Shopping for Schools: In the Land of the Blind, the One-Eyed Parent May Be Enough," *American Journal of Political Science* 42 (1998): 769–793.

4. Mark Schneider, Paul Teske, Christine Roch, and Melissa Marschall, "Networks to Nowhere: Segregation and Stratification in Networks of Information About Schools," *American Journal of Political Science* 41, no. 4 (1997), 1201–1223.

5. Kimberly A. Goyette, "Race, Social Background, and School Choice Options," *Equity & Excellence in Education* 41, no. 1 (2008): 114–129.

6. Carnegie Foundation for the Advancement of Teaching, *School Choice: A Special Report* (Princeton, NJ: Carnegie Foundation, 1992); Amy Stuart Wells, "The Sociology of School Choice: Why Some Win and Others Lose in the Educational Market Place," in

School Choice: Examining the Evidence, eds. E. Rasell and R. Rothstein (Washington, DC: Economic Policy Institute, 1993), 29–48; Kevin B. Smith and Kenneth J. Meier, *The Case Against School Choice: Politics, Markets and Fools* (Armonk, NY: M.E. Sharpe, 1995).
7. Claire Smrekar and Ellen Goldring, *School Choice in Urban America: Magnet Schools and the Pursuit of Equity* (New York: Teachers College Press, 1999).
8. Diane Reay and Stephen J. Ball, "'Making Up Their Minds': Family Dynamics of School Choice," *British Educational Research Journal* 24, no. 4 (1998): 431–448; D. Reay and H. Lucey, "Children, School Choice, and Social Differences," *Educational Studies* 26, no. 1 (2000): 83–100.
9. Valerie E. Lee, Robert C. Croninger, and Julie B. Smith, "Equity and Choice in Detroit," in *Who Chooses? Who Loses? Culture, Institutions, and the Unequal Effects of School Choice*, eds. B. Fuller and R. F. Elmore with G. Orfield (New York: Teachers College Press, 1996).
10. Christopher Lubienski, Charisse Gulosino, and Peter Weitzel, "School Choice and Competitive Incentives: Mapping the Distribution of Educational Opportunities Across Local Education Markets," *American Journal of Education* 115, no. 4 (2009): 601–647.
11. Harry Brighouse, "Educational Equality and Varieties of School Choice," in *School Choice and Outcomes: Empirical and Philosophical Perspectives*, eds. W. Feinberg and C. Lubienski (Albany: State University of New York Press, 2008).
12. The original consent decree was modified in 2004 and 2006. CPS was operating under Second Amended Consent Decree until September 2009, when a federal judge terminated the consent decree requiring CPS to use race as a factor in admissions decisions. Current CPS CEO Ron Huberman, however, has stated that race will still be used as a consideration in admissions to magnet and selective-enrollment schools; Rebecca Harris and Sarah Karp, "At Busy Board Meeting, Race Back in Mix in Magnet and Selective School Admission Policy," *Catalyst Chicago* blog, 2009, http://www.catalyst-chicago.org/notebook/index.php/entry/481/At_busy_board_meeting%2C_race_back_in_mix_in_magnet_and_selective_school_admission_policy.
13. Larry Stanton, "Chicago High Schools High School Transformation" (presentation to the Steering Committee of the Consortium on Chicago School Research, Chicago, 2006).
14. This is a conservative indication of how much "choice" there is in the system, because some students attending their neighborhood school were probably satisfied with their assignment and chose to stay in the neighborhood. Given the high number of special programs offered by neighborhood schools, a portion of students may have applied and were admitted to programs within their assigned neighborhood schools.
15. There is no limit to the number of applications one student can send. However, students can apply to only one program at any school that offers multiple programs.
16. Even though scores do not play a role in selecting students when a random lottery is used, most applications require students to send their seventh-grade scores.
17. This is how the system works in theory, but schools with open seats after April will take students.
18. Brighouse, "Educational Equality and Varieties of School Choice."
19. These interviews were collected as part of a longitudinal, multimethod research study examining students' transition from elementary to high school in CPS.
20. See the appendix online at http://www.vanderbilt.edu/schoolchoice/ for a detailed description of the sample of students and the statistical analyses.
21. Students in the top quartile of CPS test takers on the eighth-grade ISAT exam are defined as "top performers" in table 7.1. Students in the bottom quartile on the exam are labeled as "bottom performers."

22. Students in our qualitative sample were assigned to attend five different neighborhood high schools. Two of the schools contained predominantly African American students; three, predominantly Latino students. The schools ranged from the bottom to the top quartile in graduation rates.

23. For a detailed explanation of the sample of students included in our analyses, see the appendix online at http://www.vanderbilt.edu/schoolchoice/.

24. Chicago Public Schools, Office of Academic Enhancement, "Selective Enrollment High School Data," http://www.selectiveenrollment.org/apps/pages/index.jsp?uREC_ID=72696 &type=d&termREC_ID=&pREC_ID=123085&rn=6515257.

25. Twenty-seven percent of students who reported not filling out any application attended a high school outside their attendance area. This is plausible given that schools that are not oversubscribed will take students even though they did not apply before the December deadline.

26. See our appendix online at http://www.vanderbilt.edu/schoolchoice/ for a detailed description of the model and the results of this analysis.

27. The percentages in this subsection do not add up to 100 because six students did not talk about family involvement in the school choice process.

28. For a detailed description of the measures and items from the survey, see our appendix online at http://www.vanderbilt.edu/schoolchoice/. The appendix also contains a description of all the other data used in the analysis and the details of the models used.

29. Higher levels of parental support means increasing the reported parental support by one standard deviation for all students in the sample. Using the model estimates we can simulate the effects of such an increase.

30. We can simulate the effect of such an increase using the estimates from the model.

31. Strong parental support is defined as one standard deviation above the mean; weak parental support is defined as one standard deviation below the mean.

32. Amy Stuart Wells, "African-American Students' View of School Choice," in *Who Chooses? Who Loses? Culture, Institutions, and the Unequal Effects of School Choice*, eds. Fuller and Elmore with Orfield, 25–49.

Chapter 8

1. The term *Latino* is used throughout this chapter to refer to people who trace their origins to Spanish-speaking parts of Latin America and the Caribbean. It is replaced with *Hispanic* only when studies are cited that originally employed the latter term.

2. Gary Orfield and Chungmei Lee, *Why Segregation Matters: Poverty and Educational Inequality* (Cambridge, MA: The Civil Rights Project, Harvard University, 2005).

3. The majority (63 percent) of Latino children in the United States live in immigrant-led households. This figure includes foreign-born first-generation (11 percent) and U.S.-born second-generation (52 percent) children of immigrants. The remaining 37 percent of Latino children in the United States are "third generation or higher," or native-born children of U.S.-born parents; Richard Fry and Jeffrey S. Passel, *Latino Children: A Majority Are U.S.-Born Offspring of Immigrants* (Washington, DC: Pew Hispanic Center, 2009).

4. Bobby D. Rampey, Gloria S. Dion, and Patricia L. Donahue, *NAEP 2008 Trends in Academic Progress*, NCES 2009–479 (Washington, DC: National Center for Education Statistics, Institute of Education Sciences, U.S. Department of Education, 2009).

5. David C. Berliner, "Our Impoverished View of Educational Research," *Teachers College Record* 108, no. 6 (2006): 949–995; Joel I. Klein and Al Sharpton, "Charter Schools Can Close the Education Gap," *Wall Street Journal*, January 12, 2009, A13; Pedro Noguera

and Jean Y. Wing, eds., *Unfinished Business: Closing the Racial Achievement Gap in Our Schools* (San Francisco: Jossey-Bass, 2006); Richard Rothstein, *Class and Schools: Using Social, Economic, and Educational Reform to Close the Black-White Achievement Gap* (Washington, DC: Economic Policy Institute, 2004).

6. James E. Coleman, Ernst Campbell, Carol Hobson, James McPartland, Alexander M. Mood, Frederic Wienfeld, and Robert York, *Equality of Educational Opportunity* (Washington, DC: U.S. Office of Education, 1966); Orfield and Lee, *Why Segregation Matters: Poverty and Educational Inequality*; Russell W. Rumberger and Gregory J. Palardy, "Does Segregation Still Matter? The Impact of Student Composition on Academic Achievement in High School," *Teachers College Record* 107, no. 9 (2005): 1999–2045; Angela Valenzuela, *Subtractive Schooling: U.S.-Mexican Youth and the Politics of Caring* (Albany: State University of New York Press, 1999).

7. Education Commission of the States, *Open Enrollment: 50-State Report,* 2007, http://mb2.ecs.org/reports/Report.aspx?id=268; Center for Education Reform, *Charter Schools,* 2007, www.edreform.com/index.cfm?fuseAction=stateStats&pSectionID=15&cSectionID=44.

8. Cited in Sam Dillon, "Education Chief to Warn That Inferior Charter Schools Harm the Effort," *New York Times,* June 22, 2009, A10.

9. David Stout, "Obama Outlines Plan for Educational Overhaul," *New York Times,* March 11, 2009, A14.

10. National Center for Education Statistics (NCES), *Trends in the Use of School Choice: 1993 to 2003: Statistical Analysis Report* (Washington, DC: National Center for Education Statistics, 2006).

11. Lois Andre-Bechely, *Could It Be Otherwise? Parents and the Inequities of Public School Choice* (New York: Routledge, 2005); Jack Buckley and Mark Schneider, *Charter Schools: Hope or Hype?* (Princeton, NJ: Princeton University Press, 2007); Center for Education Reform, *Charter Schools*; Laura S. Hamilton and Kacey Guin, "Understanding How Families Choose Schools," in *Getting Choice Right: Ensuring Equity and Efficiency in Education Policy,* eds. Julian R. Betts and Tom Loveless (Washington, DC: Brookings Institution Press, 2005), 40–60; Jennifer Medina, "Even an Expert's Resolve Is Tested by the City's High School Admissions Process," *New York Times,* December 9, 2008, A32; Mark Schneider, Paul Teske, and Melissa Marschall, *Choosing Schools: Consumer Choice and the Quality of American Schools* (Princeton, NJ: Princeton University Press, 2000); Paul Teske, Jody Fitzpatrick, and Gabriel Kaplan, *Opening Doors: Low-Income Parents Search for the Right School* (Seattle: Center on Reinventing Public Education, University of Washington, 2007).

12. Donald J. Hernandez, "Generational Patterns in the U.S.: American Community Survey and Other Sources" (conference presentation at The Immigrant Paradox in Education and Behavior: Is Becoming American a Developmental Risk? Providence, RI, March 6–7, 2009).

13. *Integration* is preferred over the more controversial term *assimilation* to refer to the processes by which immigrants adapt to and participate in new societies and these societies adjust to receiving newcomers. For more on these theoretical concepts and the debates surrounding the term *assimilation,* see Richard Alba and Victor Nee, *Remaking the American Mainstream: Assimilation and Contemporary Immigration* (Cambridge, MA: Harvard University Press, 2003); Han Entzinger, "The Dynamics of Integration Policies: A Multidimensional Model," in *Challenging Immigration and Ethnic Relations Politics,* eds. R. Koopmans and P. Statham (Oxford: Oxford University Press, 2000); Herbert J. Gans, "Second Generation Decline: Scenarios for the Economic and Ethnic Futures of the Post-1965 American Immigrants," *Ethnic and Racial Studies* 15 (1992): 173–192; Andrew Geddes and

Adrian Favell, *The Politics of Belonging: Migrants and Minorities in Contemporary Europe* (Aldershot, UK: Ashgate, 1999); Nathan Glazer and Daniel P. Moynihan, *Beyond the Melting Pot: The Negroes, Puerto Ricans, Italians, and Irish of New York City* (Cambridge, MA: MIT Press and Harvard University Press, 1963); Alejandro Portes and Min Zhou, "The New Second Generation: Segmented Assimilation and Its Variants," *Annals of the American Academy of Political and Social Sciences* 530 (1993): 74–96; Hans Vermeulen and Rinus Penix, *Immigrant Integration: The Dutch Case* (Amsterdam: Het Spinhuis, 2000). *Educational integration* refers to the process by which immigrant parents as well as their children learn about and participate in schooling. Educational integration may be a function of immigrant families' own efforts or those of the school or district to inform them of policies, procedures, and expectations. Specific strategies to assist immigrant students in language learning or to provide other academic support are important aspects of educational integration in their own right, but they do not directly relate to this study's focus and, as such, are not addressed in this chapter.

14. Jack Buckley and Mark Schneider, "Are Charter School Students Harder to Educate? Evidence from Washington, DC," *Educational Evaluation and Policy Analysis* 27, no. 4 (2005): 365–380; John E. Chubb and Terry M. Moe, "Politics, Markets, and the Organization of Schools," *American Political Science Review* 82, no. 4 (1988): 1066–1087; Center for Research on Education Outcomes, *Multiple Choice: Charter School Performance in 16 States* (Stanford, CA: Center for Research on Education Outcomes, 2009); Frederick M. Hess and Tom Loveless, "How School Choice Affects Student Achievement," in *Getting Choice Right: Ensuring Equity and Efficiency in Education Policy*, eds. J. R. Betts and T. Loveless (Washington, DC: Brookings Institution Press, 2005), 85–100; Caroline M. Hoxby, Sonali Murarka, and Jenny Kang, *How New York City's Charter Schools Affect Achievement, August 2009 Report*, second report in series (Cambridge, MA: New York City Charter Schools Evaluation Project, 2009); Paul Teske, Mark Schneider, Christine Roch, and Melissa Marschall, "Public School Choice: A Status Report," in *City Schools: Lessons from New York City*, ed. Diane Ravitch (Baltimore: Johns Hopkins University Press, 2000), 313–365.

15. Elizabeth Frankenberg and Chungmei Lee, *Charter Schools and Race: A Lost Opportunity for Integrated Education* (Cambridge, MA: Harvard University, Civil Rights Project, 2003); Brian Gill, "School Choice and Integration," in *Getting Choice Right: Ensuring Equity and Efficiency in Education Policy*, eds. Betts and Loveless; Paul T. Hill and Kacey Guin, "Baselines for Assessment of Choice Programs," in *Choice with Equity*, ed. Paul T. Hill (Stanford, CA: Hoover Institution Press, 2002), 15–49; Amy Stuart Wells and Robert L. Crain, *Stepping Over the Color Line: African-American Students in White Suburban Schools* (New Haven, CT: Yale University Press, 1997).

16. Edward B. Fiske and Helen F. Ladd, *When Schools Compete: A Cautionary Tale* (Washington, DC: Brookings Institution Press, 2000); Dan Goldhaber, Kacey Guin, Jeffrey R. Henig, Frederick M. Hess, and Janet A. Weiss, "How School Choice Affects Students Who Do Not Choose," in *Getting Choice Right: Ensuring Equity and Efficiency in Education Policy*, eds. Betts and Loveless; Eric A. Hanushek, "Will Quality of Peers Doom Those Left in the Public Schools?" in *Choice with Equity*, ed. Hill, 121–140; Caroline M. Hoxby, "What Do America's 'Traditional' Forms of School Choice Teach Us About School Choice Reforms?" *Economic Policy Review* 4, no. 1 (1998): 47–60; Caroline M. Hoxby, "How School Choice Affects the Achievement of Public School Students," in *Choice with Equity*, ed. Hill, 141–177; Teske et al., "Public School Choice: A Status Report."

17. Anna Nicotera, Maria Mendiburo, and Mark Berends, "Charter School Effects in Indianapolis: An Analysis of Student Achievement Gains," chapter 3 of this volume; Mark Berends,

Matthew G. Springer, and Herbert J. Walberg, eds., *Charter School Outcomes* (Mahwah, NJ: Lawrence Erlbaum Associates, 2008); Buckley and Schneider, *Charter Schools: Hope or Hype?*; Center for Education Reform, *Charter Schools*; Rajashri Chakrabarti, "Can Increasing Private School Participation and Monetary Loss in a Voucher Program Affect Public School Performance? Evidence from Milwaukee," *Journal of Public Economics* 92 (2008): 1371–1393; Karen E. Ross, "Charter Schools and Integration: The Experience in Michigan," in *Getting Choice Right: Ensuring Equity and Efficiency in Education Policy*, eds. Betts and Loveless, 146–175; Salvatore Saporito, "Private Choices, Public Consequences: Magnet School Choice and Segregation by Race and Poverty," *Social Problems* 50, no. 2 (2003): 181–203; Douglas Archbald, *Magnet Schools, Voluntary Desegregation, and Public Choice Theory: Limits and Possibilities in a Big City School System* (Madison: University of Wisconsin Press, 1998).

18. David J. Armour and Brett M. Peiser, "Interdistrict Choice in Massachusetts," in *Learning from School Choice*, eds. Paul E. Peterson and Bryan C. Hassel (Washington, DC: Brookings Institution Press, 1998), 157–186; Kenneth R. Godwin, Frank R. Kemerer, and Valerie J. Martinez, "Comparing Public Choice and Private Voucher Programs in San Antonio," in *Learning from School Choice*, eds. Peterson and Hassel, 275–306; Ellen B. Goldring and Charles Hausman, "Reasons for Parental Choice of Urban Schools," *Journal of Education Policy* 4, no. 5 (1999): 469–490; Wells and Crain, *Stepping Over the Color Line: African-American Students in White Suburban Schools*.

19. Betts and Loveless, eds., *Getting Choice Right: Ensuring Equity and Efficiency in Education Policy*; Bruce F. Fuller, Richard F. Elmore, and Gary Orfield, "Policy-Making in the Dark: Illuminating the School Choice Debate," in *Who Chooses? Who Loses? Culture, Institutions, and the Unequal Effects of School Choice*, eds. B. Fuller and R. F. Elmore (New York: Teachers College Press, 1996), 1–21; Hill, ed., *Choice with Equity*; Eric Rofes and Lisa M. Stulberg, eds., *The Emancipatory Promise of Charter Schools: Toward a Progressive Politics of School Choice* (Albany: State University of New York Press, 2004); Lisa M. Stulberg, *Race, Schools, & Hope: African Americans and School Choice After Brown* (New York: Teachers College Press, 2008); Amy Stuart Wells, Janelle T. Scott, Alejandra Lopez, and Jennifer Jellson Holme, "Charter School Reform and the Shifting Meaning of Educational Equity: Greater Voice and Greater Inequality?" in *Bringing Equity Back: Research for a New Era in American Educational Policy*, eds. Janice Petrovich and Amy Stuart Wells (New York: Teachers College Press, 2005), 219–243.

20. Andre-Bechely, *Could It Be Otherwise? Parents and the Inequities of Public School Choice*; Hill, ed., *Choice with Equity*; Schneider et al., *Choosing Schools: Consumer Choice and the Quality of American Schools*; Ricardo D. Stanton-Salazar, *Manufacturing Hope and Despair: The School and Kin Support Networks of U.S.-Mexican Youth* (New York: Teachers College Press, 2001); Teske et al., *Opening Doors: Low-Income Parents Search for the Right School*.

21. Annette Lareau, *Unequal Childhoods: Class, Race, and Family Life* (Berkeley: University of California Press, 2003); Schneider et al., *Choosing Schools: Consumer Choice and the Quality of American Schools*; Teske et al., *Opening Doors: Low-Income Parents Search for the Right School*; Teske et al., "Public School Choice: A Status Report."

22. Schneider et al., *Choosing Schools: Consumer Choice and the Quality of American Schools*.

23. James Coleman, "Social Capital in the Creation of Human Capital," *American Journal of Sociology* 94 (1995) (supplement): 94–120; Annette Lareau, "Social Class Differences in Family-School Relationships: The Importance of Cultural Capital," *Sociology of Education* 60 (1987): 73–85; Lareau, *Unequal Childhoods: Class, Race, and Family Life*.

24. Edward B. Fiske, "Controlled Choice in Cambridge, Massachusetts," in *Divided We Fail: Coming Together Through Public School Choice* (New York: Century Foundation Press, 2003), 167–208; Charles Glenn, Kahris McLaughlin, and Laura Salganik, *Parent Information for School Choice* (Boston: Center on Families, Communities, Schools, and Children's Learning, 1993).
25. Glenn et al., *Parent Information for School Choice.*
26. Andre-Bechely, *Could It Be Otherwise? Parents and the Inequities of Public School Choice.*
27. Jeffrey R. Henig, "The Local Dynamics of Choice: Ethnic Preferences and Institutional Responses," in *Who Chooses? Who Loses?* eds. Fuller and Elmore, 95–117; Schneider et al., *Choosing Schools: Consumer Choice and the Quality of American Schools*; Claire Smrekar and Ellen Goldring, *School Choice in Urban America: Magnet Schools and the Pursuit of Equity* (New York: Teachers College Press, 1999); Emily Van Dunk and Anneliese M. Dickman, *School Choice and the Question of Accountability* (New Haven, CT: Yale University Press, 2004).
28. For accounts of the difficulty in accessing school-level data, see Buckley and Schneider, "Are Charter School Students Harder to Educate? Evidence from Washington, DC"; and Schneider et al., *Choosing Schools: Consumer Choice and the Quality of American Schools.*
29. Carl Bankston, Steven J. Caldas, and Min Zhou, "The Academic Achievement of Vietnamese American Students: Ethnicity as Social Capital," *Social Focus* 30 (1997): 1–16; Lisa Delpit, *Other People's Children: Cultural Conflict in the Classroom* (New York: New York Press, 1995); Cynthia T. Garcia-Coll and Katherine Magnuson, "Cultural Differences as Sources of Developmental Vulnerabilities and Resources: A View from Developmental Research," in *Handbook of Early Childhood Intervention,* eds. S. J. Meisel and J. P. Shinkoff (Cambridge, UK: Cambridge University Press, 2000), 94–111; Annette Lareau, *Home Advantage: Social Class and Parental Intervention in Elementary Education* (London: Falmer, 1989); Lareau, *Unequal Childhoods: Class, Race, and Family Life*; John U. Ogbu, *Minority Education and Caste: The American System in Cross-Cultural Perspective* (Orlando, FL: Academic Press, 1978); John U. Ogbu, "Variability in Minority Responses to Schooling: Nonimmigrants vs. Immigrants," in *Interpretive Ethnography of Education: At Home and Abroad,* eds. G. Spindler and L. Spindler (Hillsdale, NJ: Lawrence Erlbaum Associates, 1987), 255–280; John U. Ogbu, "Immigrant and Involuntary Minorities in Comparative Perspective," in *Minority Status and Schooling: A Comparative Study of Immigrant and Involuntary Minorities,* eds. M. A. Gibson and J. U. Ogbu (New York: Garland Publishing, 1991); Stanton-Salazar, *Manufacturing Hope and Despair: The School and Kin Support Networks of U.S.-Mexican Youth*; Valenzuela, *Subtractive Schooling: U.S.-Mexican Youth and the Politics of Caring.*
30. Concha Delgado-Gaitan, "Involving Parents in the Schools: A Process of Empowerment," *American Journal of Education* 100, no. 1 (1991): 20–46; Concha Delgado-Gaitan, "School Matters in the Mexican-American Home: Socializing Children to Education," *American Educational Research Journal* 29, no. 3 (1992): 495–513; Leslie Reese, Silvia Balzano, Ronald Gallimore, and Claude Goldenberg, "The Concept of *Educacion*: Latino Families and American Schooling," *International Journal of Educational Research* 23, no. 1 (1995): 57–81; Stanton-Salazar, *Manufacturing Hope and Despair: The School and Kin Support Networks of U.S.-Mexican Youth*; Guadalupe Valdes, *Con Respeto: Bridging the Distance Between Culturally Diverse Families and Schools: An Ethnographic Portrait* (New York: Teachers College Press, 1996); Richard R. Valencia and Mary S. Black, "'Mexican Americans Don't Value Education!' On the Basis of the Myth, Mythmaking, and Debunking," *Journal of Latinos and Education* 1, no. 2 (2002): 81–103.

31. Michael W. Apple, *Education and Power* (New York: Routledge, 1982); Henry A. Giroux and David E. Purpel, eds., *The Hidden Curriculum and Moral Education* (Berkeley, CA: McCutchan Publishing Corporation, 1983); Etta R. Hollins, *Transforming Curriculum for a Culturally Diverse Society* (Mahwah, NJ: Lawrence Erlbaum Associates, 1996).

32. Delgado-Gaitan, "School Matters in the Mexican-American Home: Socializing Children to Education"; Reese et al., "The Concept of *Educacion:* Latino Families and American Schooling"; Stanton-Salazar, *Manufacturing Hope and Despair: The School and Kin Support Networks of U.S.-Mexican Youth*; Valdes, *Con Respeto: Bridging the Distance Between Culturally Diverse Families and Schools*; Valencia and Black, "'Mexican Americans Don't Value Education!' On the Basis of the Myth, Mythmaking, and Debunking."

33. Lareau, *Home Advantage: Social Class and Parental Intervention in Elementary Education*; Lareau, *Unequal Childhoods: Class, Race, and Family Life*.

34. For a more detailed discussion, see Valencia and Black, "'Mexican Americans Don't Value Education!' On the Basis of the Myth, Mythmaking, and Debunking."

35. New York City Department of Planning, "Population Facts," 2007, http://www.nyc.gov/html/dcp/html/census/pop_facts.shtml.

36. New York City Department of Education, *New York City's English Language Learners: Demographics* (New York: Office of English Language Learners, New York City Department of Education, 2008).

37. New York City Department of Education, "Total Student Population," May 15, 2009, http://schools.nyc.gov.

38. Some schools host multiple programs that are organized around different curricular foci or specializations. On their applications, students list individual programs within a school unless the school has no subprograms. In that case, students list the actual high school name.

39. Clara Hemphill and Kim Nauer, *The New Marketplace: How Small-School Reforms and School Choice Have Reshaped New York City's High Schools* (New York: Center for New York City Affairs, The New School, 2009).

40. Ibid.

41. *Current Population Survey* (Washington, DC: U.S. Bureau of Labor Statistics, 2009), http://www.bls.gov/cps/cpsaat7.pdf.

42. Ibid.

43. Thomas Toch and Chad Alderman, *Matchmaking: Enabling Mandatory Public School Choice in New York and Boston* (Washington, DC: Education Sector, 2009).

44. Ati'la Abdulkadiroglu, Parag A. Pathak, and Alvin E. Roth, "Practical Market Design: Four Matches, the New York City High School Match," *American Economic Review* 95, no. 2 (2005): 364–367.

45. Hemphill and Nauer, *The New Marketplace: How Small-School Reforms and School Choice Have Reshaped New York City's High Schools.*

46. *Directory of the New York City Public High Schools, 2008–2009* (New York: Office of Student Enrollment Planning Operations, New York City Department of Education, 2008).

47. Hemphill and Nauer, *The New Marketplace: How Small-School Reforms and School Choice Have Reshaped New York City's High Schools.*

48. Ibid.

49. Ibid.

50. Art McFarland, "Hundreds Protest Schools Closing Vote," *ABC News Online,* January 28, 2010, http://abclocal.go.com/wabc/story?section=news/education&id=7240406.

51. Hemphill and Nauer, *The New Marketplace: How Small-School Reforms and School Choice Have Reshaped New York City's High Schools.*

52. All names have been changed.

53. Hemphill and Nauer, *The New Marketplace: How Small-School Reforms and School Choice Have Reshaped New York City's High Schools.*

54. See Delgado-Gaitan, "School Matters in the Mexican-American Home: Socializing Children to Education"; Reese et al., "The Concept of *Educacion:* Latino Families and American Schooling"; Stanton-Salazar, *Manufacturing Hope and Despair: The School and Kin Support Networks of U.S.-Mexican Youth;* Marcelo M. Suárez-Orozco, *Central American Refugees and U.S. High Schools: A Psychosocial Study of Motivation and Achievement* (Stanford, CA: Stanford University Press, 1989); Valdes, *Con Respeto: Bridging the Distance Between Culturally Diverse Families and Schools;* Valencia and Black, "'Mexican Americans Don't Value Education!' On the Basis of the Myth, Mythmaking, and Debunking."

55. Hemphill and Nauer, *The New Marketplace: How Small-School Reforms and School Choice Have Reshaped New York City's High Schools.*

56. Apple, *Education and Power;* Giroux and Purpel, eds., *The Hidden Curriculum and Moral Education;* Hollins, *Transforming Curriculum for a Culturally Diverse Society.*

57. Paul DiMaggio and Eszter Hargittai, "From the 'Digital Divide' to 'Digital Inequality': Studying Internet Use as Penetration Increases," working paper 15, Center for Arts and Cultural Policy Studies, Princeton University, Princeton, NJ, 2001; Daniel L. Hoffman and Thomas P. Novak, "Bridging the Racial Divide on the Internet," *Science* 280 (1998): 390–391.

58. Carola Suarez-Orozco and Marcelo M. Suarez-Orozco, *Children of Immigration* (Cambridge, MA: Harvard University Press, 2001).

59. Hemphill and Nauer, *The New Marketplace: How Small-School Reforms and School Choice Have Reshaped New York City's High Schools.*

60. Audrey Singer, *The Rise of New Immigrant Gateways, Living Cities Census Series,* (Washington, DC: Center on Urban and Metropolitan Policy, Brookings Institution, 2004).

61. Teske et al., *Opening Doors: Low-Income Parents Search for the Right School.*

62. Suarez-Orozco and Suarez-Orozco, *Children of Immigration.*

Chapter 9

1. Julian R. Betts, Paul T. Hill, and The Charter School Achievement Consensus Panel, "Key Issues in Studying Charter Schools and Achievement: A Review and Suggestions for National Guidelines," white paper NCSRP, series 2, National Charter School Research Project, Center on Reinventing Public Education, Seattle, 2006; Richard Buddin and Ron Zimmer, "Is Charter School Competition in California Improving the Performance of Traditional Public Schools?" working paper, Rand Corporation, Santa Monica, CA, 2005.

2. Jack Buckley and Mark Schneider, "Are Charter School Students Harder to Educate? Evidence from Washington D.C.," *Educational Evaluation and Policy Analysis* 2, no. 24 (2005): 365–380; K. E. Buckley and H. Hicks, "Managing Community: Professional Community in Charter Schools Operated by Educational Management Organizations," *Educational Administration Quarterly* 2, no. 41 (2005): 306–348; Marisa Cannata, "Teacher Community and Elementary Charter Schools," *Education Policy Analysis Archives,* 2007; Marisa Cannata, "Teacher Qualifications and Work Environments Across School Types," *School Choice: Evidence and Recommendations,* April 1, 2008, http://epsl.asu.edu/epru/epru_2008_Research_Writing.htm; Erica Frankenberg and Chungmei Lee, "Charter Schools and Race: A Lost Opportunity for Integrated Education," *Educational Policy Analysis Archives* 32, no. 11 (2003); Ellen Goldring and Xiu Cravens, "Teachers' Academic Focus on Learning in Char-

ter and Traditional Public Schools," in *Charter School Outcomes,* eds. M. Berends, M. G. Springer, and H. J. Walberg (New York: Lawrence Erlbaum Associates, 2008), 39–59.

3. Randall W. Eberts and Kevin M. Hollenbeck, "An Examination of Student Achievement in Michigan Charter Schools," working paper no. 01-68, W. E. Upjohn Institute, Kalamazoo, MI, 2001.

4. Betts et al., "Key Issues in Studying Charter Schools and Achievement: A Review and Suggestions for National Guidelines"; Julian R. Betts and Y. Emily Tang, "Value-added and Experimental Studies of the Effect of Charter Schools on Student Achievement: A Literature Review," working paper, National Charter School Research Project, Center on Reinventing Public Education, Seattle, 2008; Buddin and Zimmer, "Is Charter School Competition in California Improving the Performance of Traditional Public Schools?"; Gary Miron and Christopher Nelson, "Student Academic Achievement in Charter Schools: What We Know and Why We Know So Little," in *Taking Account of Charter Schools: What's Happened and What's Next,* eds. Katrina E. Bulkley and Priscilla Wohlstetter (New York: Teachers College Press, 2004); Bettie Teasley, "Charter School Outcomes," in *Handbook of Research on School Choice,* eds. Mark Berends, M. G. Springer, D. Ballou, and H. J. Walberg (New York: Routledge, 2009), 209–226.

5. Julian R. Betts, "The Competitive Effects of Charter Schools on Traditional Public Schools," in *Handbook of Research on School Choice,* eds. Berends et al., 195–208; Eberts and Hollenbeck, "An Examination of Student Achievement in Michigan Charter Schools."

6. Milton Friedman, *Capitalism and Freedom* (Chicago: University of Chicago Press, 1962), 85–107; Caroline M. Hoxby, "School Choice and School Productivity: Could School Choice Be a Tide That Lifts All Boats?" in *The Economics of School Choice,* ed. Caroline M. Hoxby (Chicago: University of Chicago Press, 2003).

7. Bryan C. Hassel, *The Charter School Challenge: Avoiding the Pitfalls, Fulfilling the Promise* (Washington, DC: Brookings Institution Press, 1999).

8. Hoxby, "School Choice and School Productivity: Could School Choice Be a Tide That Lifts All Boats?" in *Economics of School Choice,* ed. Hoxby.

9. Hassel, *The Charter School Challenge: Avoiding the Pitfalls, Fulfilling the Promise.*

10. Frederick M. Hess, Robert Maranto, and Scott Milliman, "Small Districts in Big Trouble: How Four Arizona School Systems Responded to Charter Competition," *Teachers College Record* 6, no. 103 (2001): 1102–1124.

11. Hassel, *The Charter School Challenge: Avoiding the Pitfalls, Fulfilling the Promise*; Eric Rofes, "The Catalyst Role of Charter Schools," *School Administrator* 7, no. 56 (1999): 14.

12. Hassel, *The Charter School Challenge: Avoiding the Pitfalls, Fulfilling the Promise*; Hess et al., "Small Districts in Big Trouble: How Four Arizona School Systems Responded to Charter Competition"; Rofes, "The Catalyst Role of Charter Schools."

13. Betts, "The Competitive Effects of Charter Schools on Traditional Public Schools," in *Handbook of Research on School Choice,* eds. Berends et al.

14. John Bohte, "Examining the Impact of Charter Schools on Performance in Traditional Public Schools," *Policy Studies Journal* 4, no. 32 (2004): 501–520; Kevin Booker, Scott M. Gilpatric, Timothy Gronberg, and Dennis Jansen, "The Effect of Charter Schools on Traditional Public School Students in Texas: Are Children Who Stay Behind Left Behind?" *Journal of Urban Economics,* 2008, no. 641: 123–145; Matthew Carr and Gary W. Ritter, "Measuring the Competitive Effect of Charter Schools on Student Achievement in Ohio's Traditional Public Schools," July 1, 2009, http://www.ncspe.org/list-papers.php; Hoxby, "School Choice and School Productivity: Could School Choice Be a Tide That Lifts All Boats?" in *Economics of School Choice,* ed. Hoxby; Ron Zimmer, Brian Gill, Kevin Booker, Stéphane Lavertu,

Tim R. Sass, and John Witte, *Charter Schools in Eight States: Effects on Achievement, Attainment, Integration, and Competition* (Santa Monica, CA: RAND, 2009).

15. Tim Sass, "Charter Schools and Student Achievement in Florida," *Education Finance and Policy,* 2006, no. 1: 91–122.

16. Buddin and Zimmer, "Is Charter School Competition in California Improving the Performance of Traditional Public Schools?"

17. Zimmer et al., *Charter Schools in Eight States: Effects on Achievement, Attainment, Integration, and Competition.*

18. Robert Bifulco and Helen F. Ladd, "The Impact of Charter Schools on Student Achievement: Evidence from North Carolina," *Education Finance and Policy* 1, no. 1 (2006): 50–90; George M. Holmes, Jeff DeSimone, and Nicholas G. Rupp, *Does School Choice Increase School Quality?* (Cambridge, MA: National Bureau of Economic Research, 2003).

19. Eberts and Hollenbeck, "An Examination of Student Achievement in Michigan Charter Schools"; Hoxby, "School Choice and School Productivity: Could School Choice Be a Tide That Lifts All Boats?" in *Economics of School Choice,* ed. Hoxby.

20. Eric Bettinger, "The Effect of Charter Schools on Charter Students and Public Schools," *Economics of Education Review* 2, no. 24 (2005): 133–147.

21. Yongmei Ni, "The Impact of Charter Schools on the Efficiency of Traditional Public Schools: Evidence from Michigan," *Economics of Education Review,* 2009.

22. Clive R. Belfield and Henry M. Levin, "The Effects of Competition Between Schools on Educational Outcomes: A Review for the United States," *Review of Educational Research* 2, no. 72 (2002): 279–341.

23. Kenneth V. Greene and Byung-Goo Kang, "The Effect of Public and Private Competition on High School Outputs in New York State," *Economics of Education Review,* 2004, no. 23: 497–506; Caroline M. Hoxby, "Does Competition Among Public Schools Benefit Students and Taxpayers?" *American Economic Review* 90 (2000): 1–53.

24. Belfield and Levin, "The Effects of Competition Between Schools on Educational Outcomes: A Review for the United States."

25. Greene and Kang, "The Effect of Public and Private Competition on High School Outputs in New York State"; Hoxby, "School Choice and School Productivity: Could School Choice Be a Tide That Lifts All Boats?" in *Economics of School Choice,* ed. Hoxby.

26. Danny Cohen-Zada, "An Alternative Instrument for Private School Competition," *Economics of Education Review,* 2009, no. 28: 29–37; Thomas S. Dee, "Competition and the Quality of Public Schools," *Economics of Education Review* 4, no. 17 (1998): 419–427; Caroline M. Hoxby, *Do Private Schools Provide Competition for Public Schools?* (Cambridge, MA: National Bureau of Economic Research, 1994); Christopher Jepsen, "The Role of Aggregation in Estimating the Effects of Private School Competition on Student Achievement," *Journal of Urban Economics,* 2002, no. 52: 477–500.

27. Jepsen, "The Role of Aggregation in Estimating the Effects of Private School Competition on Student Achievement."

28. Christopher R. Geller, David L. Sjoquist, and Mary Beth Walker, "The Effect of Private School Competition on Public School Performance in Georgia," *Public Finance Review* 4, no. 34 (2006): 4–32; Craig M. Newmark, "Another Look at Whether Private Schools Influence Public School Quality," *Public Choice,* 1995, no. 82: 365–373; William Sander, "Private Schools and Public School Achievement," *Journal of Human Resources* 4, no. 34 (1999): 697–709; Christopher A. Simon and Nicholas P. Lovrich, "Private School Enrollment and Public School Performance: Assessing the Effects of Competition upon Public School Student Achievement in Washington State," *Policy Studies Journal* 4, no. 24 (1996): 666–675.

29. Hassel, *The Charter School Challenge: Avoiding the Pitfalls, Fulfilling the Promise*; Hess et al., "Small Districts in Big Trouble: How Four Arizona School Systems Responded to Charter Competition"; Rofes, "The Catalyst Role of Charter Schools."

30. Buddin and Zimmer, "Is Charter School Competition in California Improving the Performance of Traditional Public Schools?"

31. Bohte, "Examining the Impact of Charter Schools on Performance in Traditional Public Schools."

32. The model used was

$$\text{Principal use of time}_i = \beta_0 + \beta_1(\text{Charter competition})_i + \beta_2(\text{School characteristics})_i + \beta_3(\text{School type})_i + \varepsilon_i$$

33. Reliability is 0.837. The factor loadings of each item are as follows: recruiting teachers (0.966), retaining teachers (0.998), attracting students (0.908), and retaining students (0.859). When the overall measure was less than 3, the principal was coded as perceiving a negative effect of competition on attracting teachers and students.

34. Bifulco and Ladd, "The Impact of Charter Schools on Student Achievement: Evidence from North Carolina"; Bohte, "Examining the Impact of Charter Schools on Performance in Traditional Public Schools"; Booker et al., "The Effect of Charter Schools on Traditional Public School Students in Texas: Are Children Who Stay Behind Left Behind?"; Buddin and Zimmer, "Is Charter School Competition in California Improving the Performance of Traditional Public Schools?"; Carr and Ritter, "Measuring the Competitive Effect of Charter Schools on Student Achievement in Ohio's Traditional Public Schools"; Holmes et al., *Does School Choice Increase School Quality?*; Robert Maranto, Scott Milliman, and Scott K. Stevens, "Does Private School Competition Harm Public Schools? Revisiting Smith and Meier's 'The Case Against School Choice,'" *Political Research Quarterly* 1, no. 53 (2000): 177–192; Newmark, "Another Look at Whether Private Schools Influence Public School Quality"; Sass, "Charter Schools and Student Achievement in Florida"; Simon and Lovrich, "Private School Enrollment and Public School Performance: Assessing the Effects of Competition Upon Public School Student Achievement in Washington State."

35. Reliability is 0.681. The factor loadings of each item are as follows: supervise clerical, cafeteria, and maintenance staff (0.622); monitor public spaces (0.710); deal with emergencies and other unplanned circumstances (0.592); work with students and their parents on discipline/attendance issues (0.768); and complete routine paperwork (0.526).

36. Reliability is 0.843. The factor loadings of each item are as follows: demonstrate instructional practices and/or the use of curricular materials (0.604), observe a teacher during classroom instruction (0.673); examine and discuss student work (0.584); examine and discuss standardized test results of students from a teacher's class (0.631); create and implement the staff development program in the school (0.621); personally provide staff development (0.555); troubleshoot or support the implementation of school improvement efforts (0.568); monitor the curriculum used in classrooms to see that it reflects the school's improvement efforts (0.782); and monitor classroom instructional practices to see that they reflect the school's improvement efforts (0.827).

37. Reliability is 0.732. The factor loadings of each item are as follows: promote the school's image in the community (0.739); communicate achievement results to the external community (0.702); attend or participate in events taking place in the community (0.646); host fundraisers or financial development efforts (0.643), and answer questions from potential students and/or their parents (0.444).

38. Bohte, "Examining the Impact of Charter Schools on Performance in Traditional Public Schools"; Buddin and Zimmer, "Is Charter School Competition in California Improving the Performance of Traditional Public Schools?"

39. Bifulco and Ladd, "The Impact of Charter Schools on Student Achievement: Evidence from North Carolina"; Paul Teske, Jody Fitzpatrick, and Tracey O'Brien, *Drivers of Choice: Parents, Transportation, and School Choice* (Seattle: Center on Reinventing Public Education, University of Washington, 2009).

40. Teske et al., *Drivers of Choice: Parents, Transportation, and School Choice.*

41. Booker et al., "The Effect of Charter Schools on Traditional Public School Students in Texas: Are Children Who Stay Behind Left Behind?"

42. Sam Dillon, "Education Grant Effort Faces Late Opposition," *New York Times*, January 19, 2010.

43. Erik W. Robelen, "Former D.C. Catholic Schools Start New Life as Charters," *Education Week*, September 10, 2008.

44. Ni, "The Impact of Charter Schools on the Efficiency of Traditional Public Schools: Evidence from Michigan."

Chapter 10

1. This chapter has benefited from the comments of Thomas Dee and Margaret Levenstein.

2. David Arsen and Yongmei Ni, "The Competitive Effect of School Choice Policies on Performance in Traditional Public Schools," working paper, Education Policy Research Unit, Arizona State University & Education and the Public Interest Center, Tempe, and University of Colorado, Boulder, 2008; Eric Bettinger, "The Effect of Charter Schools on Charter Students and Public Schools," *Economics of Education Review*, 2005, no. 24: 133–147; Robert Bifulco and Helen F. Ladd, "The Impact of Charter Schools on Student Achievement: Evidence from North Carolina," *Education, Finance, and Policy* 1, no. 1 (2006): 50–89; Kevin Booker, Scott M. Gilpatric, Timothy Gronberg, and Dennis Jansen, "The Effect of Charter Schools on Traditional Public School Students in Texas: Are Children Who Stay Behind Left Behind?" *Journal of Urban Economics* 64, no. 1 (2008): 123–145; Richard Buddin and Ron Zimmer, "Is Charter School Competition in California Improving the Performance of Traditional Public Schools?" working paper, Rand Corporation, Santa Monica, CA, 2005; George M. Holmes, Jeff DeSimone, and Nicholas G. Rupp, "Does School Choice Increase School Quality?" working paper W9683, NBER Working Paper Series, Cambridge, MA, 2003; Caroline M. Hoxby, "School Choice and School Productivity: Could School Choice Be a Tide That Lifts All Boats?" in *The Economics of School Choice*, ed. C. M. Hoxby (Chicago: University of Chicago Press, 2003), 287–341; Yongmei Ni, "Do Traditional Public Schools Benefit From Charter School Competition?" *Economic of Education Review* 28, no. 5 (2009): 571–584; Tim Sass, "Charter Schools and Student Achievement in Florida," *Education Finance and Policy*, 2006, no. 1: 91–122.

3. Caroline M. Hoxby, "School Choice and School Competition: Evidence from the United States," *Swedish Economic Policy Review* 10 (2003): 11–67.

4. Ibid.

5. Ibid.

6. A small set of hold-harmless districts, whose foundation in 1994–1995 exceeded $6,500, are eligible to levy additional local property taxes up to a cap that has increased by less than the rate of inflation since 1994.

7. However, there is a cap on the PSA foundation allowance, and this cap limits the charter schools' revenue below that of TPSs in the highest-revenue school districts. In addition, charter schools receive federal and state categorical funding on the same basis as school districts.

8. Measuring fund balance as a percentage of district current operating expenditure produced very similar results.

9. An alternative measure of charter schools' market share—total charter school enrollment in a district as a percentage of district enrollment—is less desirable as an indicator of competition, because many students attend charter schools outside the district in which they live. Indeed, more than one-third of Michigan's charter schools draw the majority of their students from districts other than the district in which the charter school is located.

10. Monk and Hussain's survey of the literature (David H. Monk and Sammid Hussain, "Structural Influences on the Internal Allocation of School District Resources," *Educational Evaluation and Policy Analysis* 22, no. 1: (2000): 1–26) distilled four key structural characteristics that their own study in turn reinforced. We incorporate these four factors in *SDstructure$_{it}$*. The factors are district enrollment size (in logarithmic form), total operating expenditure per pupil (in logarithmic form), property wealth per pupil (in logarithmic form), and the percentage of students eligible for the free or reduced-price lunch program. District enrollment size controls for scale effects on resource allocation, especially the share of spending devoted to administration, which *ceteris paribus* tends to be higher in very small districts. Operating expenditures per pupil is included to control for the fact that the share of spending devoted to support services tends to increase in districts having higher overall spending levels. Property wealth per pupil and the percentage of students eligible for free and reduced-price lunch measure local residents' wealth and income.

11. A set of year dummies, I_t, is also included to capture any systematic influence not accounted for by the observable inputs that vary over time but are common to all schools. θ_i is an unobserved school fixed effect or heterogeneity that picks up all the unobserved characteristics of a school that are stable over time, including historical reasons that influence charter location. u_{it} is the unobserved error.

12. The Michigan Department of Education requires local districts that fall into its deficit reduction program to submit a plan to balance their budgets, but the state does not prescribe the specific budgetary changes that districts must make.

13. Dan Goldhaber, Kacey Guin, Jeffrey R. Henig, Frederick M. Hess, and Janet A. Weiss, "How School Choice Affects Students Who Do Not Choose," in *Getting Choice Right: Ensuring Equity and Efficiency in Education Policy*, eds. J. R. Betts and T. Loveless (Washington, DC: Brookings Institution Press, 2005); Arsen and Ni, "The Competitive Effect of School Choice Policies on Performance in Traditional Public Schools."

14. Hoxby, "School Choice and School Productivity: Could School Choice Be a Tide That Lifts All Boats?" in *Economics of School Choice*, ed. Hoxby; Ni, "Do Traditional Public Schools Benefit From Charter School Competition?"

15. Arsen and Ni, "The Competitive Effect of School Choice Policies on Performance in Traditional Public Schools"; Goldhaber et al., "How School Choice Affects Students Who Do Not Choose," in *Getting Choice Right: Ensuring Equity and Efficiency in Education Policy*, eds. Betts and Loveless.

Chapter 11

1. Sections of this chapter also appear in Ron W. Zimmer, Brian Gill, Kevin Booker, Stéphane Lavertu, Tim Sass, and John Witte, *Charter Schools in Eight States: Effects of Achievement, Attainment, Integration, and Competition* (Santa Monica, CA: RAND, 2009). We appreciate comments from Elaine Allensworth, Julian Betts, Phil Gleason, and two anonymous reviewers, as well as financial support from the Bill & Melinda Gates, Joyce, and William Penn foundations.

2. Zimmer et al., *Charter Schools in Eight States: Effects of Achievement, Attainment, Integration, and Competition*; Atila Abdulkadiroglu, Josh Angrist, Sarah Cohodes, Susan

Dynarski, Jon Fullerton, Thomas Kane, and Parag Pathak, *Informing the Debate: Comparing Boston's Charter, Pilot and Traditional Schools* (Boston: Boston Foundation, 2009); Kevin Booker, Scott M. Gilpatric, Timothy J. Gronberg, and Dennis W. Jansen, "The Impact of Charter School Student Attendance on Student Performance," *Journal of Public Economics 91*, no. 5-6 (2007): 849–876; Eric A. Hanushek, John F. Kain, and Steven G. Rivkin, "The Impact of Charter Schools on Academic Achievement (unpublished manuscript, Hoover Institute, 2002); Caroline M. Hoxby and Sonali Muraka, "Charter Schools in New York City: Who Enrolls and How They Affect Their Students' Achievement," NBER working paper, National Bureau of Economic Research, Cambridge, MA, 2007; Tim R. Sass, "Charter Schools and Student Achievement in Florida," *Education Finance and Policy 1*, no. 1 (2006): 91–122; Robert Bifulco and Helen F. Ladd, "School Choice, Racial Segregation and Test-Score Gaps: Evidence from North Carolina's Charter School Program," *Journal of Policy Analysis and Management 26*, no. 1 (2007): 31–56; Ron W. Zimmer and Richard Buddin, "Charter School Performance in Two Large Urban Districts," *Journal of Urban Economics 60*, no. 2 (2006): 307–326; John Witte, David Weimer, Arnold Shober, and Paul Schlomer, "The Performance of Charter Schools in Wisconsin," *Journal of Policy Analysis and Management 26*, no. 3 (2007): 557–578.

3. Edward B. Fiske and Helen F. Ladd, "When Schools Compete: A Cautionary Tale," working paper, Brookings Institution, Washington DC, 2000; Casey D. Cobb and Gene V. Glass, "Ethnic Segregation in Arizona Charter Schools," *Education Policy Analysis Archives*, 1999, no 7: 1.

4. Erica Frankenberg and Chungmei Lee, "Charter Schools and Race: A Lost Opportunity for Integrated Education," *Educational Policy Analysis Archives*, 2003, no. 11: 32.

5. Ibid.; Ron W. Zimmer, "A New Twist in the Educational Tracking Debate," *Economics of Education Review* 2003, no. 22: 307–315; Ron W. Zimmer and Eugenia F. Toma, "Peer Effects in Private and Public Schools Across Countries," *Journal of Policy Analysis and Management 1*, no. 19 (2000): 75–92; Anita A. Summers and Barbara L. Wolfe, "Do Schools Make a Difference?" *American Economic Review*, 1977, no. 67: 639–652; Vernon Henderson, Peter Mieszkowski, and Yvon Suavageau, "Peer-Group Effects and Educational Production Functions," *Journal of Public Economic*, 1978, no. 10: 97–106.

6. Valerie Lee and Robert G. Croninger, "Parental Choice of Schools and Social Stratification in Education: The Paradox of Detroit," *Education Evaluation and Policy Analysis 4*, no. 16 (1994): 434–457; Amy Stuart Wells, *Time to Choose: America at the Crossroads of School Choice Policy* (New York: Hill and Wang, 1993).

7. Ted Kolderie, "Creating the Capacity for Change: How and Why Governors and Legislatures Are Opening a New-Schools Sector in Public Education," *Education Week Press*, 2004; Chester E. Finn, Bruno V. Manno, and Gregg Vanourek, *Charter Schools in Action: Renewing Public Education* (Princeton, NJ: Princeton University Press, 2000); Joseph Nathan, "Controversy: Charters and Choice," *American Prospect*, November–December 1998.

8. Mark Schneider, Paul Teske, Melissa Marshall, and Christine Roch, "Shopping for Schools: In the Land of the Blind, the One-Eyed Parent May Be Enough," *American Journal of Political Science*, 1998, no. 42: 769–793; Natalie Lacireno-Paquet, Thomas T. Holyoke, Michele Moser, and Jeffrey R. Henig, "Creaming vs. Cropping: Charter School Enrollment Practice in Response to Market Incentives," *Education and Evaluation and Policy Analysis 24*, no. 2 (2002): 145–158.

9. Henry M. Levin, "Educational Vouchers: Effectiveness, Choice, and Costs," *Journal of Policy Analysis and Management*, 1998, no. 17: 373–392.

10. Under No Child Left Behind rules, students attending schools that fail to make academic targets for two consecutive years are eligible to transfer to another school.

11. J. Powell, J. Blackorby, J. Marsh, K. Finnegan, and L. Anderson, *Evaluation of Charter School Effectiveness* (Menlo Park, CA: SRI International, 1997); J. Fitzgerald, P. Harris, P. Huidekiper, and M. Mani, "1997 Colorado Charter Schools Evaluation Study: The Characteristics, Status, and Student Achievement Data of Colorado Charter Schools," working paper, Clayton Foundation, Denver, 1998; RPI International, *The State of Charter Schools: National Study of Charter Schools Fourth Year Report* (Washington DC: Office of Educational Research and Improvement, U.S. Department of Education, 2000); Gary N. Miron and Christopher Nelson, *What's Public About Charter Schools?* (Thousand Oaks, CA: Corwin Press Inc., 2002); Erica Frankenberg, Genevieve Siegel-Hawley, and Jia Wang, "Choice Without Equity: Charter School Segregation and the Need for Civil Rights Standards," working paper, Civil Rights Project/Proyecho Derechos Civiles, UCLA, Los Angeles, 2010.

12. For more information on the geographic distribution of charter schools, see the summary of a special edition of articles in the August 2009 *American Journal of Education;* Christopher Lubienski and Jack Dougherty, "Mapping Educational Opportunity: Spatial Analysis and School Choices," *American Journal of Education,* 2009, no. 115: 485–491.

13. Bifulco and Ladd, "School Choice, Racial Segregation and Test-Score Gaps: Evidence from North Carolina's Charter School Program"; Kevin Booker, Ron Zimmer, and Richard Buddin, "The Effects of Charter Schools on School Peer Composition," working paper WR-306-EDU, Rand Corporation, Santa Monica, CA, 2005.

14. Table A-1 in the online appendix at http://www.vanderbilt.edu/schoolchoice/ lists each location, the years in which charter schools began operating, and the years for which we have data. For each student, the data include school identifiers, grade, race or ethnicity, and test scores in math and reading. Across locations, the most recent year in which we collected test score data was generally 2006–2007. Note that the appendix provides a more detailed description of each of the data, including information about any exclusions we made in the data sets and the method we used to classify schools.

15. To construct the table, we relied on information found at the Center for Education Reform Web site: http://www.edreform.com/Home/.

16. Initially the state of Ohio could authorize charter schools. But in 2005, new legislation prohibited the state from being the sponsor of charter schools. In addition, new limitations were placed on the number of charter schools that could be authorized by education service centers (ESCs). Because of these changes, a number of schools had to find new sponsors.

17. Initially, all charter schools in Texas had to target at-risk students. However, this requirement eventually was phased out.

18. The test scores in the analysis are based on scaled scores from state accountability tests or district-administered tests. To make the results comparable across grades and subjects and across geographic locations, we standardized these scaled scores relative to the districtwide or statewide distribution in each grade and subject. Therefore, scores in table 11.2 are standardized z-scores, with negative scores indicating below-average scores and positive scores indicating above-average scores. Using these scales, we present the average standardized prior math and reading scores of charter switchers and of their peers at the TPSs the switchers exited. Therefore, not only do we know whether the average scores of students switching to charter schools are above or below the average test scores of their respective district or state, but we also know whether the average standardized test scores of students switching to charter schools are above or below the average standardized scores of students in the TPSs they exited.

Note that in the table we do not indicate the statistical significance of the differences, because we do not want readers to jump to the conclusion that statistically significant differences are substantively meaningful. Our sample sizes are large, so nearly all the comparisons would be statistically significant, and that could lead readers to the wrong conclusions.
19. Bifulco and Ladd, "School Choice, Racial Segregation and Test-Score Gaps: Evidence from North Carolina's Charter School Program"; Booker et al., "The Effects of Charter Schools on School Peer Composition."
20. These averages give equal weight to each jurisdiction rather than weighting by the number of students or schools.
21. Bifulco and Ladd, "School Choice, Racial Segregation and Test-Score Gaps: Evidence from North Carolina's Charter School Program."

Chapter 12

1. See, for example, Fordham Institute, *Fund the Child: Tackling Inequity and Antiquity in School Finance* (Washington, DC: Thomas B. Fordham Institute, 2006).
2. TIMSS stands for Trends in Mathematics and Science Study. See http://nces/ed/gov/timss/results03_fourth03.asp. PISA refers to the Program for International Student Assessment sponsored by the Organization for Economic Cooperation and Development. See http://pisa.acer.edu.au.
3. UNICEF, *Child Poverty in Perspective: An Overview of Child Well-being in Rich Countries* (Florence, Italy: Innocent Research Center, 2007). The UNICEF scale for child well-being uses six measures: material well-being, health and safety, educational well-being, family and peer relationships, behaviors and risks, and subjective well-being.
4. Edward B. Fiske and Helen F. Ladd, *When Schools Compete: A Cautionary Tale* (Washington, DC: Brookings Institution Press, 2003); Julie Berry Cullen, Brian A. Jacob, and Steven Levitt, "The Impact of School Choice on Student Outcomes: An Analysis of the Chicago Public Schools," *Journal of Public Economics* 89, no. 56 (June 2005): 729–760; David N. Plank and Gary Sykes, eds., *Choosing Choice: School Choice in International Perspective* (New York and London: Teachers College Press, 2003).
5. Kevin Booker, Ron Zimmer, and Richard Buddin, "The Effect of Charter Schools on School Peer Composition," RAND working paper WR-306-EDU, Santa Monica, CA, 2005; Robert Bifulco and Helen F. Ladd, "School Choice, Racial Segregation and Test-Score Gaps: Evidence from North Carolina's Charter School Program," *Journal of Policy Analysis and Management* 26 (2007): 31–56; Brian P. Gill, Mike Timpane, Karen Ross, and Dominic Brewer, *Rhetoric Versus Reality: What We Know and What We Need to Know About Vouchers and Charter Schools* (Santa Monica, CA: RAND Corporation, 2001).
6. Salvatore Saporito, "Private Choices, Public Consequences: Magnet School Choice and Segregation by Race and Poverty," *Social Problems* 50 (2003): 181–203; Lawrence D. Bobo, "Prejudice as Group Position: Microfoundations of a Sociological Approach to Race and Race Relations," *Journal of Social Issues* 55 (1999): 445–472; Karl Tauber and David James, "Racial Segregation Among Public and Private Schools," *Sociology of Education* 55 (1982): 133–143; Amy Stuart Wells and Robert Crain, "Do Parents Choose School Quality or School Status? A Sociological Theory of Free Market Education," in *The Choice Controversy*, ed. Peter W. Cookson Jr. (Newbury Park, CA: Corwin Press, 1992), 174–196.
7. Robert Bifulco, Helen F. Ladd, and Stephen Ross, "Public School Choice and Integration: Evidence from Durham, North Carolina," *Social Science Research* 38, no. 1 (2009): 71–85
8. Ibid.

9. Countering this prediction is the possibility that when there are high levels of residential segregation, the introduction of choice programs that break the link between place of residence and schooling options may lead to less segregation than would arise with neighborhood schools. This mechanism, called the *liberation theory* (Douglas Archbald, "School Choice, Magnet Schools, and the Liberation Model: An Empirical Study," *Sociology of Education* 77 (2004): 283–310), is most applicable when members of the disadvantaged group are restricted in their choice of residential location by discrimination or other barriers.

10. In many ways the privately operated Dutch schools are similar to publicly funded charter schools in the United States. The main difference is the far larger role that the privately operated schools play in the Dutch system.

11. Strictly speaking, Article 23 applies only to the right to found new schools. In practice, however, it has been interpreted as also giving parents the right to choose the school that their child will attend.

12. Why pillarization persisted in education after it disappeared in other areas of Dutch life is a complicated question. One common explanation is the desire of many Dutch parents to enroll their children in schools in which the teaching coincides with their family values broadly defined. Another has to do with finances. Some religious school boards had accumulated financial endowments that they have been eager to maintain in the post-pillarization Dutch society. In a 1995 article Jaap Dronkers lists a number of other explanations, including the fact that religious schools are attractive to some parents because of their "generally middle educational conservatism compared to the generally more progressive tendency of public schools" (Jaap Dronkers, "The Existence of Parental Choice in the Netherlands," *Educational Policy* 9, no. 3 (1995): 227–243). Three national organizations that oversaw the interests of the three traditional pillars continue to receive public funding for education-related activities such as training, conferences, and the development of teaching materials.

13. These school boards should not be confused with U.S. school boards. Dutch school boards are typically self-perpetuating boards that are responsible for one to more than one hundred schools. In some ways they are comparable to the charter management organizations that operate groups of charter schools in the United States.

14. Eddie Denessen, Geert Driessen, and Peter Sleegers, "Segregation by Choice? A Study of Group-Specific Reasons for School Choice," *Journal of Education Policy* 20, no. 3 (2005): 347–368, table 3.

15. Ibid.

16. For a full analysis and discussion of this policy of weighted student funding, see Helen F. Ladd and Edward B. Fiske, "Weighted Student Funding for Primary Schools: An Analysis of the Dutch Experience," working paper, Sanford School of Duke University, Durham, NC, 2009, and Fiske and Ladd, *When Schools Compete: A Cautionary Tale*. We document in the 2009 paper that the additional resources in the schools having large proportions of weighted students enable them to hire 57 percent more teachers per pupil than schools with few or no weighted students.

17. These same three points are highlighted by Sjoerd Karsten, Charles Felix, Guuske Ledoux, Wim Meijnen, Jaap Roeleveld, and Erik Van Schooten, "Choosing Segregation or Integration? The Extent and Effects of Ethnic Segregation in Dutch Cities," *Education and Urban Society* 38, no. 2 (February 1, 2009): 228–247.

18. This section relies heavily on the OECD background report on immigrant education in the Netherlands: Lex Herweijer, *OECD Thematic Review on Migrant Education: Country Background Report for the Netherlands* (The Hague: The Netherlands Institute for Social Research, 2009).

19. Indonesians are not identified as non-Western immigrants because of their long exposure to Dutch culture and to the Dutch language. In addition, immigrants from Japan are not treated as non-Western immigrants.

20. Herweijer, OECD *Thematic Review on Migrant Education: Country Background Report for the Netherlands,* table 12.

21. Sjoerd Karsten, Guuske Ledoux, Jaap Roeleveld, Charles Felix, and Dorothe Elshof, "School Choice and Ethnic Segregation," *Educational Policy* 17, no. 4 (September 1, 2003): 452–477; Karsten et al., "Choosing Segregation or Integration? The Extent and Effects of Ethnic Segregation in Dutch Cities."

22. Sako Musterd and Wim Ostendorf, "Spatial Segregation and Integration in the Netherlands," in *Residential Segregation and the Integration of Immigrants: Britain, the Netherlands, and Sweden,* ed. Karen Schonwalder (Berlin: Social Science Research Center, 2007), 41–60.

23. Karsten et al., "Choosing Segregation or Integration? The Extent and Effects of Ethnic Segregation in Dutch Cities."

24. Geert Driessen and Michael Merry, "Islamic Schools in the Netherlands: Expansion or Marginalization?" *Interchange* 37 (2006): 201–223.

25. Karsten et al., "Choosing Segregation or Integration? The Extent and Effects of Ethnic Segregation in Dutch Cities."

26. J. Broekhuizen, M. Jansen, and J. Slot, *Segregatie in het basisonderwijs in Amsterdam* [Segregation in primary education in Amsterdam] (Amsterdam: Dienst Onderzoek en Statistiek Gemeente Amsterdam, 2008); Peter Wolfgram (with help from Jan Tito and Guido Walraven), *Leerlingen, bassisscholen en hun buurt* [Primary students and their neighborhood] (Rotterdam: The Knowledge Center, January 2009). One exception is N. Van Nimwegen and I. Esveldt, *Beleidsvraagstukken in Nederland anno 2006; Grote steden in demografisch perspectief* [Policy issues in the Netherlands in the year 2006; Big cities in demographical perspective] (Den Haag: Nederlands Interdisciplinair Demografisch Instituut, 2006), a long report on Dutch demographics that includes a few pages about primary school segregation based on isolation and dissimilarity indexes.

27. Wolfgram et al., *Leerlingen, bassisscholen en hun buurt.*

28. Because we are using information reported for the purposes of school financing, our measures of segregation in this section apply to schools regardless of the number of locations the school has. Although most schools have only one location, some have more than one, in part as a consequence of school consolidations in the 1990s. We have also done some comparable analysis based on other data on immigrant status that are available at the level of the school location, but only for the years 2003–2006. Despite the use of an immigrant measure that does not specifically adjust for disadvantage, the results are virtually the same as those reported in the text. We had initially hoped to use this other data source—referred to as country-of-origin data—to extend our analysis to 2008–2009. Unfortunately, based on our initial examination of the data as reported by the schools and provided to us by the Central Agency for the Funding of Schools, we concluded that the data are not reliable for the years after 2006; hence we were not able to use data for those years. Specifically, the school-level data generated large year-to-year declines after 2006 in the proportions of immigrant pupils—declines that were inconsistent with city-level trends in the proportions of school-aged non-Western immigrant pupils. Officials at the Ministry of Education have since confirmed our conclusion that the post-2006 data appear to be incorrect, but officials cannot do anything about it until the new pupil-level identifiers are operational. We hypothesize that when the immigrant criterion for the school funding weights was eliminated in 2006, either schools became less careful in reporting the country-of-origin information or the ministry became less vigilant in checking to see that the schools reported it correctly.

29. This measure, which can be interpreted as the percentage of disadvantaged immigrants in the school of the typical disadvantaged immigrant, is calculated as follows:

$$I = \Sigma_i \left((DI_i / DI_{city}) \times (DI_i / N_i) \right)$$

where DI_i is the number of disadvantaged immigrants in school i, N_i is the total number of students in the school, and DI_{city} is the number of disadvantaged immigrants in the city. It differs from the previous two measures in that it is based on all disadvantaged immigrants in the city rather than only those in the most highly disadvantaged schools.

30. The index ranges from 0 (complete balance) to 1 (complete segregation) and is often interpreted as the fraction of pupils who would need to be moved among schools to attain balance. This measure is calculated as follows:

$$DIS = 0.5 \; \Sigma \left[\, (DI_i/DI_{city}) - (AO_i/AO_{city}) \, \right]$$

where DI_i is as defined earlier, and AO_i and AO_{city} refer to all other pupils in the school and in the city, respectively. The square brackets denote absolute values. Hence the measure is the average deviation (independent of sign) across schools between the shares of the city's total pupils who are disadvantaged immigrants and those who are more advantaged.

31. If disadvantaged immigrant students were evenly distributed among schools, the typical advantaged student would attend a school with the average proportion of disadvantaged students in that city. Call that ratio R. The segregation index measures the gap between that maximum ratio and the actual exposure ratio (E) of advantaged students to disadvantaged immigrant students expressed as a fraction of the maximum ratio. Again, the range is 0 to 1. A value of 0 indicates that there is no imbalance in the sense that the proportion of disadvantaged immigrants is similar across schools and equal to the citywide proportion, whereas a value of 1 indicates complete imbalance.

32. The dissimilarity index is usually higher than the segregation index, but the two measures are quite highly correlated. For example, in a sample of 715 public school districts in the United States the correlation between the two measures was 0.86 (Charles T. Clotfelter, *After Brown: The Rise and Retreat of School Segregation* (Princeton, NJ: Princeton University Press, 2004), 205).

33. These thirty-two cities form a group that often works together to promote its specific interests with the national government. Two-thirds of the cities have populations greater than 100,000, with the largest being Eindhoven, which has about 210,000 residents. The analysis on which this paragraph is based is available at www.nienkeruijs.nl/laddfiskeruijs.

34. Charles T. Clotfelter, Helen F. Ladd, and Jacob Vigdor, "Federal Oversight, Local Control and the Specter of Resegregation," *American Law and Economics Review* 8 (Summer 2006): 1–43.

35. Clotfelter, *After Brown: The Rise and Retreat of School Segregation*, table 2.3.

36. The CBS defines non-Western immigrants as first- and second-generation persons born in Turkey, Africa, Latin America, or Asia, excluding Japan and Indonesia. Note that this definition is broader than that used for the school analysis in that it includes all persons, not only children, and it includes not only disadvantaged non-Western immigrants (those in households for whom the adults have limited education) but also those who are more advantaged. We were not able to restrict the analysis to the four major non-Western groups, almost all of whom are disadvantaged, because that breakdown was available only after 2003. To ensure consistent definitions over time, we report data only for 1999 and 2003–2008. Finally, excluded from the analysis are all neighborhoods having fewer than fifty total residents, because data for those neighborhoods are withheld for confidentiality. That exclusion

has little influence given that 80 percent of the relevant neighborhoods have more than one thousand inhabitants.

37. Karsten et al., "Choosing Segregation or Integration? The Extent and Effects of Ethnic Segregation in Dutch Cities."

38. The term *polderizing* has its origins in the long-standing and continuing Dutch challenge of containing the sea. The construction and maintenance of *polders,* which are low-lying tracts of land enclosed by dikes, was a community effort that gave birth to the political tradition of polderizing.

39. F. Ledoux, C. Felix, and D. Elshof, *Z"Bestrijding van segregatie in het onderwijs in gemeenten: Verkenning van lokaal beleid anno 2008* [Combating Educational Segregation in Cities: Exploration of Local Policies in the Year 2008] (Utrecht: FORUM, 2009).

40. Ibid.

41. Ministerie van Onderwijs, "Tegengaan van Segregatie in het Basisonderwijs" [Reducing Segregation in Elementary Education], 2008, http://www.forum.nl/paoo/artikelen/BriefDijksma-segregatie13mei2008.pdf.

42. D. Peters, M. Haest, and B. Walraven, *Gemeenten in actie tegen segregatie in het basisonderwijs: Een inventarisatie bij de G31 en vier andere gemeenten* [Municipalities in Action Against Segregation in Primary Education: An Inventory of the G31 and Four Other Municipalities] (Utrecht: FORUM, 2007).

43. "Een school dichtbij" [A school nearby], June 24, 2009, www.eenschooldichtbij.nl.

44. Ministerie van Onderwijs, "Tegengaan van Segregatie in het Basisonderwijs" [Reducing Segregation in Elementary Education], 2008, http://www.forum.nl/paoo/artikelen/BriefDijksma-segregatie13mei2008.pdf.

45. Ibid.

46. Ibid.

47. Gemeente Nijmegen, "Inrichting en start van het centraal aanmeldpunt primair onderwijs in Nijmegen" [Organization and start of the central subscription moment primary education in Nijmegen], 2009, http://www2.nijmegen.nl/gemeente/gemeenteraad/politieke_avond/politieke_avonden_2009/vergaderstukken_2009/4_maart_2009.

48. "Gemeente Nijmegen, Centrale aanmelding basisonderwijs Nijmegen" [Central subscription primary education Nijmegen], 2009, http://www.gemengdescholen.nl/documenten/Uitleg%20centrale%20aanmelding.pdf.

49. Gemeente Nijmegen, "Inrichting en start van het centraal aanmeldpunt primair onderwijs in Nijmegen."

50. Ledoux et al., *Z"Bestrijding van segregatie in het onderwijs in gemeenten: Verkenning van lokaal beleid anno 2008.*

51. Peters et al., *Gemeenten in actie tegen segregatie in het basisonderwijs.*

About the Editors

Mark Berends is Professor of Sociology, director of Notre Dame's Center for Research on Educational Opportunity, and director of the National Center on School Choice. He also serves on several editorial boards, technical panels, and policy forums and recently ended his term as vice president of the American Educational Research Association's Division L, Educational Policy and Politics. Professor Berends' research focuses on the ways school organization and classroom instruction are related to student achievement, with special attention to disadvantaged students. Within this agenda, he has applied a variety of quantitative and qualitative methods to understand the effects of school reforms on teachers and students. He is the author or editor of numerous articles and books, most recently including *Examining Gaps in Mathematics Achievement Among Racial-Ethnic Groups, Charter School Outcomes, Leading with Data: Pathways to Improve Your School,* and *Handbook of Research on School Choice.*

Marisa Cannata is senior research associate in the department of Leadership, Policy, and Organizations and associate director of the National Center on School Choice at Vanderbilt University. Her research interests focus on school choice and teacher quality policies, including induction, teacher career decisions, work experiences, and hiring. Dr. Cannata has a PhD in Educational Policy from Michigan State University.

Ellen B. Goldring is Patricia and Rodes Hart Chair and Professor of Education Policy and Leadership, and chair of the Department of Leadership, Policy and Organizations, at Peabody College of Vanderbilt University, where she has received the Alexander Heard Distinguished Professor award. Professor Goldring's two primary research foci are school reform efforts that connect families, communities, and schools, with a focus on schools of choice; and the changing roles of school leaders and leadership effectiveness. Her books include *School Choice in Urban America, Leading with Data: Pathways to Improve Your School,* and *From the Courtroom to the Classroom: The Shifting Landscape of School Desegregation.*

About the Contributors

David Arsen is Professor of Educational Administration and Education Policy in the College of Education at Michigan State University. He received his PhD in economics at the University of California, Berkeley. Dr. Arsen's research focuses on school finance, school choice, and school facilities.

Kevin Booker is researcher at Mathematica Policy Research, Inc. Dr. Booker specializes in longitudinal analysis of student test score data. His policy research interests include charter schools, value-added modeling, teacher and school accountability, and teacher incentives and retention.

Xiu Cravens is Research Assistant Professor of Education Policy at the Department of Leadership, Policy, and Organizations, and holds an administrative appointment as Peabody College's assistant dean for international affairs. She conducts research in the areas of school leadership and school choice.

Nada Eissa is Associate Professor of Public Policy and Economics at Georgetown University and research associate at the National Bureau of Economic Research (NBER). Her research focuses on the economics of the public sector and empirical methods.

Edward B. (Ted) Fiske, formerly education editor of the *New York Times,* is an education writer and consultant who has written on topics ranging from U.S. higher education to school reform in Cambodia. He is also author of the *Fiske Guide to Colleges,* an annual publication that has been a standard part of college admissions literature for more than twenty-five years, as well as numerous other books on college admissions.

Brian Gill is senior social scientist at Mathematica Policy Research in Cambridge, Mass. He has extensively studied the effects of school choice in general and charter schools in particular. Currently, Dr. Gill is directing the National Study of the Effectiveness of Charter-School Management Organizations and is principal investigator on the first nationwide evaluation of the effects of the KIPP schools.

Babette Gutmann is vice president at Westat. She has extensive experience in research related to early childhood and to elementary and secondary education at the federal, state, and local levels. She has designed, managed, and conducted randomized experiments and program evaluations for services to at-risk children, primarily children receiving Title I services.

Charles S. Hausman currently serves as associate professor in the Department of Educational Leadership & Policy at Eastern Kentucky University. His research focuses on the educational consequences of school choice for students, families, teachers, and principals.

David W. Johnson is research assistant for the Consortium on Chicago School Research at the University of Chicago, where he is also a doctoral student. A former public school teacher, he conducts research on predictors of public school students' academic performance, gender disparities in student outcomes, and school practices that help students successfully transition to high school.

Brian Kisida is senior research associate in the Department of Education Reform at the University of Arkansas. He provides technical and analytic expertise for both the School Choice Demonstration Project (a national research team conducting an independent longitudinal multimethod evaluation of the Milwaukee Parental Choice Program) and the DC Opportunity Scholarship Program impact evaluation.

Helen F. Ladd is Edgar Thompson Professor of Public Policy Studies and Professor of Economics at Duke University. Most of her current research focuses on education policy. With her husband Edward Fiske, she is coeditor of *Handbook of Research on Education Finance and Policy* and coauthor of books on school reform in New Zealand and South Africa.

Elisabeth S. Larsen is an advanced graduate student in the Department of Sociology at Brigham Young University, with a focus on the sociology of education. Her research interests include school desegregation and school choice.

Stéphane Lavertu is a doctoral candidate in the Department of Political Science at the University of Wisconsin-Madison. His research interests include bureaucratic politics, American political institutions, public administration, and policy analysis and evaluation, including the ways these topics apply to K–12 education.

Maria Mendiburo recently received her doctorate in Leadership and Policy Studies from Vanderbilt University's Peabody College of Education and Human Development. She is currently a member of the research faculty in the Department of Electrical Engineering and Computer Science at Vanderbilt University. Her research concentrates on using technology to enhance students' conceptual and procedural understanding of mathematics and on understanding the effects of charter schools on student outcomes.

Yongmei Ni is currently assistant professor in the Department of Educational Leadership and Policy at the University of Utah. Her research interests focus on school choice, finance and governance, and school effectiveness.

Anna Nicotera is research and evaluation director for the National Alliance for Public Charter Schools. Prior to joining the Alliance, Nicotera was a predoctoral research fellow with one of the Institute of Education Sciences (IES) of the U.S. Department of Education training programs at Vanderbilt University. Her research includes program evaluations of whole school reform models and professional development initiatives in urban school districts.

Paul E. Peterson is Henry Lee Shattuck Professor of Government and director of the Program on Education Policy and Governance at Harvard University, and editor-in-chief of *Education Next,* a journal of opinion and research on education policy. His research covers areas such as No Child Left Behind, school vouchers, and charter schools.

Kristie J. R. Phillips is assistant professor in the Department of Sociology at Brigham Young University. Her current research interests include school choice, school desegregation, the social contexts of education, and teacher quality. Her research combines elements of sociological theory, social geography, and education policy, all of which provide context for the range of social and academic experiences of students, teachers, and administrators within school settings.

Michael Puma is an expert in program evaluation with more than thirty-five years of experience in conducting major national studies in education, child and youth development, nutrition assistance, human services, income security, and employment and training. His current research activities include serving as principal investigator for the nine-year National Head Start Impact Study and senior researcher on the experimental evaluation of the D.C. school voucher program.

Louis Rizzo is senior statistician at Westat. With extensive experience in a range of survey methodologies and survey areas, he has authored or coauthored a number of refereed journal articles, one book chapter, and numerous proceedings reports on estimation, sampling, weighting, and other issues in survey statistics.

Nienke Ruijs is a PhD student at the Top Institute for Evidence Based Education Research (TIER) at the University of Amsterdam. She recently completed a research master's in Educational Sciences and a master's in Clinical Developmental Psychology.

Carolyn Sattin-Bajaj is PhD candidate in International Education at New York University's Steinhardt School of Culture, Education and Human Development and research assistant at the Institute for Globalization and Education in Metropolitan Settings (IGEMS). Her research interests focus on immigrant integration in various national and institutional settings.

Marc L. Stein is education researcher at Johns Hopkins University. Dr. Stein's research interests lie in the quantitative analyses of the social contexts surrounding schools and schooling and the role that these contexts play in the enactment of educational policy, with special emphasis on racial–ethnic and socioeconomic inequalities.

W. David Stevens is sociologist and senior research analyst for the Consortium on Chicago School Research at the University of Chicago. His research focuses on high school reform and instructional development. Currently he is leading a three-year mixed-methods study of the transition to high school that follows a cohort of students from eighth grade into their second year in high school.

Marisa de la Torre is senior research analyst for the Consortium on Chicago School Research at the University of Chicago. Her research has focused on the Chicago High School Redesign Initiative and student mobility issues.

Martina G. Viarengo is the current PEPG postdoctoral research fellow and fellow of the Women and Public Policy Program at the Harvard Kennedy School. Dr. Viarengo holds a PhD from the London School of Economics. Her research interests within education policy include the effects of school characteristics on students' performance, an evaluation of charter schools in the United States, and a study on school choice in Western Europe.

John F. Witte is Professor of Political Science and Public Affairs at the University of Wisconsin-Madison. His research and teaching interests include democratic theory, American politics and public policy, and organizational theory.

Patrick J. Wolf is Professor of Education Reform and 21st Century Endowed Chair in School Choice at the University of Arkansas in Fayetteville. Professor Wolf is principal investigator of the DC Opportunity Scholarship Program Impact Evaluation and also leads a collaborative multimethod longitudinal evaluation of voucher and charter school choice in Milwaukee.

Ron Zimmer is Associate Professor of Public Policy and Education in the Peabody College at Vanderbilt University and is currently serving as associate editor of *Economics of Education Review*. Dr. Zimmer's research focuses on school choice and school finance. Currently, Dr. Zimmer is coleading an IES-funded study of reform efforts and programs in a major urban district, and an evaluation of the impact of Chicago's charter schools on long-term educational attainment.

Index

absenteeism, 61, 69–70, 72
academic engagement, 61, 69–70
academic quality
  as priority in school choice, 112, 114–116
  variation in meaning of, 123
acceptance policies as barrier to access, 125
accountability
  for charter schools, 37
  national standards (Dutch), 236
achievement models, 45–47
actively involved families, 139
added needs instruction, 200, 203, 204,
    205–206
Adequate Yearly Progress (AYP), 49–50, 77,
    90, 116–119, 122
admissions criteria
  for NYC high schools, 156–157
  for selective-enrollment schools, 128
adult support
  importance to application process,
    141–145
  by school counselors, 139–141
advantaged families, 234–235
African American students. *See also*
    desegregation; segregation by
    educational disadvantage
  charter school effects, 45, 46, 47
  in charter school populations, 218, 227
  switching patterns of, 109, 230, 231, 232
Amsterdam (Netherlands)
  non-Western immigrants in, 239–240
  residential segregation trends, 248–250
  school and student data, 237, 238
  segregation by disadvantage in, 244–247
application process
  as barrier to access, 135–137, 144
  competitive, for charter schools, 37

importance of adult support, 141–145
need for improvement in, 145
oversight of, in NYC, 157–158
parental involvement in, 137–139, 143
role of elementary schools in, 142–143
at-risk provisions, 225
attainment analysis, 25, 26
attention in class, 61, 69–70, 72
attrition rates
  selection bias and, 56–57
  student compliance and, 74

Ballard, Gregory, 36
barriers to access
  choice participation and, 85, 86
  for disadvantaged families, 235
  for Latin American immigrant families,
    148–149, 168–171
  study of, 125–145
    in application process, 135–137, 144
    data collection, 128–130
    discussion of results, 144–145
    higher-performing schools, 130–133
    importance of adult support, 141–143
    parent involvement and, 137–139
    role of school counselors, 139–141
    school choice and, 126–127
    transaction costs, 133–135
    variety of options, 127–128
basic needs instruction, 200, 203, 204
Big Picture Company, 111
bilingual guidance counselors, 163–164, 169
"black schools" (Netherlands), 239, 241–
    242, 243
Bloom adjustment, 20
Bush, George W., 17